UNLEARNING EXERCISES

Art Organizations as Sites for Unlearning

Casco Art Institute: Working for the Commons

Minor Compositions / Autonomedia

CONTENTS

Foreword: UNLEARNING TO UNLEARN

Kerstin Stakemeier and Marina Vishmidt

At the UK university where I work as a lecturer, there's a program called "Learning to Learn." It's intended for incoming students whose experience of education up to that point failed to prepare them for the basics of university instruction. Of course, some of these deficiencies are predictable: a ludicrously marketized university system that aggressively recruits in East Asia mustn't grumble when students arrive having been educated in a manner that's not exactly compatible with the ostensible Western tradition, neither in form nor in content.

German art academies work on the flipside of this situation. Here, studying is still not predicated upon gathering fees that monetarize the education of those who can afford it. The skills of self-monetarization taught here are also considerably more limited than those which UK universities predicate their curricula on today. In some places, like the one I teach at as a professor, studies are still entirely free of charge. But while one would hope that this invites a more diverse student body into aesthetic forms of praxis, this is rarely true: the social group feeling addressed by such an institution, the group prepared to be aesthetically "unlearned" in the (relative) absence of monetarization, is the group able to temporarily extricate themselves from being subjected to it, from being subjugated by it. While art academies pride themselves on their non-academic character it's only the subjects of learning who find themselves in a position to unlearn.

Institutions of education, while important for the project as a whole as well as for Annette Krauss' praxis as a researcher and artist, are not the only "sites of unlearning" that will feature in what is to follow. The learning to be unlearned in question is not so much the divestment of specific skills but of a *habitus*. In the characteristic mix of acquiescence and entrepreneurship envisioned by the autonomic nervous system of the knowledge economy, "life-long learning" demands the disposition to acquire skills, the speculative orientation to flexibility, and constant bootstrapping. Thus, what is to be unlearned are all the presuppositions that sustain those dogmas of learning, primarily divisions of labor (waged/unwaged, mental/manual, productive/re-productive, gender, racial, and legal status). But that is hardly all, since it is also those institutions that dwell at an angle to the workplace, the school, and the training facility—namely art institutions—that find themselves reproducing those habits in the pursuit of critical reflection, the entrenched split between action and representation, subject and object. Yet, even when reflecting on entanglement itself becomes a norm, if not a convention, practicing this critique at the level of the everyday reproduction of the small arts institution runs immediately into an interesting, even electrical, problem. Where is the institution? How would its borders have to be drawn in order for us to say, in a future anterior: this will have been changed, with these and these effects?

But while the limits of the institutions are all but transient right now—or maybe just from the inside out but not from the outside in—they can serve as spheres of "breaking my habits" (as per Genesis Breyer P-Orridge),[1] and the habitus they come with. Workers who documented their strike in Nanterre in 1968 took their factory over from the unions, who they began to see as critical *to* the process of capital, rather than critical to its *disintegration*. Commoning meant to defy their consistent representation. They formed and documented "strike committees," which one could understand as militant spaces of com-muning: they were to function as "worker's states in the factory," as one worker explained. Positioned right at the (re)productive center of capitalist machinery. But because they were not critical *for* the process of capital but for their own practical *unlearning*, we do not know of them through the mass distribution of their films and those produced by others, such a the Medvedkin Group between

1   Simon Ford, *Wreckers of Civilization*
     (London: Black Dog Publishing, 1999), 113.

1967 and 1976. That distribution became marginal after the 1970s, after the strikes in much of Europe were nationalized, regionalized, and professionalized—segregated into conflicts of interest. We know of those workers because Claudia von Alemann integrated part of their self-documentation in her own 1969 documentary, "This is Only the Beginning—the Struggle Continues," a film student's attempt at agitational film: a documentation of sites of attempted self-dispossessions via a redistribution of information, of public and mutual learning.

The absence of this situation today emerges when one of Casco's interlocutors says, "I'm not sure how we can practically change something in a physical space when it comes to property relations because I imagine you can change narratives about it and get a different perspective on it, but I don't see a way of actually doing it yet."[2] She is pointing to the immanence of temporality and scale in any action undertaken by a group to alter its conditions. If these are conditions of its reproduction, what is the entity to be reproduced? This might be the stake of "learning to unlearn" which is so very tangled, and potentiated to the degree it is tangled, the "double" trajectory of prefiguration discussed in the following pages. The institution commons itself in a way that both presupposes and projects the dissolution of the institution as currently constituted. Yet in order to do so, it must both have and provide infrastructure. So, what is the institution? Is it a concatenation of habits, of possibilities, and ethics plus the power to put them into operation? The relationship of this experiment to the forces that traverse it, the institutions that sustain it, is the friable medium of all efforts insofar as the question of scale never ceases to torment, as it is the vector of relation back to violent real abstractions (nation, capital, class, gender, and race). As Mariarosa Dalla Costa and Selma James noted in another context, "To demand a communal canteen in the neighborhood without integrating this demand into a practice of struggle against the organization of labor, against labor time, risks giving the impetus for a new leap [to the managers of poverty] so that we will then have the possibility at lunchtime of eating shit collectively in the canteen."[3] Close to home, the trial

2   See: "Unlearning Exercises," in *Unlearning Exercises: Art Organizations as Sites for Unlearning*, Binna Choi, Annette Krauss, Yolande Zola Zoli van der Heide eds. (Amsterdam: Casco Art Institute/Valiz, 2018), 44.

3   Mariarosa Dalla Costa and Selma James, *The Power of Women and the Subversion of the Community* [1971], 3rd ed. (Bristol: Falling Wall Press, 1975), 21.

of the Universal Basic Income in Utrecht is a learning scenario. We are always faced with a recursion: "The dissolution of the whole social relations" (as per Rifkin)[4] that identifies and enables us as the (collective) subjects *of* and *for* this dissolution.

The question of reproduction arises from the pages of these texts, as the shared site of debates, of antagonism, of divided labor, of group process, and of becoming critical of and for our (self-) institutions. A couple of years ago the two of us wrote about this context, hoping not least that its autonomization, its processes, could spur a deinstitutionalization of art as a field of segregated aesthetic practice, could socialize it through the terms of its reproduction. Right now, it seems that reproduction itself has to go through deproduction and that socialization has to passage through desocialization. The exclusivities which we attack are in no way external to us. Who are we to reproduce, to self-affirm our own form? Unlearning might be turning into the site of our deproduction. And this shared deproduction in fact might be the source of our commoning. We are hoping to be unlearning *ourselves*.

4   Adrian Rifkin, "Inventing Recollection," in *Interrogating Cultural Studies: Theory, Politics and Practice*, ed. Paul Bowman (London: Pluto, 2003), 114. As quoted in Andrea Phillips, "The Imperative for Self-Attainment: From Cradle to Grave," in *Unlearning Exercises: Art Organizations as Sites for Unlearning* Binna Choi, Annette Krauss, Yolande Zola Zoli van der Heide eds. (Amsterdam: Casco Art Institute/Valiz, 2018), 97.

INTRODUCTION

Liz Allan and
Yolande Zola Zoli van der Heide

Who has not been institutionalized or organized at some point? Who, as a result, has not internalized the divide between reproduction and production, and the devaluation of reproductive labor for economic gain? And to that end, what can be done to address this experience, to engage in the grueling and imaginative process of unlearning, to construct more commoning spaces where our embodied experiences are the subject of each other's learning and unlearning—whilst keeping in mind the ground of inequity, on which we tread and are bound by in the global division of labor? How can one keep sharp, and organize differently amidst neoliberal working conditions?

Unlearning Exercises: Art Organizations as Sites for Unlearning follows a pathway of collective endeavor over four years (since 2014) and is a collection of exercises, inter-organizational conversations, and theoretical texts that identify and protest the challenges

faced by institutions across the board, and especially those (art) institutions who are dedicated to the commons while building alternatives. We believe that *institutional critique* as an artistic genre and the ensuing *new institutionalism* as a key artistic discourse of the last decades could move similarly by activating both the front and the back sides of an institution, including their visible and invisible layers, to operate *in tandem*. To institute *as* you (re)present!

The publication is woven through multiple nodal points and new encounters made during the trajectory of the collaborative project *Site for Unlearning (Art Organization)*. A series of UNLEARNING EXERCISES form a red thread throughout the book and have been developed by the shifting team at Casco Art Institute and artist Annette Krauss from conversations, exhibitions, meetings, study meetings, and (un)learning experiments in order to bring awareness and, in the best-case scenario, get rid of competitive organizational structures and working relationships, while bolstering cooperative forms of interaction. We offer you these imperfect and modest tools as the concrete evidence of our commoning process for your uptake, intervention, and further imagining.

Offering their introductory insights in retrospect in UNLEARNING TO UNLEARN, Marina

Vishmidt and Kerstin Stakemakier astutely point out that it is the subjects of higher education that find themselves in a position to unlearn, further calling attention to the tangled nature of "becoming critical of and for our (self-)institutions." Indeed, criticism became a constant companion throughout the journey of *Site for Unlearning (Art Organization)*, and external questioning often focused on the art status of and funding sources for the project. We are often asking ourselves how privilege might be playing out in our daily lives, and so it became apparent during a mid-project editorial meeting that, up until that point, not one of the fourteen exercises explicitly addressed decoloniality. Had we overlooked this as a team all this time? Surely not, given how implicated and entrenched we are in the decolonial project day-to-day, as we engage with reproductive labor and the effect that its devaluation and depoliticization has on the poor, the marginalized, and people of color, and also as some of us in the group are people of color ourselves.

Moreover, when we worked to address this now glaring omission at a time where decolonialization is widely spoken about and less often practiced—so as to engage with the latter—we would come to learn how patchily this subject has been addressed within the arts as opposed to, for instance, the academy. The work of Nancy Jouwe's SITES FOR

UNLEARNING IN THE MUSEUM brings together several vignettes from personal accounts over ten years during which the Dutch cultural archive (as per Gloria Wekker) has omitted or obscured her black subjectivity from conversations. Jouwe notes a number of recently-founded black initiatives in the Netherlands, where "a decoloniality of aesthetics, knowledge, and being is proposed." This comparatively recent instituting of decolonial thinking could dovetail well with the unfinished potential of the unlearning exercises, which we offer as a set of proposals to be taken up by others in the understanding that institutions live within us as well. Binna Choi and Yolande Zola Zoli van der Heide reach into the cinematic archive to reveal the framework of our present day modern-colonial matrix in DECOLONIZING ART INSTITUTES FROM A LABOR POINT OF VIEW. This forward thinking text draws together the political urgencies of arts institutions with practices of unlearning to focus on how new labor relations can be cultivated. The authors draw upon their experience of thinking differently as part of the Arts Collaboratory network to provide an innovative model for how counter-hegemonic (arts) funding structures can be collectively built.

The economic focus on art, instituting, and learning is further studied in LIFELONG LEARNING

AND THE PROFESSIONALIZED LEARN-ER. It presents scholarship by Annette Krauss on the ideology of lifelong learning and its institution into European policy papers since 2000. Krauss highlights (mis)connections between the formation of pedagogical and artistic subjects as role models for the knowledge economy. Andrea Phillips' incisive essay THE IMPERATIVE FOR SELF-ATTAINMENT: FROM CRADLE TO GRAVE sets this research into a wider frame through a re-embodiment of the phantom notions of meritocracy and self. In the process of disentangling life-long learning from the notion of education, Phillips pinpoints the challenges that unlearning will face in the field. Together, these companion pieces reveal the structural, often economic, forces at play in our conceptions of (un)learning.

Site for Unlearning (Art Organization) also reaches out to sister organizations and scholars in Casco Art Institute's networks in a three-part conversation series entitled TOILET (T)ISSUES, which was ignited by the question of who buys the toilet paper, or, who performs taken-for-granted labor in one's organization. Reflections on day-to-day operations from the field of art, culture, and social organizing across Indonesia, the Netherlands, the United Kingdom, and Mexico provide first-hand accounts of successful experiences

13

with collective processes, while also voicing personal frustrations with the reproductive site with humor and openness.

The practice of unlearning is thus not one of denying any particular skill set but is instead rooted in questioning the habits and privileges assumed through accumulative learning processes. At best, it is thus a question of dismantling structures of op-pression, and not only to examine how they work. Binna Choi and Annette Krauss reflect on this pathway in their afterword HAVE YOU HAD A PRODUCTIVE DAY? Writing together, they look back on *Site for Unlearning (Art Organization)* and explain how studying the "spatio-temporal, embodied, and material relationalities inherent in the institution of Casco" became crucial for collectively engaging in unlearning. In other words, we needed to think and work through how we can overcome the divisions that uncommon us on a daily basis. The collaborators share research and anecdotes from the project's micro-history to show how the desire for "deep understanding" builds stronger connections between theory and prac-tice, and how organizational forms become forms of organizing. Indeed, when we first started unlearning we wanted to unlearn the feeling of being busy at the expense of deep time, deep understanding, or study. This came with the realization that, by valuing study

over cleaning or maintenance, we too had fallen into the tendency of devaluing reproductive labor. None of us, after all, are exempt from repeating the very same capitalist logic that thrives off of the back of the poor, minorities, and invisibilized people.

It will then come as no surprise to find that Annette Krauss and Binna Choi's text is to be found by the glossary, bibliography, and COLOPHON, next to the lists of people and concepts that most often make up the less visible components of a publication. The addition of an extended colophon supports an en-deavor towards collective authorship, as both a form of genealogy and (never complete) road map, naming (insofar as we can) the people, branches, and byways that have grown and intertwined as part of the Casco Art Institute, unlearning, and commoning journeys. Looking further towards the back, the GLOSSARY OF TERMS provides a small selection of key termsthat emerge from these experiences and that keep resonating between our practices as common values.

All the while, the collective endeavor has been guided by a character we call Nina bell Federici (Nina bell F.) who arose from our admiration for Nina Simone, bell hooks, and Silvia Federici and their artistic, black, feminist, and political engagements. We propose that these engagements connect the unlearning project

to future experiments in other sites (institutional frameworks) beyond Casco Art Institute. Nina bell F. articulate(s) a proposition that is yet to be taken up for future experiments. In "working for the commons" we want to practice and understand the commons as more than a pool of resources, but as a value system, set of governing principles, and a way toward counter-hegemonic relations.

We give thanks. We give thanks to the workers: the generosity of conversation partners who shared their wisdom on leadership and the burdens, sacrifices, and triumphs of (self-)organization; we give thanks to the writers, the firm and faithful hands of the editors, publisher, and designer. We give thanks to the full contingent of Casco Art Institute's team members, former and current, and to those active in our ecosystem.

Sincerely (and back to you),
Your Art Laborers

UNLEARNING EXERCISES

The Shifting Team
at Casco and Annette Krauss

In the following section, the Casco Art Institute team and Annette Krauss share fourteen proposals that actively intervene in and possibly reshape the art institutional and organizational habits that they want to unlearn. Taking Casco Art Institute as a concrete site for research and subject for change, our unlearning evolved around "busyness," the familiar state and prevalent mode of "business." Running a business, in particular the business of an art institution, is irrevocably tied up with the anxiety and stress of habitually "being busy." While focusing on presentation and publishing practices and making things visible in competitive conditions, we have found ourselves undervaluing what often remains invisible; so-called reproductive labor such as cleaning, fixing, and caring.

Unlearning Exercises have been developed over the long-term during practice-oriented study gatherings. This process has been experimental and has involved trial and error, discussions, and adaptions; some of which can be traced in the following pages. We encourage anyone who shares similar issues to consider this approach and to keep in mind the underlying questions of the project:

How can we actively practice the commons together in our everyday work and life?

What is the purpose of art, and the role of the artist in all of this?

What is the relationship between an art institution's vision and engagement in cultural production, and its administrative and managerial ethos?

Why are we always so busy?

How do we dismantle the feeling of always being too busy?

How can we value reproductive labor as an essential part of productivity?

How can we unlearn the form of productivity that feeds on busyness?

How can we feed the collective imagination towards unlearning capitalism?

*How would we relate to each other, think, live and work with each other, if we started counting from two instead of one, not pretending that we know where and how things start, but that our selves are always already two, if not multiple...?

2.
MEETING

UNLEARNING EXERCISE
Besides the regular weekly team meeting on Monday, we have been trying to have our "unlearning" meeting regularly too, which we were not really successful at, especially in the hectic weeks leading up to exhibitions or other activities. After several attempts, we have established a "three week cycle," each week having one of three types of unlearning meeting: 1. general meeting with all participants; 2. working group meeting when research strand groups meet; and 3. the collective study wherein a major issue arising from unlearning is intensively studied by the team, with invited guests or in public.

WHAT TO UNLEARN
Structural forms that prevent common rhythms and which don't enable collaborative research and a sense of structurelessness.

Transcript (excerpt)
11 May 2015: Annette, Binna, Carlijn, Ika, Jason, Sanne, Staci, Suzanne, Ying, and Yolande.

Suzanne
For me though, it's not only about the Monday [annoyance is felt due to the significant amount of time the team spend on the weekly team meeting and unlearning meeting every Monday], I like to start things on that day, get on track. On the other hand, it's very good to hear what's coming up and what everyone is doing on Mondays. So it's double, actually.

Binna
Maybe we should change the time?

Jason
Yeah, it's rough on Monday mornings with all the weekend's e-mails.

Binna
There's a general issue about working hours though. The nice thing about Mexico City-based artists' collective Cooperativa Cráter Invertido, Jakarta-based art organization ruangrupa, or KUNCI Study Forum & Collective from Yogyakarta is that their

time is very fluid. But that's not what I am advocating. In the case of Suzanne, her time is not fluid, but we also know it very well so we have an easiness about it. The time does not change much — we know what it is, we share the rhythms. What do we miss if we just make a certain time that is super necessary for us all to be there and otherwise leave it super open?

Suzanne
It's really good to have time just to meet, not by appointment, but just because we are there. You can say, "Hey, shall we sit for ten minutes and do this?" And during these open conversations we went deep into certain issues.

Note
We also get tired of meetings and confused as to whether they need to be efficient or as open as possible to keep conversation flowing. We adopted a stronger structure by appointing a time-keeper, facilitator, and action-point maker, to the point that the structure is similar to that of our board meetings. We miss the open conversations during which we went deep into certain issues.

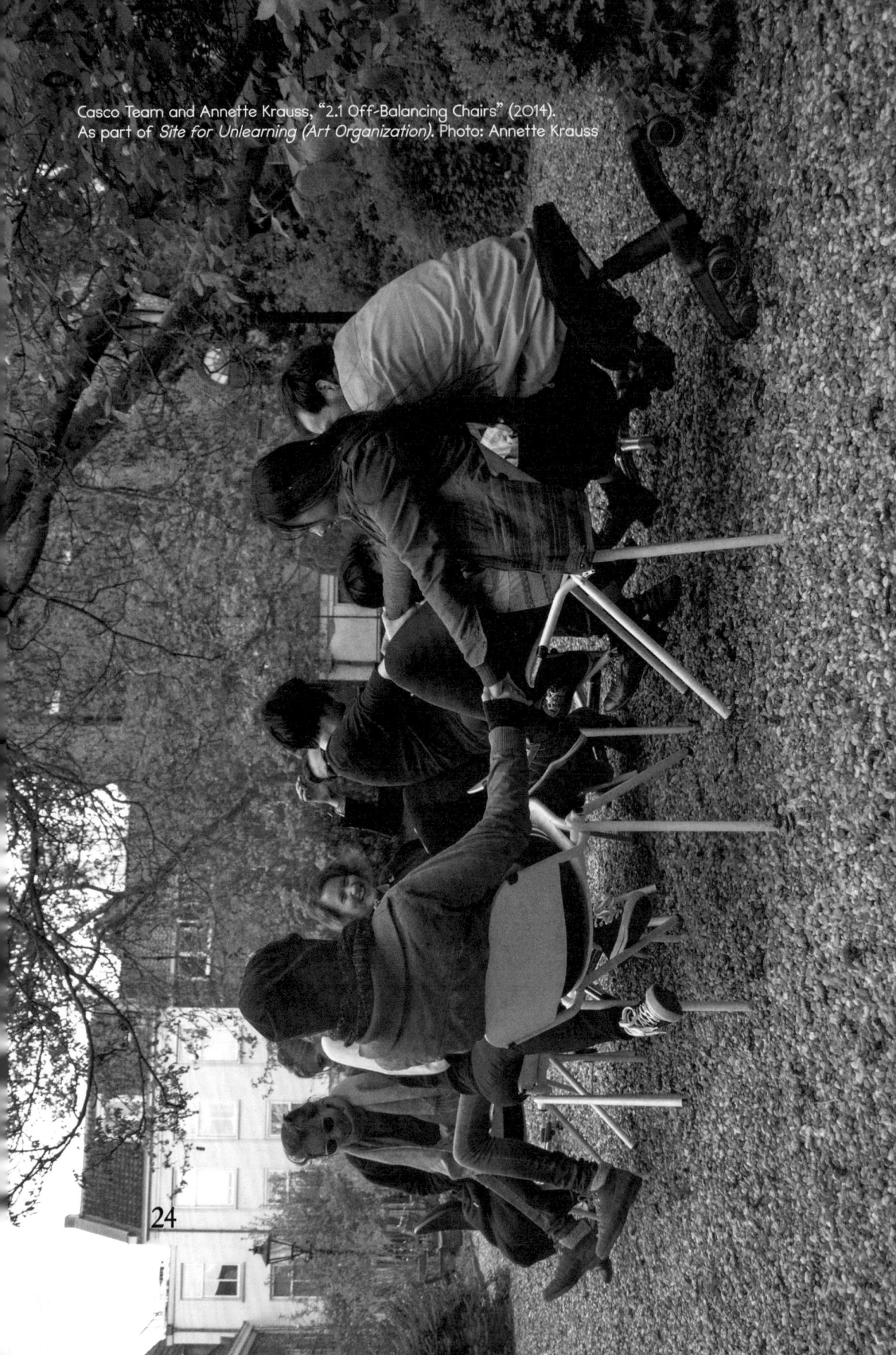

Casco Team and Annette Krauss, "2.1 Off-Balancing Chairs" (2014).
As part of *Site for Unlearning (Art Organization)*. Photo: Annette Krauss

24

2.1
OFF-BALANCING CHAIRS

UNLEARNING EXERCISE
While having a meeting, we sit in our (office) chairs balancing on two legs by holding each other.

WHAT TO UNLEARN
Non-physicality of meetings that tend to be focused on the verbal and in which we remain in the same standard posture; taking for granted the horizontality of roundtable discussions; and routines of "meeting culture."

Extension
Another version of this unlearning exercise was developed as part of a seminar given by Casco Art Institute for the Critical Studies program at the Sandberg Institute in 2014. Tired of a lengthy discussion, a proposal was made to silently look at a tiny part of a big old tree that grows in Casco Art Institute's courtyard, for ten minutes.

Transcript (excerpt)

14 April 2014: Annette, Binna, Carlijn, Deborah, Ester, Janine, Jason, Malcolm, Sanne, Suzanne, Ying, and Yolande.

Janine
If this were true, that this were an alternative space in which participation is necessarily voluntary, production wouldn't be a task. Given my slight refusal of the balancing chairs exercise, because I don't like wobbly chairs, I feel we should have the opportunity to change the task. It never seemed that there were rules at the beginning of this process. It kind of confuses me as to why we now have them. The initial exercise was to sit on chairs differently, what would that mean for you?

Annette
I think it is possible to retreat, pull away from the participation. This of course is a really interesting point. As for my own position, I would also have anxieties about that.

Janine
To me it is not a vilification of the project, but the suggestion of accommodating all individuals.

Annette
When I was thinking about the production process, I was simply putting forward the issue of money. With the question as to how far this hour would be compensated in terms of participants being paid, which anyway can only be a symbolic payment.

Janine
But also how this can be made transparent and appreciated, instead of us becoming neglectful proponents of precarity. Sorry I am speaking like this, I don't know why. Possibly because it is a Monday—it's something about trying to recognize what it is we are doing presently.

Acknowledgement

This exercise was developed in Tower Hamlets, London, 2013, during a Hidden Curriculum workshop with Krauss and students from St Paul's Way Trust School including Murad Mohammed Ahmed, Nozir Ali, Sayidul Alum, Rukshana Bhanu, Jaber Chowdhury, Opeyemi Fakunie, Sayeeda Firdaus, and Aniqua Islam.

2.2
ASSEMBLY

UNLEARNING EXERCISE
The general team meeting for discussion and planning of the future program takes place at home if possible, with meals and time for conversation.

WHAT TO UNLEARN
Lack of common understanding of programming and planning, and top-down programming or programming led by one person.

Note
The scope and scale of assembly has been extended beyond the team to be inclusive of all interested publics. This way we also experiment with the convention of membership towards temporary yet committed participation. The function of the assembly changed, becoming a reflexive moment for commoning institutions that set a broader collective agenda and action plan, including the formation of a collective pot and its use and distribution.

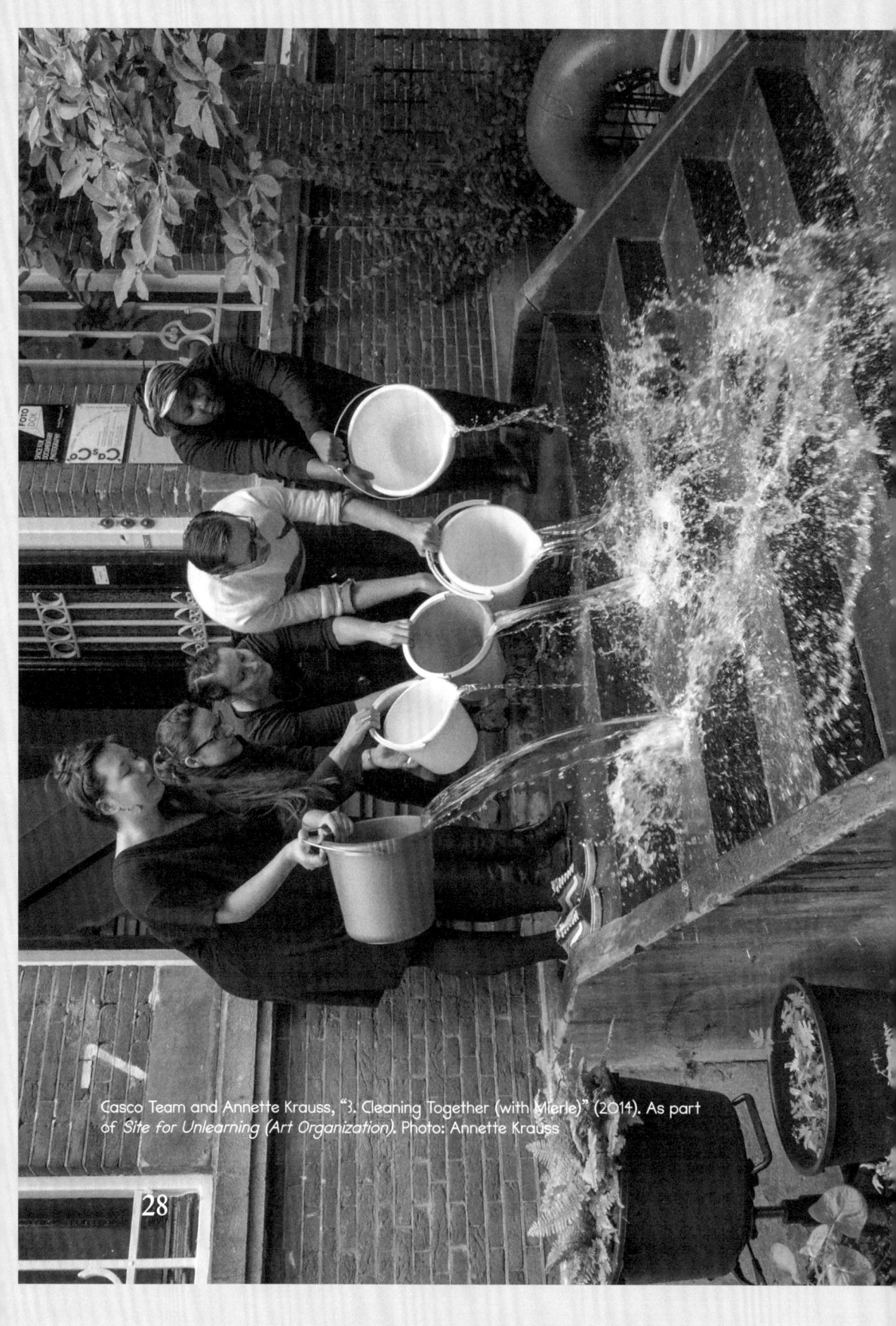

Casco Team and Annette Krauss, "3. Cleaning Together (with Mierle)" (2014). As part of *Site for Unlearning (Art Organization)*. Photo: Annette Krauss

3.
CLEANING
TOGETHER

UNLEARNING EXERCISE
We clean our office together every Monday morning after the team meeting. We divide the tasks, put on music (sometimes), and set the timer for around thirty minutes. It's important to begin cleaning together and feel we are collectively responsible.

WHAT TO UNLEARN
Undervaluing reproductive labor; hierarchies and un-equal division of domestic labor in terms of who does what; and making reproductive labor the last priority and not finding any satisfaction in it.

Transcript (excerpt)

6 October 2014: Annette, Binna, Björn, Ester, Jason, Lara, Sanne, Suzanne, Ying, and Yolande.

Ying
So, we have cleaned collectively a few times, because we would like to unlearn undervaluing reproductive labor. Through collective cleaning, do we try to revalue it? How has it worked?

Ester
It hasn't. I already value cleaning a lot, so it didn't change anything for me.

Suzanne
Well, for me I think I value that we did it collectively. It was a team effort.

Lara
It depends. Okay, as an intern, I clean when you do the important stuff. That's when this labor starts to make no sense to me. I think it's a really powerful thing to do this together.

Ying
That points to the collective aspect of it, which is crucial to revaluing it. I agree that maybe, individually, I feel the same about cleaning as a job, or cleaning in general. But doing it collectively does something to the implications of the work of cleaning within an institution.

Yolande
Yeah, I also think we are forgetting that. We're trying to think about the things that we internalize, because even if I value cleaning as an activity, I still make it a last priority.

3.1
DIGITAL
CLEANING

UNLEARNING EXERCISE

We exchange with designers, researchers, and accountants whose occupations involve digital maintenance. Alongside this we develop our own method and habit of organizing and cleaning digital files on our desktops, laptops, and in our archives, allocating time for digital cleaning as part of our weekly cleaning and visualizing this activity toward common recognition and validation of cleaning.

WHAT TO UNLEARN

Sticking to physical cleaning as a recurring metaphor for reproductive labor, for instance, by extending it to include the maintenance of digital files in computers and other digital archives, and beyond (see 3.2 Rewriting Maintenance Manifesto).

Transcript (excerpt)
23 March 2015: Annette, Binna, Carlijn, Jason, Sanne, Simone, Suzanne, Ying, and Yolande.

Yolande
I think we all define cleaning in different ways. Cleaning and maintaining the space, and here I mean maintaining the physical space, is the most visible and obvious thing, of course. But there's other work that I would also deem cleaning work that happens behind glowing computer screens. This is invisible labor and falls under maintenance work as well.

Annette Krauss, *Digital Cleaning* (2015). Collage-drawing

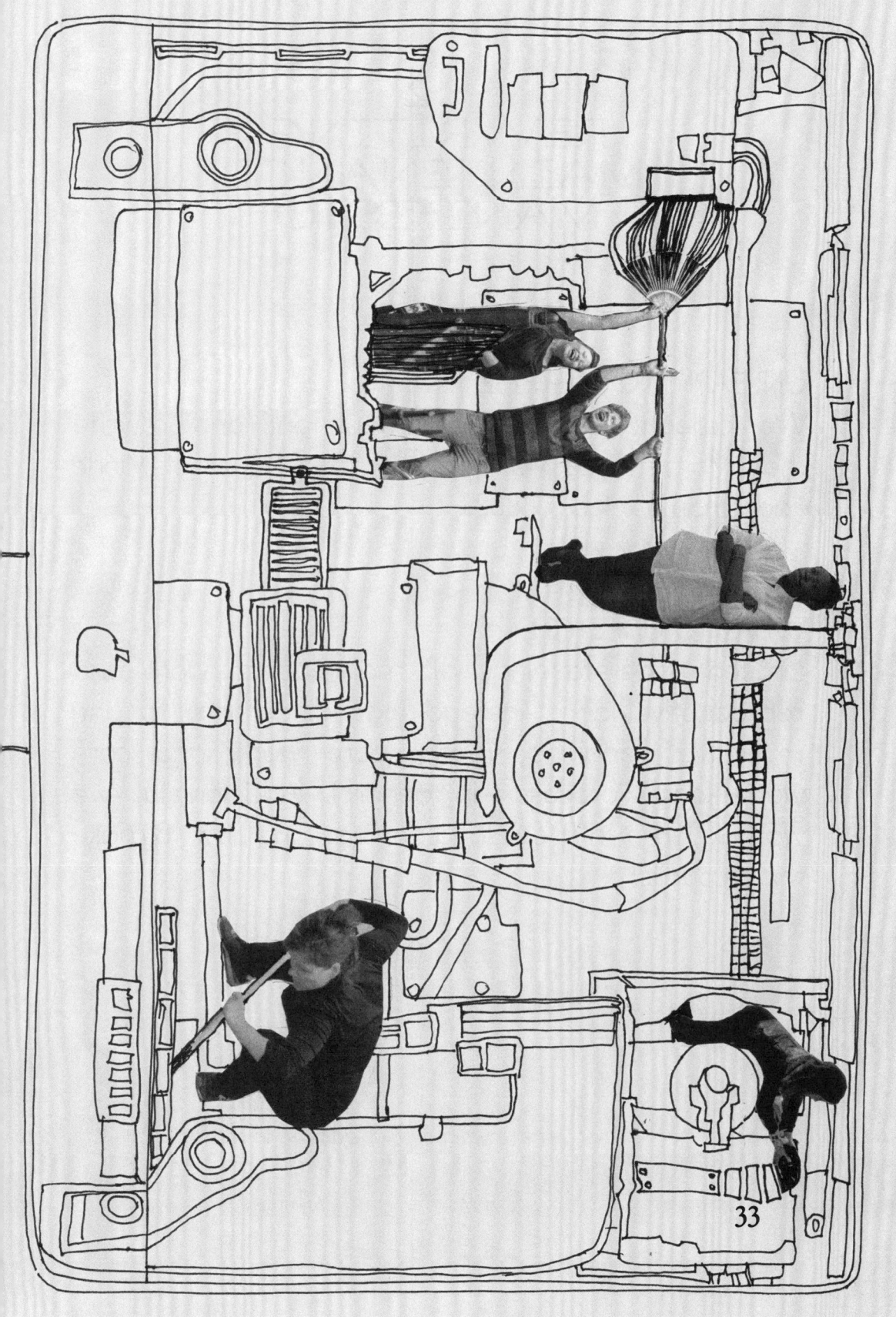

33

3.2
REWRITING
MAINTENANCE
MANIFESTO

UNLEARNING EXERCISE
We collectively read, comment on, and rewrite the "Maintenance Manifesto" written by artist Mierle Laderman Ukeles in 1969.

WHAT TO UNLEARN
Limited understandings of maintenance work and reproductive labor, instead extending them to any repetitive, repairing, fixing, care work, and care work—and "process" in general. Additionally, we want to learn to speak loud and far, and how to make things public!

MAINTENANCE ART

Proposal for an exhibition

MIERLE LADERMAN UKELES

© 1969

[handwritten:] MANIFESTO!

[handwritten:] director carbs
[handwritten:] who goes to the execution?
[handwritten:] "CARE" vs. PROCESS ORIENTED MALE: FLUXUS SITUATIONISTS "MALE" GARDE-ARTISTS AVANT-GARDISTS

IDEAS

I.

A. The Death Instinct and the Life Instinct:
The Death Instinct: separation; individuality; Avant-Garde par excellence; to follow one's own path to death—do your own thing; dynamic change. *[handwritten: Devour]*
The Life Instinct: unification; the eternal return; the perpetuation and MAINTENANCE of the species; survival systems and operations; equilibrium. *[handwritten: Mother / the]*

[handwritten:] Freud Lacan Psychoanalysis

B. Two basic systems: Development and Maintenance. The sourball of every revolution: after the revolution, who's going to pick up the garbage on Monday morning?
[handwritten: AVANT GARDISTS ARE RIGHT:]
Development: pure individual creation; the new; change; progress; advance; excitement; flight or fleeing.
[handwritten: IN ORDER TO ACHIEVE THIS WE NEED TO:]
Maintenance: keep the dust off the pure individual creation; preserve the new; sustain the change; protect progress; defend and prolong the advance; renew the excitement; repeat the flight;

[handwritten: WHEN DOES OUR GARBAGE GET PICKED UP?]

C. Maintenance is a drag; it
The mind boggles and
The culture confers lo
minimum wages, hous

clean your/desk, wash
wash your clothes, wa
diaper, finish the repo
fence, keep the custom
garbage, watch out do
shall I wear, I have no
litter, save string, was
go to the store, I'm out
he doesn't understand
work, this art is dusty,
flush the toilet, stay yo

[handwritten:] do your emails / clean your desktop / do your "likes" / keep track on your # / wash your clothes / finish the report finish / the application / do the reading / water the plants (water the reading / have you done your reading) be a good host / connect with

[handwritten:] reproductive labor

D. Everything I say is Art is
Art is Art. "We have no
well." (Balinese saying

Avant-garde art, which ch
by strains of mainten
and maintenance ma
Conceptual & Process art
and change, yet emp

[right column top:]
show your work—sh
keep the contempor
keep the home fires

Development systems a
room for change.
Maintenance systems a
room for alteration.

E. The exhibition of Mainte
on pure maintenance, exh
yield, by utter opposition,

[handwritten:] Silvia Federici: unpaid work

[handwritten:] domestic space

[handwritten:] she's addressing an art audience.

4.
READING
TOGETHER

UNLEARNING EXERCISE
Whenever a text appears relevant to our common interest, we propose to read it together in a meeting. We each read sections aloud until it is finished, and then discuss and/or analyze the content.

WHAT TO UNLEARN
Individualized research and the division of labor by intellectuals or non-intellectuals in order to practice studying together.

References

We have been reading: Marina Vishmidt's "All Shall Be Unicorns: About Commons, Aesthetics and Time" (2014); Manuela Zechner's "Barcelona en Comú: the city as horizon for radical democracy" (2015); Mierle Laderman Ukeles' "Manifesto for Maintenance Art, 1969!" (1969); Manuela Zechner's "A Politics of Network-families?" and "Care Network Exercise" from the *Nanopolitics Handbook* (2013); Sara Danius, Stefan Jonsson and Gayatri Chakravorty Spivak's "An Interview with Gayatri Chakravorty Spivak" (1993); Donna Haraway's "Situated Knowledges: The Science Question in Feminism and the Privilege of Partial Perspective" (1988); and J. K. Gibson-Graham's "Take Back Work: Surviving Well" in *Take Back the Economy* (2013). Full references with publication details are available in the bibliography at the end of this book.

Note

Furthermore, reading aloud is a gentle way of getting to know each other's differences (accents, pace, rhythm) and moving in the direction of negotiation and mutual learning processes.

5.
CARE
NETWORK*

UNLEARNING EXERCISE
We map the care relations that hold our group together.
What kind of relating and interactions can we identify
as care relations? To whom and to what are we related
in terms of care in our working environment?

WHAT TO UNLEARN
Understanding the team as just a functional body
or a combination of different functions; the notion
of objective, not affective, working relations; and independence within the idea of professionalism.

* Care Network is inspired by Paolo Plotegher et al. *Nanopolitics Handbook:
The Nanopolitics Group* (2013).

Transcript (excerpt)

20 October 2014: Annette, Binna, Björn, Jason, Lara, Sanne, Suzanne, and Ying.

Suzanne
But then I'm also wondering what care relations are in our office. For instance, is baking a cake for someone's birthday, sitting down, eating it, having a chat, etc., the same as collectively cleaning the office? We clean it collectively because we want to give it value together. But, at the same time, it's also some-thing you do for the space, for the institution, while these other small things don't feel that way, because they're not necessarily jobs.

Ying
I don't really agree, because the intention of cleaning together is also to share the burden, which wasn't shared in the beginning.

Binna
It is interesting to consider why we need to differentiate care relations from domestic labor, or if we can think of them together.

Sanne
...maybe, for me, they relate to one another because both are often undervalued.

Annette
Can we connect these to bigger structures and the hierarchies that might then come in? Take care relations. Does it eventually become obvious that the same person is always doing this work? At home, for example, who takes care of the relations? If you look into heterosexual relationships, the women are very often the ones who take time to take care of the relations: talking to the relatives, friends, neighbors. Kind of maintaining a social life. The devaluing comes in when women are stereotyped as chatty when they are sustaining relations. It's a vicious circle...

5.1
MOOD COLOR

UNLEARNING EXERCISE
At the beginning of a week or a day, we pick a color or a few out of a set we think represent(s) our current state of mind and feeling. We create a moment in which to discuss why people have chosen which colors. You can choose to share your motivation or not. This helps us to address the affective climate in the team as well as open up ways to support each other if someone asks for that.

WHAT TO UNLEARN
Holding on to negative feelings individually or not voicing unspoken tensions within the group; the inability to share or discuss; and the idea that the workplace is no space for emotions.

Transcript (excerpt)

6 February 2017: Anne, Annette, Binna, Judith, Niek, Suzanne, and Yolande.

Anne
Shouldn't we delete the mood color exercise? It seems to lack a certain depth.

Suzanne
It was never functional; we never actually did it.

Yolande
We did it a few times.

Suzanne
No, come on.

Binna
If the subject is still relevant isn't it better to leave it in and say that we didn't manage, rather than take it out.

Suzanne
The reason we didn't follow it through is that there was way too much discussion before the staff meeting, "Oh, I feel like orange." "Oh, that's not good." "No, it's good to me!" "Orange is not good to me." "Why do you feel that way?" "I don't want to talk about it." "Oh, but I do." [*Laughter.*]

Niek
Seriously.

Binna
Maybe we should think of Melanie Gilligan's [2014, sci-fi mini series] work that Casco produced, *The Common Sense*, in order to introduce emotions that we know how to read.

Annette
Are we missing a certain way of coding the colors, then?

Yolande
Only as part of the discussion. For me, the discussion is more important than the code. [...] The strength of this exercise is that it allows for ambiguity and addresses tensions, or a certain kind of vibe in the room.

Suzanne
It would be good if the ongoing tension between the personal interpretation of colors and the creation of a framework became clear.

Binna
This exercise is difficult because
there is an institutional culture that
doesn't really allow us to think or
facilitate these vibes and emotions
in the room.

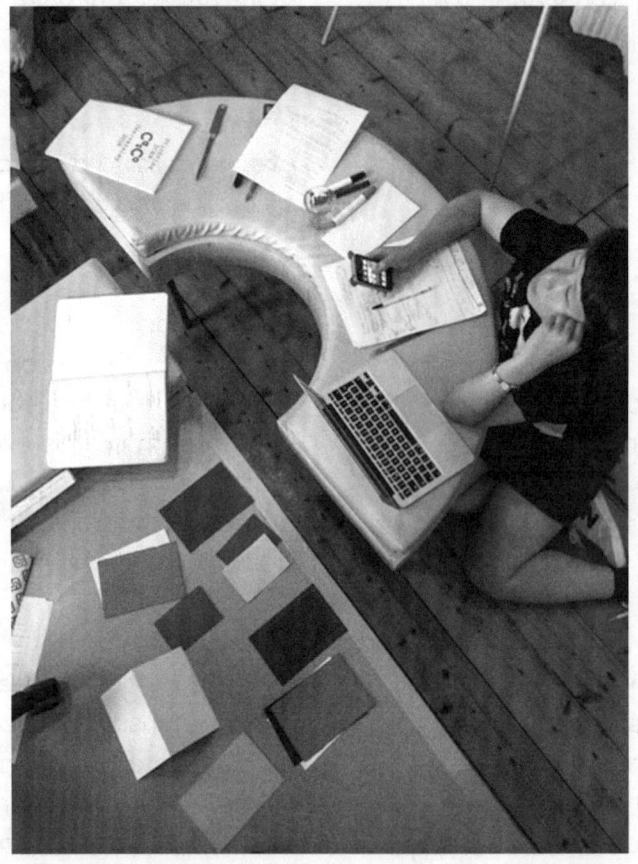

Unlearning meeting: practicing "5.1 Mood Color." As part of *Site for Unlearning (Art Organization)*,
Casco Art Institute, Utrecht, 2015. Photo: Casco Art Institute archive

6.
PROPERTY
RELATIONS

UNLEARNING EXERCISE

We identify things we own—from electronics to intangible capital and possible heritage. We elaborate on the ways these have become our property and how they are entangled with our relationships to objects and work vis-à-vis security, care, and solidarity. Concretely, we rethink the wage system and employment contract that, as a given, binds our work to duty, and move toward the possibility of material commons.

WHAT TO UNLEARN

Focusing only on an affective approach to the commons, weakness in political economic thinking, and unlearn invisiblizing the material condition of our work.

Transcript (excerpt)
26 February 2015:
Annette, Binna, Carlijn, Ester,
Jason, Sanne, Suzanne, and Ying.

Ester
Uh, for me it doesn't make
sense to look into property.
I understand property literally
as what you own in a materialistic
way. Personally, what would
it matter for commons and
unlearning? I can't understand.
What would it matter that I
have a bike and twenty books.

Sanne
We are not only looking into
what we have, but how we got
these things—things we pay for,
are still paying for, and things
that we haven't paid for but
nevertheless have. For instance,
things you have or own through
partnership, bought, inherited,
stole, and got as a present...

Jason
It's not about you having a bike,
three plates, and a boyfriend.
What we try to get at is that
property is not about material
things in the first place. It's the
rules that govern our relationship
with objects and people. So

immediately this became essential
to understanding the rules by
which we relate to each other.

Ying
Phew, it's so much about language
as well. It's a narrative that you
start to believe in, so you need to
focus on what kinds of narratives
exist. I'm not sure how we can
practically change something in
a physical space when it comes
to property relations because I
imagine you can change narratives
about it and get a different
perspective on it, but I don't see
a way of actually doing it yet.

6.1
WORK AND
WELL-BEING

UNLEARNING EXERCISE
We try to recognize how "diverse forms of work contribute to our individual well-being, and [...] impact on the well-being of our planet."* We do this as a way to study our own work within the wage structure. We have checked and scored our ecological footprints against J. K. Gibson-Graham's five categories for well-being (material, occupational, social, community, and physical), rating each on a scale from poor to excellent.

WHAT TO UNLEARN?
Capitalist understandings of waged labor starting from the cultural sector and moving beyond; the exclusion of well-being; tensions between paid work, "duty work," and "joyful or desirable work"; and the evasion of cross-training.*

*From Chapter 2, "Take Back Work:
 Surviving Well," in J. K. Gibson-Graham et al.,
 Take Back the Economy (2013).

Transcript (excerpt)

8 January 2016:
Annette, Binna, Ika, Steyn,
Suzanne, Ying, and Yolande.

Ying
So, if sufficient in the scorecard
means I have everything I need,
then how is that not excellent?

Binna
It's not excellent because I
don't know the currency rate
or how it will fluctuate. I only
have basic insurance. I don't
own a house (I rent). My living
situation depends on market
change, which is immensely
fluctuating and unreliable. So
I don't know, with the money
I have, what it means for the
future.

Steyn
I also didn't put excellent there.
I wasn't thinking of the future,
but more about this comparison
that forces itself upon you.
My wage is fine and I'm happy
with it. I basically have all I need
and want, but societally speaking
it's not an excellent wage.

Ying
But it's about your individual
well-being, this is what we're
trying to grade here.

Binna
But that's really curious. I worry
a bit about your short term
thinking and how easily you get
satisfied and disappointed.

Annette,
The comparison between wage
and well-being could also be seen
differently. Silvia Federici says that
in the 1970s they were all working
for three days per week and the
rest was activist work, and it was
perfectly fine. How come?

Yolande
I'd identify this as not worrying,
that is, if push comes to shove
your parents would step in. That's
how I would define luxury.

Annette
You point to most of our middle-
class upbringings!

Ika
My mother is rich, but if she
stepped in financially it means I
have to say yes to certain things.

Ying

What is missing in general is a strong support network, community, or social network whereby, if you go down the drain, you have people you can count on because you did enough labor, you did enough for the community. I know that if I ever get screwed over I have a group of people that will help me out.

Binna

So, when you put excellent on the scale then you do still consider some idea of security. Well-being is always about a future too.

Note

Most of the employees at Casco Art Institute are waged workers, thereby seemingly inevitably subjected to the capitalist wage labor system. Most perform different types of paid and unpaid labor for the institution. Some argue that cultural workers' jobs and lives are inseparable and so while our work is potentially great, it is also potentially self-exploitative. Could Casco Art Institute handle income differently to the productivist-driven economy? If we allowed for a different understanding and practice of work and well-being could our organizational structure change?

WELL-BEING SCORECARD*

INDIVIDUAL	1 poor	2 sufficient	3 excellent
Material			
Occupational			
Social			
Community			
Physical			

47

| PLANETARY | 1 | 2 | 3 |

6.2
(COLLECTIVE)
AUTHORSHIP

UNLEARNING EXERCISE

In our work we repeatedly make acknowledgements, credits, and colophons more thorough. We unpack the politics of citation. We study the "we" in working processes and discuss its shifting roles. We identify mechanisms that lead to authorship in (institutional) working processes by asking which work is authored, which isn't, and why? And at what point does a process move from reproductive to authorial labor, and vice versa.

WHAT TO UNLEARN

The fixed and conditioned notions of invisibilizing, hierarchical, and individualized authorship as a driving force in current knowledge economies; instead we strive for collective authorship as a common(ing) gesture through collaborative embodiments (like Nina bell F.) and inclusive forms of attribution.

Transcript (excerpt)
17 and 31 October 2016:
Anne, Annette, Binna, Niek,
Suzanne, Staci, Whitney, and
Yolande.

Whitney
This binary differentiation of
single and collective authorship
is a false binary. It will not lead
to transformative change.

Annette
Still, how can collective authorship
become a political gesture? How
do we politicize the process?

Yolande
Let me play devil's advocate.
In her editing Janine [Armin] is
careful not to spill over into an
authorial position as a firm
rule because she cannot take
responsibility for the ideas.
Those borders are helpful, right?

Annette
Certainly! And vice versa for
the importance of recognizing
project spillovers. While Nina
emerged through the working
group, she/they will take on a
life of her/their own that will not
necessarily be connected to
unlearning.

Suzanne
I understand this empowerment
spill-over is about indirect
outcomes, but I'm still unsure
how it connects with authorship.

Staci
It's another form of
acknowledgement, that of
process and the group's
importance. Nina is just one
example.

Binna
Who is Nina bell? Do I belong
to Nina bell or not? I find
these questions very productive
as a means to think of what an
institution is and does.

Annette
She/they challenge the
attribution of authorship in art
contexts, which is an institutional
habit that we perform.

Yolande
Can we list ethical principles
for collective authorship?
For me, it's being open to new
members.

Staci
Always incomplete.

Yolande
Would that be an openness determined by collective study?

Binna
So study and change? Study for change?

Note
The figure of Nina bell Federici (Nina bell F.) stems from our admiration for Nina Simone, bell hooks, and Silvia Federici and their artistic, black, feminist, and political engagements. Her/their collective persona inspires *Site for Unlearning (Art Organization)* to move beyond the (institutional) frameworks of Casco Art Institute and artist Annette Krauss.

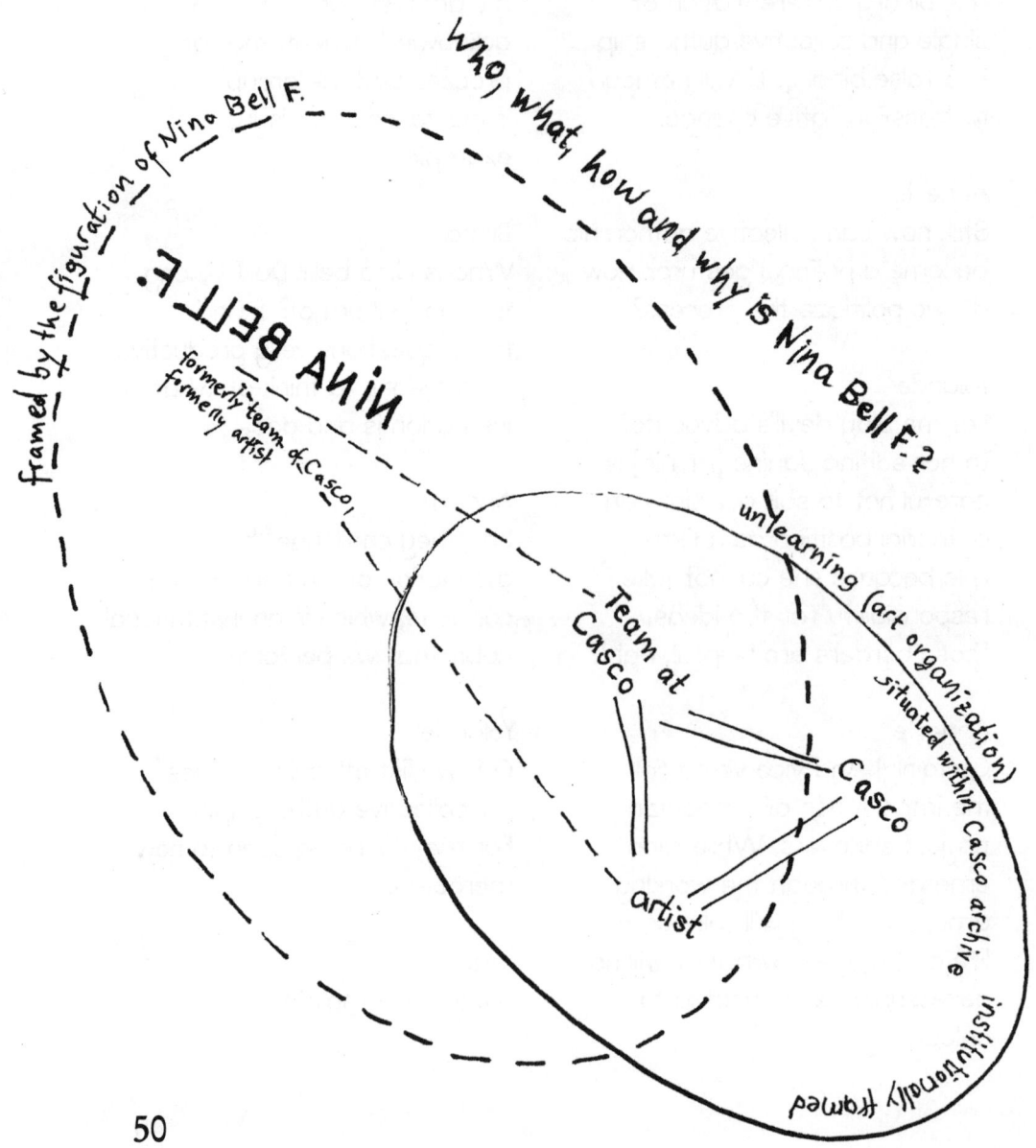

7.
TIME DIARY

UNLEARNING EXERCISE
For a limited period (a few days to a few weeks), every team member makes a record of their day beyond set working hours by noting down what they are doing from time to time. Together we try to distinguish categories; invisible, care, productive, communicative, and "intellectual" for different activities and analyze this by identifying our working habits, breaking down logics of efficiency and productivity, and recognizing other values. We also read aloud together, revaluing our day-to-day activities, especially with respect to what are normally considered unproductive moments, as a means to arrive somewhere else.

WHAT TO UNLEARN
Ways of dealing with time and planning based on logics of efficiency and productivity while undervaluing, or even attempting to kill reproductive time; entanglement between no time, busyness, and business; and struggles with different ways of working and rhythms.

Transcript (excerpt)

16 March 2015:
Annette, Binna, Carlijn, Jason, Sanne, Simone, Suzanne, Ying, and Yolande.

Binna

So we documented what we do every day for two weeks. I think what we enjoyed in common was appreciating each step of the working process, realizing that reproductive dimensions are constantly generated within the productivity regime. You get annoyed when something goes wrong and you have to fix it—that's reproduction. If we are able to appreciate this reproductive labor as part of the process, part of what do, we may feel happier, have less frustration.

Ying

Politically, I am not so sure. Still, it made sense to formalize cleaning. But does it make sense to formalize these other things? Or does it take away their value? Not to forget the control issue.

Annette

It's about abusing this form of tracking or not, no?

Note

There's some fear attached to sharing this diary. In fact, it could be considered a general exercise/method used in big institutions and companies to control their workers and make them more efficient. It's important to articulate again and again the purpose of writing this diary. There's no fundamental necessity to share them, though this allows for the recognition of differences and collective analysis of the personal as the political. We are also looking for a more affective and easy way of doing and sharing this diary.

ACTION	CONTEXT	Self	Friends	Family	Team	Community
Getting ready						
Care						
Cleaning						
Laundry						
Grocery shopping						
Cooking						
Fixing						
Transition btw. places						
Execution						
Deviation						
Daydream						
Shopping						
Eating						
Physical Exercise						
Break						
Networking						
Meeting						
E-mail						
Telephone						
Hosting						
Lobbying						
Writing						
Performance						
Planning						
Infrastructure						
Logistics						
Coordination						
Study						
Research						
Reading						
Report						
Fundraising						
Application						
Designing						
Administration						
Archiving						
TOTAL TIME - CONTEXT					53	
of which combined time: (done at the same time)						

8.
PASSION
AND OBSTACLE

UNLEARNING EXERCISE
Each of us writes down their passions for what they do around the workplace and obstacles that hinder that passion. Afterward, we find links between the different passions and obstacles to deepen our analysis (time was a common obstacle). We are aware that every obstacle could become a passion, and every passion an obstacle.

WHAT TO UNLEARN
Work because of "duty" (externally given); doing without awareness of purpose; and opposition between passion and obstacle. Through this unlearning, we learn to focus, make choices, and carefully discern between things, and intensify or concentrate instead of simply accelerating for the sake of doing many things.

Transcript (excerpt)

11 May 2015:
Annette, Binna, Carlijn, Ika,
Jason, Sanne, Staci, Suzanne,
Ying, and Yolande.

Suzanne
I think working together is maybe
number one for me with exhibition
making, because that's what we
do together and that's the main
thing, as well as mentoring interns.
I think I really like to do that. And
the hindrance: the life/work divide,
which still feels like a struggle. I've
found a good way to deal with it,
but it does come up often. How to
manage different schedules and
demands—family and work. And
time management, for sure. A lot
of small, little tasks that I see as
a huge hindrance to the things that
I think need my attention. But that's
like a basic hindrance in life, no?

Annette
Of course everyday life seems
like a big obstacle. At the same
time I'm completely fascinated,
maybe because I wonder, "How
can it be such an obstacle?!"
Of course, part of it is the time
issue again. But it is also about
positionality. And what's my own
position in that and how can

I shape it? This relates again to
the moment of working together,
sharing. Maybe shaping is the
desire, the passion for shaping
a situation, shaping a position. The
desire for shaping a position that
works with these other desires.

Note
This exercise was applied in an Arts
Collaboratory Assembly in Senegal, April
2015 as part of the process of building
a common future for the network.

TOILET (T)ISSUES #1

Toilet Tissue and Other Formless Organizational Matters

A public conversation on how commons-orientated organizations work in the field of art, culture, and social practices across Indonesia, the Netherlands, and England. In discussing the benefits and challenges of working collectively, participants find themselves addressing the unrecognized reproductive work found in practical organizational matters, such as who purchases the toilet paper.

Participants include: Antariksa, Syafiatudina, and Ferdiansyah Thajib (members of KUNCI Study Forum & Collective, Yogyakarta), Emily Pethick (then the director at The Showroom, London, an exhibition space and collaborative program; currently director at Rijksakademie, Amsterdam), and Binna Choi (director at Casco Art Institute, Utrecht). The conversation was held on January 31, 2015 at KUNCI Study Forum & Collective.

Syafiatudina (Dina)

In Indonesia, OTB [Organisasi Tanpa Bentuk, or organizations without a form] was a term used by the government during the Suharto regime as a name for a group of people who were conducting illegal or illicit activities related to Communism or other forbidden ideologies. These groups were un-registered, so they didn't have a legal status. From the late 1990s to 2000s, many art (and other) organizations started registering themselves as legal organizations and adapted formal structures, such as a director, a manager, an accountant, and a board as required by the government. We have been talking about how these positions or job titles affect how these collectives or groups of people operate—that's also what we decided to name this conversation. Before, it was quite horizontal, everyone chipped in in a way that they believed in and contributed however they could. But after the legalization process what has changed, and what is still happening? For example, Antariksa mentioned the expression *hanya di atas kertas*, or "only on paper." On paper there is a director and there is a manager, but in the reality of daily practice the structures are still collective and fluid. But is this really fluid? There is a tension between structure and non-structure in organizations.

Binna

Over the last week, we've visited and been having conversations at various organizations including Forum Lenteng [a group of artists and researchers who work on media, art, and community development] and ruangrupa [an artists' initiative with a focus on urban issues and collaborative projects] in Jakarta, Lifepatch [a citizen initiative in art, science, and technology] and Teater Garasi [a theatre group who focus on performance studies and culture] in Yogyakarta, and KUNCI, of course. The focus of our conversations has been on "how" they are organizing in terms of their organizational structure, physical space, finance, and process of working while they are programming. The usual approach to understanding an organization is to hear about the program as the visible result.

Instead, we aimed to gain in-sight into shifting organizational structures, the economy, relations, and conflicts within these parts and how this conflict interacts with their programming. I think this interest comes from various experiences and

58

one, which Emily mentioned, is the Cluster network which is a network of eight visual art organizations ranging from a museum just outside of Madrid, to spaces like Casco, Tensta Konsthall (Sweden), and the Israeli Centre for Digital Arts in Holon. We all operate quite differently from other museum practices and most of us are located in residential areas and on the "periphery," so we started asking how we are different, what are we actually doing differently from others, and what are our values?

Emily

One of the things we did as Cluster was to visit each other to get to know each other's work, which included walking around each other's neighborhoods, as well as understanding what was inside the organizations and looking at how each is constituted through the relations with our environments and what this can produce in terms of an organizational environment.

Binna

One of the commonalities amongst the situations of these organizations is what you might call "community works": that they are working with a community of concern and community, or a place nearby, is a very important factor. This kind of practice, although it could be easily co-opted, is something that is not always valued by the cultural policies of the countries in Europe where we are, and that's part of the thing that brought us together in 2008 when the global financial crisis that affected many countries in Europe had a knock-on effect of funding cuts. Organizations like us are the best target of those cuts because we are in between art and social practice, our identities in terms of "art" aren't clear. So, by working together we not only secured certain financial supports for our programs, but our positions in the field as well. The Showroom and Casco informally became sister organizations, sharing practices.

In speaking about that shared history, and although we never labeled this as such, feminism is a very important struggle, theory, and practice that shapes us and our work, and relates to this interest in organizational matters. One could compare an organization to a house and a household, where mostly mothers are still in charge and there are "jobs" that are rarely made visible and not considered to be public work, just something that enables public work. The gap could

be even more intense in our type of practice. So, I think another reason for this investigation is to have a feminist reading and validation of the work that we do, one that goes against the capitalist mode of validation. But when we were at Bumi Pemuda Rahayu [a learning center for environmental sustainability in Yogyakarta] two days ago, there was a sense that we'd better not talk about "capitalism."

Antariksa

More or less, yes. I think most people there didn't really want to talk about capitalism in an abstract way.

Binna

But I have to say, I think capitalism—being patriarchal in its nature—is really infiltrating everywhere, so we are really thinking and acting through its idiom. The tendency to only see and think of the product belongs to that idiom. If our organizations are working for an alternative to such rules of capitalism then I think it's important to speak of the language and mode of our organizational practice, I would say, as part of anti-capitalist struggles. That's why we have begun this research and the series of meetings

at various organizations last week, which were very inspiring!

Ferdianyah Thajib (Ferdi)

What interested me from our last conversation is when you asked us how we do our daily conduct, and also when you shared what happens in your own organizational practice. A lot of it had affective aspects to it and these are unaccountable—almost unaccountable. This kind of investment, friendship, and passion for work and producing what we are producing is something that is not actually valued by funding bodies. We are actually creating values not just among ourselves as organizations, but also with the communities that we are engaging with. But we always seem to fail to translate that into quantitative terms. I don't know how Hafiz would do it when he wants to approach policy or if any structure would be able to value these other kinds of immaterial values.

Emily

In fact, for the "Common Practice" conference we are holding next week, we will shift our focus from value to values, and how to hold these at the center of our work. [Common Practice is an advocacy group working for the recognition and

fostering of the small-scale contemporary visual arts sector in London.] This is something that links the three organizations represented here today. We are all working with very diverse communities, but it's happening in an intimate way through long-term engagements, which is difficult work to assign a value to. The communities range from the Researchers' Affects team who are in residence here [at KUNCI] this week, students that come here and engage with the organization, and the communities who you work with in the *kampungs* [a word for both urban and rural villages in Indonesian and Malay languages].

It's the same with The Showroom. On one hand we are bringing in academics, hosting PhD research groups and holding theoretical discussions. On the other hand we also work with artists, students, and with a wide range of local groups. Then we are also part of networks such as Cluster and Common Practice. These are all different communities that we are closely engaged with in ways that are long-term and open-ended. Once we have finished a project we often don't just move on. Once a relationship is formed, you can actually do more because you trust each other, you have a friendship, you can understand each other's needs and desires and where something productive can take place.

Binna
Lifepatch is another example to consider. Everyone in the group has particular skills that they bring, and it's not like one person is in charge of PR and the other of fundraising, but everyone is doing something in relation to a project and bringing their respective knowledge into what they do. The same goes for KUNCI. You went through this structural change where you decided to call everyone a member. ruangrupa, who now has more than thirty-five members, just went through restructuring. Before, they had a somewhat abstract, conceptual division of their work, such as their "Research and Development Division." Now they've gotten rid of this kind of division and structured the whole team around projects with a "coordinator" for each project, while they still keep the directorship and the board "on paper." All of these changes show how professionalization or standardization is the way of truth, and how informality that is inclusive of the affective aspect of an

organization is an important value to protect. And besides the articulation of these values, I think we should also work in common, let's say "organizing" ourselves as organizations, working together within the organizations.

Dina
I will reflect on my experience at KUNCI. Two years ago, Ferdi proposed to either make us all directors or make us all members, and the response was that we should all be members and that everyone would be responsible for a project. So, for this project I will be the project officer and someone will be the researcher, and on another project Antariksa will be the project officer and I will help, maybe as a researcher. I think this shift is an example of working collaboratively or "in commons" where everyone supports each other. But in this very loose term of member there are not really clear divisions for the job of how to run the space. For example, we are all members but does it mean we are all responsible for replacing the toilet tissue when it runs out? Or is everyone responsible for buying Cepha's [KUNCI's dog] food when it runs out? It's already empty!

Ferdi
It's your responsibility, Dina! [*Laughter.*]

Dina
No, it's Wok's.

Antariksa
Yes, it's in your contract Dina. [*Laughter.*]

Dina
And then as I contemplate this responsibility while I am in the supermarket buying toilet tissue, I wonder what it would be like if we had someone specifically in charge of buying toilet tissue, buying Cephas' food, and checking that we still have water. We have a finance manager who pays the electricity and the internet bill, but if we had a person in charge of small errands for the domestic work, would I, as an intellectual, write more? Would I produce better quality projects because I have more time to think? Because I worry that if I start to think this way, then I will start to downsize the quality or potential of domestic work or "mothers" work for more engaging "masculine" intellectual work. Now, I am interested in working with the mothers of this neighborhood, but

how will I approach the mothers if I see domestic work as a burden to my intellectual life? Maybe this is something outside of our conversation but I know that I'm not alone. For example, Lifepatch is a collective but they are also living together. How does this separation work between who produces the idea and who enables the production of this idea to come about? Is it being separated or not? To give another example, MES 56 [a cooperative space for art in Yogyakarta] also has a manager.

Wok the Rock (Wok)
I feel guilty now. [Wok lives at KUNCI] I feel like a parasite here. I don't buy toilet paper, I don't buy water, I just live here. I only pay rent and maybe lock the door at night, because I have to take care of another collective [MES 56].

Binna.
And are you buying toilet paper for them?

Wok
Yeah!

Dina
We are in the same position for different spaces. I don't know if anyone wants to talk more about who produces the intellectual property and who enables this intellectual property to be produced by doing the domestic work in these sorts of organizations?

Edwina
This reminds me of my time in public institutions in Australia. On one of my first days interning as a nineteen year old in Sydney I was so petrified and nervous, and I was standing in the staff kitchen where there were all these dirty plates, and I thought I would be a good little intern and stack the dishwasher, this fancy pull-out dishwasher. So, I asked this really hard-nosed curator how to turn it on and she glared at me and replied, "Can't you ask somebody else who actually has time!" The next person to come into the kitchen was actually the cleaning lady, so I asked her and she said, "Oh, you don't need to worry about that, but you just press this button under here." So it was one button, but this curator didn't have that time. I thought afterwards that it was probably also code for the cranky curator not actually knowing how to turn the dishwasher on.

I think it's interesting once you get deeper into those big institutions

because you realize that no one actually knows what they are working for. There isn't a common vision. So, I really like what you said, Binna, about using the organizational structure to also define your values as an organization and what you are actually working for. That's really the worry of big institutions; nobody knows how their cogs fit together anymore.

Binna
Actually, at Casco we have recently started cleaning together and the picture we put on Facebook for this event is a photograph documenting our second session. Somewhere in the *Grand Domestic Revolution Handbook* is the reference to artist Mierle Laderman Ukeles' *Maintenance Manifesto*, from which we took our idea for the picture.

She cleaned in front of museums as a series of performances and wrote a manifesto for maintenance art where she contrasts maintenance with development. Whereas Ukeles did this cleaning performance alone, at Casco we did it together. And it was not only a symbolic represent-ation: we'd had exactly that same dilemma about who is cleaning and who is not. For example, two staff members had sarcastically signed off an email to the rest of the team with, "Thank you, Your Lovely Housewives." While we are working with domestic workers in the Netherlands, many of whom come from Indonesia, it is in fact a global structural problem that we can find in all our own houses, and organizations as well. Hence, we decided to clean our office every Monday all together after our regular general team meeting. At first, we cleaned for an hour or even more. Now, as we do it every Monday it doesn't take as long, and we set a rule not to clean for longer than thirty minutes. It's manageable and it also brings a kind of physical relation to our space, so we feel more "ownership" I guess, to use an economic term.

Emily
The Showroom also works with a domestic workers union in London (Justice for Domestic Workers), who lobby around immigration issues. One of the domestic workers told me about how a politician had complained to her about unskilled labor in relation to immigration. Upset by the comment, the worker responded that their work was highly skilled: "We can cook, we can clean, we can look after children, we can

organize." They are campaigning for a different kind of value in order to shift the social perception of their work. I think that's something that one can keep in one's own consciousness in relation to what is a valuable use of time. Some of the work that is more about caring for things, like feeding the dog, is important to what this organization is and does.

Antariksa

I have to admit that KUNCI wasn't designed as a modern organization. It was started more from a circle of friendship, which I think happens everywhere in Indonesia although I don't know if it also happens in Europe. But we started hanging out and sharing ideas together and then came the question of "well why don't we make this together?" It was as easy as that. But then after one or two years we thought that to be able to become a proper research center we needed to have a physical space, a library, and an office so all these "needs" then also constructed our way of working. We needed to have this new inorganic system and so we just followed this "new culture of organization," where you need to have budgets, annual planning, and that kind of stuff and at the end

of the year you need to have an annual report. Suddenly having this organization was no longer fun.

Binna

Well I think we should have, not in a progressive way but by occasion, a shift from organization to organizing. So, to repeat what Hafiz told us earlier about negotiation— I think he used the word negotiation in almost every sentence!—was that together he and Ade started organizing this nationwide collective, the Artists Coalition, which brought them to the Jakarta Arts Council, which represented a great shift in Jakarta Arts Council policy. This gave them contact with the ministry, and then the ministry asked them to write the policy paper. This move is very interesting and it is also similar to what we experienced at Casco when we had a crisis; the power of organizing.

Ferdi

If I may beg to differ to what Antariksa was saying earlier, I actually see a cultural value or an organizational value at KUNCI that has existed from the beginning, which is our culture of *ngeyel*, or resilience. Because we don't use negotiation that much, or we use it

65

in the sense Antariksa mentioned, where we are always reporting back but reporting back in the way we want to, in the time that we want to, whether the funding body is happy or not. If the funding body is knocking on our door asking for that report we still say, "wait, we are still doing something else." So, that's also a culture which sticks. Even the decision to not buy a piece of land for our office building, for instance, because we knew that once we bought a piece of land we would be committing to something big; and we aren't even buying a piece of land for ourselves so why would we buy this piece of land for this institution? Because we know that maybe one day the organization will dissolve and we don't want to be burdened by that. And I think that this positioning that Emily was talking about is also important. We are good at "not negotiating," and at the same time we are also good at putting forward what we think is important. Even when we're commissioned to do something, usually we say yes in the beginning, but it's actually just for the beginning as later on we develop it to something that is more suitable to our process of development. Of course at the end of the day,

a compromise is still needed. But usually we use this opportunity to clarify why we modified certain things, such as the reasoning behind it, as we always see the need to adapt to unfolding processes. So, for me it is not a matter of what is organic or inorganic anymore.

Emily
Maybe it's just pragmatism. I wonder whether there is an issue of leadership—do you not want to be leaders? You have this flat membership model, but actually if you have a space and have created this context, you also can't avoid being leaders. Hafiz has been quite strategic in this respect, entering into policy and taking leadership in that system on behalf of others.

Edwina
Actually, I wanted to ask a bit about the role of mentoring. There are sort of built-in social hierarchies in Indonesia. For example, if Antariksa meets a senior from his university it's always very polite, and if one of Antariksa's juniors from university meets with him it's the same. While KUNCI's structure is a lot flatter now, do you think there is still a form of hierarchy based on age and experience? I just wondered, you

know, as a younger person seeking informal mentoring or as an older person having a responsibility to lead—and in following on from what Emily was saying about leadership as well.

Dina

Well, based on my experience I would say there is never really any direct mentoring from KUNCI, they sort of push me to the hill.

Ferdi

Everyone is pushed.

Dina

Everyone has a specific skill and we believe that each person here has a specific skill or perspective that can enrich our being collective, or being together, so in a sense it's also quite horizontal. The tension, or the question of regeneration is also part of the discussion in many other organizations, but I have never felt there is a need for regeneration and I, with the younger generation, will continue this heritage.

Ferdi

There is an "organizational age" though, that is, it matters when you joined the organization. I'm not saying what went on is a kind of

knowledge transfer, because we believe everyone has their own knowledge and then they bring that to the collective. But it's more a transmission of awareness of what we are doing. That is something that is a bit tricky. Of course, a lot of people come here just to hang out because this place is cool or whatever, but actually there is more to it than that, there is a kind of a shared value that ties us together.

Binna

Many organizations we talked to responded to the question about membership that they have no formal procedure. It's all based on "hanging out." And then in the case of the artist Jompet Kuswidananto, Teater Garasi found out by reading an interview with him that he'd said that he was part of the group, which they were surprised about as they didn't consider him to be a member. I wonder whether KUNCI can tell us a negative case, because I know you have a history of having other members who have left. Besides personal reasons, inevitable personal reasons, are there other cases?

Antariksa

Oh yes, we tried having this kind of formal regeneration so we did a series

of interviews with people and it was even worse actually, they left the organization within six months, not even a year. So, we decided that wasn't a good way to have new members.

Binna
I have had exactly the same experience. Interviews and open calls rarely work.

Antariksa
And even when a member left KUNCI, it was never really official. They just disappeared little by little. First, they came to the office once a month, then next it was once a year, and then they suddenly disappeared, but we still actually have friendships and relationships with them, and we also always ask them to come to KUNCI. So, we have a common ground when, for example, you are no longer an official part of KUNCI.

Christine Wagner
Do you have an aim to grow? Or is it like you have to sustain the people to do the work? Is there an interest in growing actually?

Dina
Growing the number of people?

Antariksa.
We never really think about that. Well, sometimes we need more people.

Ferdi
We always need more people. Because there are always more demands than we can meet, but it's always quite pragmatic in the beginning, and if people decide to stay then of course we will welcome them, but it's really open. A lot of these commissions, or demands, are project-based and involve salaries, but then when the project ends we have said, "Hey, we can no longer pay you, if you want to continue to hang out here we would be very pleased, but if you want to go elsewhere and come back here again when there is a project, that's also fine."

Dina
In my case I actually want to have more KUNCI members, because I need someone to buy toilet paper.

Raquel Ormella
You need more KUNCI members like you!

Dina
Well, actually, one of the changes in the arts and cultural landscape in Yogya is that it is becoming more

and more professionalized and the professionalism can overturn friendships. It is becoming more competitive and, like professionals do, people are now saying things such as, "This curator will meet me, but will not meet you." This kind of competition can also make you feel quite excluded or lonely, so [I keep questioning] who is my ally and who can I work with? The nature of friendship is also changing among most cultural practitioners in Yogya, so I think in a sense, for me to have more KUNCI members is to have more allies, but I am also not just looking for registered members of KUNCI, I also am looking for comrades—ooh, that also sounds very war-like—but I'm looking for more friends and colleagues in these arts and culture fields to work together, so not just at KUNCI but partners, or types of co-operation, not membership, but a working network perhaps.

Binna
A certain looseness has been possible it seems because the living costs are very low here. So, you can also compare yourselves with organizations in the Jakarta arts scene, for example, where living costs are much higher and that's

why they are more "professionalized" and why ruangrupa had this division and that division. But it's coming here to Yogya as well, right?

Dina
Yes.

Hans Knegtmans
And that's one of the risks when you're growing.

Binna
And when the city is growing.

Hans
Even the organization gets bigger with more partners, more comrades, then you build walls and compartmentalize. That's the risk.

Antariksa
The problem is that this growing system is becoming more and more oppressive. They push us to do things that sometimes we don't want to do. So, the challenge for growing organizations is how to make them in a way where they will not only survive but also be unique and able to maintain their own principles. That's why the notion of the sustainability of ideas was really interesting. How do we deal with this?

69

Emily

I would like to ask about the sustainability of a political position. Most of the organizations we met with talked about this moment in 1998, building networks around shared activism, and how after the fall of a dictatorship suddenly there was a moment when you could set up organizations. A lot of the organizations we met are trying to understand where they are now through looking at the past, after all of these shifts and turbulent times, where a lot of things changed and were redefined, and people were redefining themselves. How do you locate yourself in relation to this now? What is the consciousness of the organization now?

Binna

Hafiz said the enemy became horizontalized. So, house, family, and media all became their enemies whereas before their enemy was the Suharto regime. That's why they started Forum Lenteng, which has a focus on alternative media.

Emily

In the UK, London is being taken over by corporate interests to the point where it's hard to continue small projects that are carving a small space for something else. The public sector is shrinking, and the dominant culture is that of spectacle. We work a lot within our neighborhood, collaborating and entering into conversations with local residents, through which we have been able to read the political on a micro-scale.

I see this here at KUNCI through what you're doing in the *kampung*, or the other kinds of research happening here. When we were talking, you skirted away from having to define it. In a way KUNCI can be defined by the different things that you do, but when you look at the library with its different sections of discourse—feminism, post-colonial discourses, European philosophy—you can see how you're maintaining a complex position of intersecting discourses.

Ferdi

I'm always referring back to the individual aspirations that we project onto the collective. For me it's about working against normativity, and that actually allows us to go in different directions. Right now, for instance, people talk a lot about collaboration or relational art and these practices are increasingly becoming a new norm in what art

values, so then for us it's necessary to actually find a niche, to position ourselves as a counterbalance to these new social norms. The only word that we can pull out of these experiences is "criticality," but of course criticality itself is a bit over-rated. Critique for its own sake has never really been our interest, but for us to be able to articulate how normativity works so that we can see our own positioning in the discourse, we either speculate for it or against it. But again, this is still my individual projection on the collective. Of course, Antariksa or Dina would have a different perspective, and these collective perspectives are perhaps what define us. At the same time, not all interests could directly translate into a common ground. So that is why if I don't find something to be suitable for KUNCI, I do it elsewhere, like in the Researchers' Affects Project. Not all of our individual interests are accommodated by the collective, I think it is important to accept that.

Binna
I wonder whether there are common causes shared among organizations or in an organization in Indonesia though. As Emily said, all the organizations we met talked about

1998, which is not long ago. It seems to be quite particular for the Indonesian art scene.

Antariksa
Yes, of course there are. I believe there is a common cause but I also want to bring this idea in, well maybe it's very Indonesian or very Yogya, but I am wondering whether is it possible to understand KUNCI, for example, through the idea of family? Families don't really need a common cause. They just happen like, you're my brother, you're my sister, you're my mother, and you're my father and we don't really need a common cause. We cannot really express how it's possible, it's really difficult but somehow things happen and we work together for different reasons and I feel like KUNCI is kind of my extended family.

Ferdi
Awww.

Antariksa
If you see it in this way... and sometimes you need to escape from your own family. So, of course, we have these values that you can position in the political history of Indonesia, especially because we were founded just after 1998 amidst

this freedom and of course, we are against certain values such as censorship. But it could be difficult to formulate our values in a very solid form. It's really difficult.

Binna
Why?

Antariksa
I feel like I have a second home, a place to stay and work and sleep—safely.

Dina
I agree with what Antariksa said about KUNCI being a safe space for everyone and about being a family and that we take care of each other, but I think the forms of family do not eliminate the common cause. I was driven to this family because I have common causes that are shared with the rest of the family. So, it's an ideologically-driven family. It's not like this family with geese and that family with cats. But also, maybe, and this might be coming from my position within an activist [immediate] family, but my common cause moving into this field of arts and culture is to fight inequality. It sounds quite abstract and quite heroic in this time of chaos and crisis, but I think this has driven

me to move closer toward criticality. I am also interested in intellectual works as modes of thinking and doing in practice, not only just in theory but also in life, on a daily basis—for example, in my attitude to local politics. In this way I feel I can move closer to KUNCI as my family or my safe house from the places I feel rejected from.

Brigitta Isabella (Gita)
I would actually prefer a KUNCI gang rather than a family.

Wok
Woah, so tough!

Gita
I was also interested in talking about membership and I was thinking to myself, is it possible to be an ex-member of KUNCI? I thought, even if I have a different vision to what KUNCI is doing now, as Ferdi also said, I can accommodate it outside of KUNCI whilst also still investing something in KUNCI. You don't see KUNCI as a working place anymore but a place that you invest in and for that reason, for me, as long as you have a shared vision you cannot be an ex-member. Unless of course you did something really bad and someone kicked you out. Everyone always says

72

that we have a very informal bond and I think that this unstructured structure is stronger because of that, rather than from having made more solid and committed stuff. Regarding the diverse interests, I also see it that way. Ferdi has his own research on queer issues, Antariksa has his own interest in history, and I have my own interest in philosophy. I think what also makes us stronger is that we have so many different perspectives and we can accept more jobs! Sometimes I don't do some of KUNCI's projects because I'm abroad or I'm engaged in other projects, but you are still a member of the team although you don't really work. For example, Nuning [Nuraini Juliastuti is KUNCI's co-founding member] has been doing her PhD for four years but always has an emotional engagement with the whole vision of the organization.

Dina
This formula is very specific to KUNCI but it's also not proven to be successful yet. For example, we still find it hard to decide who will buy toilet tissue.

Gita
OK Dina, I'll buy the toilet paper. I'm sorry! [*Laughter.*]

"Toilet Tissue and Other Formless Organizational Matters" is an excerpt from "Curating Organizations (Without) Form," which was originally published on *Open! Engagement* on April 6, 2015. Online: www.openengagement.info/tag/casco (Accessed September 29, 2018). It has been edited for the purpose of this second publication. Transcription by Edwina Brennan.

Local artists and art workers also joined the conversation, including Edwina Brennan, Brigitta Isabella, Hans Knegtmans, Raquel Ormella, Wok the Rock, and Christine Wagner.

LIFELONG LEARNING AND THE PROFESSIONALIZED LEARNER

Annette Krauss

In this text, I turn towards European policy papers on lifelong learning to outline their connections with the formation of a pedagogical subjectivity intertwined with the advancement of an artistic subject as a possible role model for the new economy. Lifelong learning functions here as an example of a progress-orientated accumulative model of learning that pervades institutions and subjectivities today. The detrimental effects of the commodification of art, education, and research made it inevitable that I better understand the discourse of lifelong learning promoted by European policies as a prevalent model for learning in the framework of European knowledge economies. Equally as important, this text articulates nodal points that contribute to an understanding and practice of unlearning against and within the seemingly overwhelming regime of capitalist appropriation.

In European policy papers since 2000, learning is central to the conceptualization of society and the formation of the individual. The papers I review here aim to reshape Europe as a learning society, and not least as a *learning economy.*[1] Lifelong learning is a dominant discourse engendered through education policy in the last decades, a general description can be derived from the *Lisbon Memorandum for Lifelong Learning* (2000): "all learning as a seamless continuum from cradle to grave."[2] And, from its follow up *Making a European Area of Lifelong Learning a Reality* (2001): "Learning from pre-school to post-retirement, lifelong learning should encompass the whole spectrum of formal, non-formal and informal learning."[3] In this vein, lifelong

learning addresses and wants to include all forms of life, expanding the scope of education outside the gates of the nursery, school, universities, and the like including distance, work-based, and home-based learning. Both papers are seen as being among the most important policy documents in the area to be launched by the European Commission since 2000.[4] Sixteen years later, lifelong learning remains the vehicle for major developments in primary, secondary, and tertiary education in Europe.[5]

In *Struggles for Living Learning*, artist and scholar Lina Dokuzović draws a line between the advent of European policymaking on lifelong learning and how capitalist market economies in the age of knowledge-based economies in Europe have become the dominant growth model in Europe since the 1990s.[6] Dokuzović concurs with a vast body of literature that the emergence and implementation of lifelong learning is tightly interwoven with the commodification of education.

The 1972 UNESCO report *Learning to Be* (the "Faure" report) put lifelong learning on the international agenda. The report linked lifelong learning, globalization, and economic growth, focusing on international development in the Global South. In 1996 UNESCO followed it with a second report *Learning: The Treasure Within* (the "Delors" report). Both tried to establish lifelong learning as a global educational master concept. Since the early 1990s, policy-

1   Jan Masschelein et.al, "The Learning Society from the Perspective of Governmentality: An Introduction," *Educational Philosophy and Theory* 38, no. 4 (2006): 417–30.

2   Commission of the European Communities. Commission Staff Working Paper: A Memorandum on Lifelong Learning. Brussels, 30.10.2000 SEC(2000)1832: Luxembourg Publication Office, 2000. Online: www.arhiv. acs.si/dokumenti/Memorandum_on_Lifelong _Learning.pdf (Accessed December 3, 2016).

3   Commission of the European Communities. Communication from the Commission: Making a European Area of Lifelong Learning a Reality, Brussels, 21.11.01 COM (2001) 678 final. Directorate-General for Education and Culture; Directorate-General for Employment and Social Affairs, Brussels, 2001. Online: www.viaa.gov.lv/files/free/48/748/pol_10_ com_en.pdf (Accessed September 29, 2016), 3.

4   Lina Dokuzović, *Struggles for Living Learning: Within Emergent Knowledge Economies and the Cognitivization of Capital and Movement*, Pdf. (Vienna: transversal texts, 2016). Online: www.transversal.at/books/livinglearning (Accessed June 7, 2018), 78; Andreas Fejes, "Lifelong Learning and Employability," *Challenging the 'European Area of Lifelong Learning,'"* ed. George K. Zarifis and Maria N. Gravani, (Dordrecht: Springer, 2014), 99–109; and Jan Masschelein et al. "The Learning Society from the Perspective of Governmentality: An Introduction," *Educational Philosophy and Theory* 38, no. 4 (2006): 417–30.

5   In 2015 the European Platform for Lifelong Learning (EUCIS-LLL; www.lllplatform.eu) celebrated its tenth anniversary and announced further implementation of lifelong learning strategies and policies in primary, secondary, and tertiary education.

making bodies and political parties, such as New Labour in the UK and the European Commission, have increasingly embraced debates on lifelong learning with the goal of strengthening Europe's knowledge-based economy.[7] Agendas such as the 1996 declaration of the "European Year of Lifelong Learning" and the *Lisbon Memorandum on Lifelong Learning* in 2000, have been among many implementation policies.

As political strategy, the notion of lifelong learning claims to be "a key element of the strategy, devised at Lisbon, to make Europe the most competitive and dynamic knowledge-based society in the world."[8] Since 2000, debates around knowledge and economy have introduced both lifelong learning policies and massive waves of reform in higher education (namely the Bologna Process).[9] More recent programs have integrated its agendas into higher education and research,[10] highlighting the combined impacts of lifelong learning, mobility, and economy. For the last decade, the EU has promoted lifelong learning as the essential component of the "overarching Growth Strategy for the European Union (in the Lisbon Strategy (2000–10) and more importantly

6   Dokuzović traces the economization of tertiary education back to the model of growth and wealth in the eighteenth and nineteenth centuries: "That modern university model [namely, the Wilhelm van Humboldt model, 1810] which united institutions of higher education with the state, began a process that shifted the understanding of the wealth of nations from the model proposed by Adam Smith in 1776 of land-based resources or of population growth, towards [...] competitions of nations through wealth of knowledge." This expansion has helped to lay the basis for new types of accumulation, production, and exploitation, which, after Moulier-Boutang (Yann Moulier-Boutang, *Cognitive Capitalism*, trans. E. Emery (Cambridge, MA: Polity Press, 2011), 57), Dokuzović summarizes as follows, "human capital has become a crucial factor in defining the new wealth of the nations." Lina Dokuzović *The Limits of Capital and its New Frontiers*, PhD diss. (Vienna: Academy of Fine Arts Vienna, 2015), 236–39.

7   Penny Jane Burke and Sue Jackson, *Reconceptualising Lifelong Learning: Feminist Interventions* (New York: Routledge, 2007), 10–11.

8   Commission of the European Communities, *Making a European Area of Lifelong Learning a Reality*, 2.

9   The Bologna Process has introduced a far-reaching transformation within European higher education since 1999. European member states have agreed on the instalment of standards regarding bachelors, masters, and doctoral degrees in order to ensure comparability of higher-education qualifications in Europe.

10   The *Lisbon Memorandum* led to European tertiary education policies, such as Erasmus+ and Horizon 2020, with the imperative of making lifelong learning one of the strongest pillars in the knowledge economy. Together with the Bologna Process these have introduced major developments in the field.

in the Europe 2020 Strategy (2010–20)."[11]

Since the 1970s these policies have reorganized Europe's cultural funding landscape. They have been referred to in Casco Art Institute team meetings as effecting increased working hours and pressure in art organizations. My work, research, and study at art institutions and academies are situated within the reorganization of higher education that result from these policies.

How Not to be Governed at Such Costs[12]

Scholars in education have linked the political agenda of lifelong learning policies to neoliberal strategies.[13] Here, neoliberalism is understood as the dominant economic model of the late twentieth into the twenty-first century, where economizing all spheres of life and the "liberalization" or deregulation of the market is the primary means of governance. Political scientist Wendy Brown terms this "the conversion of non-economic domains, activities and subjects into economic ones [...]. Neoliberalism construes subjects as market actors everywhere."[14] Most importantly, as an advanced form of capitalism, neoliberalism is a logical unfolding of the historical conditions of Empire that made the university possible.[15] Neglecting capitalism's structural continuities in neoliberalism risks separating the modern project of education from its colonial enterprise. In this regard, modern education cannot be addressed as emerging solely from European history; a study of the modern-colonial matrix

11   European Civil Society Platform on Lifelong Learning (EUCIS-LLL), *Twelve Years After: A Call for a Renewed Memorandum on Lifelong Learning*. Brussels: EUCIS-LLL, 3 September 2012. Online: www.lllplatform.eu/lll/wp-content/uploads/2015/10/A-call-for-a-renewed-Memorandum-on-Lifelong-Learning-EUCIS-LLL1.pdf (Accessed October 15, 2016), 1.

12   Michel Foucault, "What is Critique?" in *The Politics of Truth*, ed. Sylvère Lotringer and Lysa Hochroth (New York: Semiotext(e), 1997), 193.

13   Mark Olssen, "Understanding the Mechanisms of Neoliberal Control: Lifelong Learning, Flexibility and Knowledge Capitalism," in *Foucault and Lifelong Learning. Governing the Subject*, ed. Andreas Fejes and Katherine Nicoll (New York: Routledge, 2007); Andreas Fejes, "Lifelong Learning and Employability."

14   Wendy Brown, "Sacrificial Citizenship: Neoliberalism, Human Capital, and Austerity Politics," *Constellations* 23, no. 1 (2016): 3.

15   Vanessa de Oliveira Andreotti, et al. "Mapping interpretations of decolonization in the context of higher education," *Decolonization: Indigeneity, Education & Society* 4, no. 1 (2015): 34; Marina Vishmidt, *Speculation as a Mode of Production in Art and Capital*, PhD diss. (London: Queen Mary University of London, 2012), 37–9.

of power needs to take into account the modes of control of social life, economic, and political organization that have been engineered in the colonies and the entanglements between capitalism and colonialism.[16] These technologies have shaped Western institutions, our ways of learning and relating to each other. Historian Craig Steve Wilder shows how many of the US' most esteemed universities developed under and were nurtured by an economy built on the work of enslaved people.[17] How are we to interrupt the logic of separation and address coloniality and modernity as "one field of analysis"?[18]

→ skills → flexibility → employability →
adaptation → skills →

The vocabularies around lifelong learning come from a market-driven discourse. Its terms are interwoven with discourses that shift lifelong learning towards economization and profitable efficacy. The iteration of, and emphasis on, *skills* in policy papers on lifelong learning is omnipresent. The "acquisition of skills"—whether they are "new basic skills," "knowledge, skills, and competences," "social skills," or "soft skills"—is described as providing the best preparation for the challenges of a fast-changing society and economy. "New basic skills" are skills in foreign languages and digital literacy required for active participation in the knowledge society and economy. "Social skills," identified as self-confidence, self-direction, and risk-taking are seen as increasingly important for a labor market that shifts responsibilities from business and government to individuals. "Soft skills" are almost exclusively brought together with creative capacities and innovation. Educational theorist Katarina Popovic

16   Anibal Quijano, "Coloniality of Power, Eurocentrism and Latin America," in *Nepentla: Views from the South 1* (2000); Achille Mbembe, *Kritik der schwarzen Vernunft* [critique of black reason], trans. Michael Bischoff (Berlin: Suhrkamp, 2014).

17   Craig Steve Wilder, *Ebony and Ivory, Race, Slavery and the Troubled Histories of American Universities* (New York: Bloomsbury Press, 2013).

18   Ann Laura Stoler, *Race and the Education of Desire: Foucault's History of Sexuality and the Colonial Order of Things* (New York: Duke University Press), xi.

characterizes skills as the "chimera of modern education."[19] Originally associated with manual work, skills are now also linked to cognitive and intellectual work. Skills are the personal capacity to carry out specific tasks with predetermined results or according to certain procedures. Tracing the importance of skills in human capital theory,[20] Popovic largely ascribes their discourse to the realm of labor. According to writer and critic Marina Vishmidt, as a form of subjectivation, human capital is seen as an excessive form of (self-)valorization, where a constant calculation assesses the best from those capacities that the subject believes constitute her basic values—her human assets:

> The idea of human capital is essentially that of applying cost:benefit analysis to "intangibles" such as education, family, health or cultural interests and viewing them as rational investments made by individuals in their employability, social mobility and financial security.[21]

Through their acquisition, enhancement, and training skills promise to get a grip on human assets that are subsequently measured as human capital. Their attachment to labor makes skills highly appealing for the discourse around lifelong learning because they can function as the missing link between education and the labor market. Put differently, skills are techniques amenable to the learner that aim to minimize the time lag between learning and employment. In learner-centered, self-directed pedagogical processes skills promise to prepare the individual for economic and technological change. They seem to be measurable and transferable, and in the economic logic within education

19 Katarina Popovic, "The Skills: A Chimera of Modern European Adult Education," *Challenging the 'European Area of Lifelong Learning,'"* ed. George K. Zarifis and Maria N. Gravani (Dordrecht: Springer, 2014), 17.

20 Gary S. Becker, *Human Capital: A Theoretical and Empirical Analysis with Special Reference to Education* (Chicago: The University of Chicago Press, 1993); Michel Foucault, *The Birth of Biopolitics: Lectures at the College de France 1978–79,* trans. Graham Burchell (Basingstoke and New York: Palgrave Macmillan, 2008).

21 Marina Vishmidt, *Speculation as a Mode of Production in Art and Capital,* 42.

these features provide important and quantifiable proof. An emphasis on learner-centeredness and self-determination, referred to as the skill of self-management, is complemented in the policy papers by referencing record keeping and audit culture, demonstrating established learning and acquired skills. Conversely, these quality controls indicate certain deficiencies in the individual that could hamper success in the labor market or education, with the implication of requiring further updating of skills in the interest of (finally) being equipped for employment. This produces—in the spirit of Stefano Harney and Fred Moten—a truly professional learner:

> Students must come to see themselves as the problem, which, counter to the complaints of restorationist critics of the university, is precisely what it means to be a customer, to take on the burden of realization and always necessarily be inadequate to it. Later, these students will be able to see themselves properly as obstacles to society, or perhaps, with lifelong learning, students will return having successfully diagnosed themselves as the problem.[22]

In a similar vein, education researcher Andres Fejes interrogates the specific language around "employment" used in the lifelong learning policy papers and observes a shift from speaking about "employment" to "employability." This tiny change in language emphasizes, firstly, a process of individualization, as *employability* is aligned with the individual's responsibility instead of the state's or employers' who are "construed as enablers";[23] secondly, *employability* emphasizes future employment as forms of postponement and speculation written into learning to prepare for the job market. In a highly economized learning industry, this speculation becomes the nexus for further investments in oneself. As Vishmidt reminds us, speculations are "mediated by financial rather than welfare state institutions and in the subjective parameters of 'human capital'

22   Stefano Harney and Fred Moten, *The Under-commons: Fugitive Planning & Black Study* (Colchester: Minor Compositions, 2013), 29.

23   Andreas Fejes, Katherine Nicoll eds. *Foucault and Lifelong Learning: Governing the Subject* (New York: Routledge, 2007), 8.

ideology."[24] Vishmidt's thoughts translate to lifelong learning's relation to capital and labor as the "developmental tendency" of lifelong learning and education "not only appears more and more, but is experienced as a moment of capital."[25] The epitome of this mechanism is the debt politics implemented in university systems, colleges for further education, and vocational training that lifelong learning addresses. Following feminist scholar Silvia Federici, Vishmidt describes debt's force in disguising "capital relation of exploitation as 'self-investment.'"[26] What has been invented as "human capital" obscures conditions of workers, students, learners in the contemporary neoliberal structures. Debt is another fierce mechanism through which the subject's relation to capital has been individualized.

Let's continue investigating the language of policy papers on lifelong learning. The notion of a "flexible" workforce thoroughly frames the vocabulary, though the terminology itself is not as frequently applied as terms like adaptation and mobility. Flexibility, as the adaptability of workers and learners, is judged on their mobility in the labor market and between businesses, institutions, and/or freelance workplaces. This moving or being moved readily from place to place, across time, of being available 24/7 requires a high level of "workforce versatility"[27] enabled by the addition of new and potentially short-term skills to already-acquired high levels of technical training. What is this all for? The policy papers provide an answer: adaptation!

> Lifelong learning has a key role in promoting a skilled, trained and adaptable workforce… individuals have to adapt to changes… Europe's education and training systems must adapt to the new realities… improving employability and adaptability of the workforce… the ADAPT program: a European

24 Marina Vishmidt, *Speculation as a Mode of Production in Art and Capital*, 119.

25 See also Morgan Adamson, who specifies that the "novel aspect of the invention of human capital is not merely that it measures the capacity of human labour […]. In essence, the technology of human capital produces its object, *human ability* conceived of as a *fixed form of capital*, in order to measure it." "The Human Capital Strategy," *Ephemera: Theory & Politics in Organization* 9 no. 4 (2009, emphasis added): 272.

26 Silvia Federici, *Revolution at Point Zero: Housework, Reproduction, and Feminist Struggle* (Oakland: PM Press, 2012); and Marina Vishmidt, "The Politics of Speculative Labour," *Transformative Art Production*, 2012. Online: www.transformativeartproduction.net/the-politics-of-speculative-labour/ (Accessed November 12, 2016), 4.

27 Mark Olssen, "Understanding the Mechanisms of Neoliberal Control," 38.

network for education and training... employers demand adaptation to new challenges and situations... adapt to new market conditions and new work patterns... the employability and adaptability of citizens is vital for Europe becoming the world leading knowledge economy.[28]

It is important to take note of the policy papers' suggestion that it is the pressure of the markets that force adaptation, skill management, and flexibilization.[29] In addition to what I have already argued, I present another perspective: the policies on lifelong learning—with their mechanisms of flexibilization, skills management, speculation, and adaptation—have greatly helped to engineer the very market these policies urge us to follow. In other words, with its explicit focus on individual, economized learning processes and orientation in the labor market, lifelong learning is a distinct capitalist technology. The force that speaks through lifelong learning is a collective power that is exercised through and over individuals. It is precisely that which links policies of lifelong learning to Michel Foucault's concept of govern-mentality, described by Mark Olssen as: "a model of governing individuals in their relation to the collective."[30] As a discursive filter, the concept of governmentality allows for an understanding of the double move in shifting authority from the collective to the individual. In this sense, lifelong learning is a force that attempts to individualize *and* totalize; it shapes both individuals and populations. The emphasis of lifelong learning on the self-organizing, self-responsible, self-investing individual is a means to enact and endorse market-driven neoliberal structures. From this perspective, lifelong learning has to be understood as a market discourse that *pedagogizes* the individual into a form of capital. This constitutes an intricate web between the learning individual, labor, and capital, or respectively education, enterprise society, and the growth model of the knowledge economy.

28 Quotes are taken from Commission of the European Communities, Communication from the Commission: Making a European Area of Lifelong Learning a Reality, Brussels, 21.11.01 COM (2001) 678 final; see also Katarina Popovic, "The Skills: A Chimera of Modern European Adult Education."

29 It is here that I see the most vulnerable moment for concepts of unlearning taken as a shallow placeholder for flexibilization that suggests a key to social financial success (closely attached to the realm of labor).

30 Mark Olssen, "Understanding the Mechanisms of Neoliberal Control," 36.

A Question of Self-Determination

The unambiguous emphasis on learner-centered pedagogies, self-determination, and in- and non-formal learning in lifelong learning policy papers has provoked scholars to make parallels to critical pedagogies from the 1970s and 1980s.[31] What was radical then seems to be incorporated and rendered harmless in the discourse on lifelong learning.[32] These critical pedagogies attempted to analyze the role of education, knowledge, and especially learning in all spheres of life and processes. Following the work of Paulo Freire, Ivan Illich, and bell hooks, a move away from learning within hierarchical, authoritarian educational structures towards the learner herself was made. Freire's insistence on *self-determined* learning no longer sees the learner as a passive container exposed to education, while hooks and Freire both emphasize the mutuality of learning and its impact on learner *and* (academic) teacher, with the potential to de-hierarchize classroom relationships. Both certainly stress self-determined learning but they can only be understood in their radicality when they are thought together with their inseparable quest for social equality and justice. hooks has dedicated her practice as scholar, educator, and activist to transgressing the status quo of education and teaching.[33] She not only critiques practices of domination in learning and teaching, but relentlessly points out how a "white supremacist capitalist patriarchy" attempts to structurally consolidate its position of power through education.[34] This is in line with

31 Stewart Martin, "The Pedagogy of Human Capital," *Mute: Culture and Politics after the Net* 2, no. 8 (2008): Online: www.metamute.org/editorial/articles-pedagogy-human-capital (Accessed June 7, 2018); Anna Tuschling and Christoph Engemann, "From Education to Lifelong Learning: The Emerging Regime of Learning in the European Union," *Educational Philosophy and Theory* 38, no. 4 (2006); Jan Masschelein et al. "The Learning Society from the Perspective of Governmentality: An Introduction."

32 One of many examples for the use of self-directed learning in the policy papers: "The regular (traditional) system [...] should be adapted to accommodate modular programmes, non-sequential study and qualification trajectories, open and distance education and self-directed learning programmes." Commission of the European Communities, Commission Staff Working Paper: A Memorandum on Lifelong Learning, Brussels, 30.10.2000, SEC (2000), 32.

33 bell hooks, *Teaching to Transgress: Education as the Practice of Freedom* (London: Routledge, 1994).

34 bell hooks, *Feminism Is for Everybody: Passionate Politics* (Cambridge: South End Press, 2000), 4; and *Talking Back: Thinking Black* (Boston: South End Press, 1989), 113.

decolonial scholar Sylvia Wynter who asks in the open letter "No Humans Involved" (1994) what "conception of the self" is presupposed in *self*-determined learning and education. Wynter directs our attention to a radio news report right after the acquittal of the police officers involved in the Rodney King beating.[35] This report stated:

> Public officials of the judicial system of Los Angeles routinely used the acronym N.H.I. to refer to any case involving a breach of the rights of young Black males who belong to the jobless category of the inner-city ghettoes. N.H.I. means "no humans involved."[36]

Wynter directly relates the production of these racist categorizations to education and traces the consequences that they produce. The category "human," Wynter warns us, means to be "White, of Euroamerican culture and descent, middle-class, and college-educated."[37] In the same article she relates the category of the human to conceptions of the self, and asks who is excluded from this self.

Let's raise this question in the context of lifelong learning and self-determination. Who and what is excluded from the "self"? The policy papers focus on "economic growth," "competitiveness," and "workforce adaptability." The struggle against oppression, the quest for social justice, and re-distribution of wealth are lacking throughout. Whereas critical pedagogues promote an active individual that seeks to intervene in societal oppression, lifelong learning promotes an individual that seeks to actively augment her attributes to feed "a powerful engine for economic growth."[38] Interestingly enough, after the *Lisbon Memorandum* concerns were raised "that the employment and labor market dimensions of lifelong learning were too dominant."[39] In response,

---

35 Rodney King was an African-American taxi driver, who was violently beaten by Los Angeles police officers after a high-speed chase in 1991. A bystander videotaped the beating and sent the footage to a local broadcast that was then shown nationwide. The officers were acquitted of charges.

36 Sylvia Wynter, "No Humans Involved: An Open Letter to My Colleagues," *Forum N.H.I.: Knowledge for the 21st Century* 1, no. 1 (1994): 1.

37 Sylvia Wynter, "No Humans Involved," 1.

38 Commission of the European Communities, Commission Staff Working Paper: A Memorandum on Lifelong Learning, 6.

39 Commission of the European Communities, Communication from the Commission: Making a European Area of Lifelong Learning a Reality, 5.

lifelong learning's objectives have been expanded beyond a sole focus on market-driven economics and employment, to "personal fulfilment, active citizenship, social inclusion and employability."[40] However, this is hardly more than lip service as the overall framework and rhetoric of the policy papers did not change. On the contrary, what was a point of contention for lifelong learning in 2001, was in 2016 rendered an economic conceptual device for labor markets and employment, and has now become the unambiguous goal for educational policies in Europe, namely "to boost growth and competitiveness [...] to increase productivity."[41]

What cultural theorist Angela McRobbie[42] observes for many reports promoting creative economies during the UK's New Labour government is equally apparent for the policy paper on lifelong learning: work or labor conditions are virtually invisible across the documents. The market-driven perspective drastically reorganizes the role of the learning subject as it deprives learning of its politicizing dimension. The policies on lifelong learning are infused with the language of student-centered pedagogy, context-specificity, and transformation that focuses on an atomized individual. This rhetoric is a form of de-politicization that either (following Wynter) structurally excludes people from entering the category of the "self," or renders structurally-generated conditions personal problems. Political and economic decisions get displaced into individual failings and responsibilities.[43] Philosopher Stewart Martin summarizes the "pedagogy of human capital" as the shift towards lifelong learning and its market orientation that shows "capitalism's appetite for self-directed activities."[44]

In contrast to this, the conception of self-directed learning in critical pedagogies is inseparably interwoven with an analysis of control and power,

40   Commission of the European Communities, ibid, 9.

41   Life Long Learning Hub: Creating a Space for Lifelong Learning. *EU Handbook and Glossary.* Updated version, April 2016. Online: www.lll-hub.eu/wp-content/uploads/2015/05/lllhub_handbookUPDATED_FINAL.pdf (Accessed February 2, 2017), 23.

42   Angela McRobbie, *Be Creative: Making a Living in the New Culture Industries* (Cambridge: Polity Press, 2016), 60–66.

43   Judith Walker, "Towards Alternative Lifelong Learning(s): What Freire Can Still Teach Us," *Rizoma Freireano* 3 (2009). Online: www.rizoma-freireano.org/index.php/towards-alternative (Accessed June 8, 2018).

44   Martin Stewart, "The Pedagogy of Human Capital," 11.

with the aim to prepare subjects to fight oppression. Or to put it differently, any self-directedness requires the analysis and negotiation of the political conditions that bring the "self" into place. Against this backdrop, my aim is to approach and activate what has been left out and unconsidered in these appropriations of, and perspectives on, critical pedagogies. In a nutshell, what is at the core of critical pedagogies, namely the inseparability of self-determined learning *and* the quest for social equality and justice, has not been appropriated.

A Question of De-institutionalization

The focus on self-directed activities demands a closer look into the role of institutions in lifelong learning documents and critical pedagogies. The documents on lifelong learning pay attention to forms of learning that are both non-formal processes that are distant from (educational) institutions, and informal, unrecognized forms of learning in institutions. Taken together with the conception of self-directed lifelong learning, this focus could be understood as "a campaign for the de-institutionalization and de-bureaucratization of education"[45] seemingly orientated against educational institutions that provide a dominant, over-directed learning structure. Such aspects strongly resonate with the claim of "softening the institutions" made in the UNESCO report *Learning to Be* from 1972,[46] and the "soft law politics"[47] of the EU since the beginning of 2000, which subsequently informed policy papers on lifelong learning.[48]

The rigid and authoritarian educational structures that obstruct meaningful learning were also critiqued by radical pedagogue Illich in his 1971 text *Deschooling Society*. There, he developed a concept for a democratic educational system that destabilizes a fixed and disciplinary educational system in favor of a more horizontal mode of address, central to which were:

---

[45] Anna Tuschling and Christoph Engemann, "From Education to Lifelong Learning: the emerging regime of learning in the European Union:" 451–69.

[46] Faure et al. UNESCO Report. *Learning to Be: The World of Education Today and Tomorrow.* (known as the Faure Report), Ward. Paris: UNESCO (1972). Online: www.unesco.org/education/pdf/15_60.pdf (Accessed October 4, 2016), 251.

Educational webs, which heighten the opportunity for each one to transform each moment of his living into one of learning, sharing, and caring. We hope to contribute concepts needed by those who conduct such counterfoil research on education—and also to those who seek alternatives to established service industries.[49]

What might today sound like fashionable wording around lifelong learning was deeply rooted in radical (student) movements of the 1960s and 1970s that took up Illich's thoughts and actions. The discourse around self-determination in critical pedagogies has to be also situated in the demands of student movements to introduce greater autonomy into universities in that era. These movements struggled for a more egalitarian society and less hierarchical structure in the university, with more democratic participation in decision-making processes. This concerned both the "autonomy of persons" (less hierarchical relationships between student, lecturer, and professor) and

47 The term "soft law" refers to a quasi-legal instrument in the EU. It was established around 1993 as a form of governance to both regulate and encourage the cooperation between the EU member states on a voluntary basis. Soft law politics is a mechanism to distribute policies among the EU states without direct regulation. In return member states draft their own proposals for meeting EU objectives. Nafsika Alexiadou and Bettina Lange, "New Forms of European Union Governance in the Education Sector? A Preliminary Analysis of the Open Method of Coordination." *European Educational Research Journal* 6, no. 4 (2007): 322. The implementation of the Bologna Process is an example of soft law politics. Local adaptations can "include differences in tuition fees, the level of cooperation with the private sector, or the level of austerity measures imposed, the financial role of the individual state or the number of students accepted per term." Lina Dokuzović, *Struggles for Living Learning: Within Emergent Knowledge Economies and the Cognitivization of Capital and Movement* (Vienna: Transversal Texts, 2016), 78.

48 The "Lifelong Learning Handbook" by the European Commission dedicates several sections to definitions of soft law and soft law policy measures: Life Long Learning Hub, "Creating a Space for Lifelong Learning. EU Handbook and Glossary."

49 Ivan Illich, *Deschooling Society* (Hardmondsworth: Penguin Books, [1971] 1978), 1.

"autonomy of units" (division into faculties with a greater say in decisions).[50] The demands were formulated on the basis of a rejection of the "ivory tower" of the university and its separation from society. Actors such as sociologist Michel Crozier, a consultant in administrative and social reform in France, sensed that once the anti-institutional critique of student movements was deprived of revolutionary references, then the implementation of its remaining critique would allow market influences.[51] In many cases, parts of the movement's revolutionary demands were channeled into modernizing the university. Conservative actors in the university meanwhile opposed the egalitarian demands but agreed with the critique of a too-hermetic university system and the plea for self-determination.

Let's look at the effect of lifelong learning policies on public higher education and current institutional processes. According to the European Higher Education Area (EHEA), lifelong learning has been crucial for implementing the Bologna Process.[52] Concomitantly, the Bologna Process has been critiqued for its active role in further converting Europe into a knowledge economy by enhancing its competitiveness while cutting costs.[53] Whereas this vision has become the bottom line in university education, it has reached different dimensions in different states of the EU due to soft law policies. For example, in recent years the protests by student movements in continental Europe have not necessarily been sparked by high tuitions fees as in the UK, Canada, and the US. Student protests in Amsterdam in 2015, for instance, addressed program and staff cuts effected by the dwindling funding allocated

50   Luc Boltanski and Ève Chiapello, *The New Spirit of Capitalism*, trans. G. Elliott (London: Verso, 2005), 191.

51   Boltanski and Chiapello, ibid, 212.

52   Policies on lifelong learning in the Bologna Process are directly connected to a widening access to higher education: creating more flexible, student-centered modes of delivery; improving the recognition of prior learning, including non-formal and informal learning; developing national qualifications frameworks; and improving cooperation with employers (EHEA 2014).

53   For more on the modularization of education through Bologna, see Gerald Raunig, *Factories of Knowledge: Industries of Creativity*, Semiotext(e) Intervention Series (Cambridge: MIT Press, 2013); on the Bologna Process and student movement, see Lina Dokuzović, *Struggles for Living Learning: Within Emergent Knowledge Economies and the Cognitivization of Capital and Movement* (Vienna: Transversal Texts, 2016).

by the state per student, comparing the university to a "'cookie factory', churning out students on the cheap."[54]

This means lifelong learning intends for no disorganization or dismantling of national educational systems. Softening institutional processes and valorizing non-formal learning get promoted as devices that render fixed and slow institutions more malleable and porous to outer institutional processes and the market. These processes are successfully obscured by policies on lifelong learning that seek to flexibilize the given frameworks of education in order to bring non-formal learning, direct education, and socio-economic developments closer. This again indicates that lifelong learning is a late-capitalist, neoliberal tool and resonates with what Brown called the "double standard":

> In the economic realm, neoliberalism aims simultaneously at deregulation and control. It seeks to privatize every public enterprise, yet valorizes public-private partnerships that imbue the market with ethical potential and the public realm with market metrics. With its ambition for unregulated and untaxed capital flows, it undermines national sovereignty while intensifying preoccupation with national GNP, GDP, and other growth indicators.[55]

Demands of university activists, now, address the financialization and market-driven economies that universities implement in the form of private-public partnerships, research-on-demand, self-management of students and staff. Dokuzović argues:

> Where demands were made for an autonomy of intellectual thought and decision-making, the "autonomy" that universities were granted in many cases rather gave way to the precarization of the university as part of a larger precarization of the labor market.[56]

54 Sven Lütticken and Jorinde Seijdel, "Common Knowledge: A Virtual Round Table on the Crisis in Higher Education," *Open! Platform for Art, Culture & the Public Domain*, May 23, 2015. Online: www.onlineopen.org/common-knowledge (Accessed February 2, 2017), 3.

55 Wendy Brown, *Undoing the Demos: Neoliberalism's Stealth Revolution* (New York: Zone, 2015), 49.

56 Lina Dokuzović, *Struggles for Living Learning*, 3.

The forms of precarization due to the deregulation of labor markets extend into multiple dimensions of the academic world,[57] including employment conditions of staff with short-term contracts, contracts, and increased teaching loads and administrative tasks. For the students, the rationale behind these tertiary education programs is not necessarily to "find people who can be made to work, [...] but rather people who can be made to pay."[58]

Lifelong learning, together with the Bologna Process, has introduced a learning industry that reduces higher education to an income-generating promise. The narrow economic focus in higher education has turned students, teachers, and all staff at the universities into producers and consumers. What looks like collateral damage of lifelong learning policies—precarization, debt politics, end of critique—are actually at the heart of it. Precarization affects large groups of people who inhabit universities and academies. That does not mean old inequalities disappear. Cleaners and other maintenance workers demand better working conditions and fight against precarious contracts that feed economically and ethnically hierarchized global divisions of labor. Inequalities remain regarding, on the one side, access for black, minority ethnic, and working-class students and teaching staff, and, on the other side, the predominance of curricula that are to a large extent white, Western, and male.

My point is that the demands by university activists and student movements did not dissolve. We need to pay attention to complex and overwhelming entanglements between precarious conditions of work, and old and new inequalities that linger in forms of representation and the global division of labor.

57   With precarization, I follow Isabell Lorey's work on the distinction between precariousness, precarity, and precarization. Lorey expands Foucault's concept of governmentality by emphasizing "how state governance and individualized self-governing are intertwined in governing through insecurity," especially the concept of autonomy has played a crucial role in these governmental techniques until today. Isabell Lorey, "Autonomy and Precarization," *Mobile Autonom: Exercises in Artists' Self-Organization*, ed. Nico Dock and Pascal Gielen (Amsterdam: Valiz, 2015), 49.

58   Ben Rosenzweig, "International Student Struggles: Transnational Economies, Guest Consumers and Processes of Restructuring," *Mutiny* 48 (2010). Online: www.jura.org.au/files/jura/Mutiny%2048%20WebV3.pdf (Accessed October 4, 2016).

Who Is a Model for the New Economy?

Be creative! The demand and the desire to be creative, the commitment to innovation, and a transformative subject position form important pillars of the creativity paradigm, and deeply influenced understandings of labor and subjectivity in late capitalism.[59] "Artists" function as role models who impersonate a certain form of bohemian freedom and independence that dissolves borders between art and life and consequently between work and non-work.[60] Interestingly, the vocabulary around creativity in the policy papers was rather reluctant in the early 2000s. By 2010, the term "soft skill of creativity" had become apparent, mentioned frequently in the European Lifelong Learning Hub handbook and accompanying documents.[61] Searching for and unfolding "the potential for creativity and innovation in all spheres of learning" is a recurring phrase closely tied to entrepreneurship in the policy papers.[62]

Luc Boltanski and Éve Chiapello's sociological analysis of management discourses since the 1960s identifies the appropriation of countercultures and subcultures in the arts through "the new spirit of capitalism."[63] They use the term "artistic critique" to frame a particular form of anti-capitalist critique of alienation often voiced by cultural producers (including artists, philosophers, and so forth) in the twentieth century based on the demands for autonomy, authenticity, and freedom.[64] In a much criticized move, they contrast—and therefore separate—artistic critique and social critique that demands solidarity, security, and equality.[65] For Boltanski and Chiapello, artistic critique was

59   Angela McRobbie, *Be Creative: Making a Living in the New Culture Industries*; Marion von Osten, "Unpredictable Outcomes / Unpredictable Outcasts. A Reflection after some Years of Debates on Creativity and Creative Industries," *Eipcp* 11 (2007). Online: www.eipcp.net/transversal/0207/vonosten/en (Accessed October 10, 2016); "STOP MAKING SENSE: Some Reflections on Educational Reforms," *Intersections: At the Crossroads of the Production of Knowledge. Precarity, Subjugation and the Reconstruction of History, Display, and De-Linking*, ed. Lina Dokuzović et al. (Vienna: Löcker Verlag, 2009); and Marina Vishmidt, "Speculation as a Mode of Production in Art and Capital."

60   Luc Boltanski and Éve Chiapello, *The New Spirit of Capitalism*, trans. G. Elliott (London: Verso, 2005).

61   Life Long Learning Hub, "Creating a Space for Lifelong Learning. EU Handbook and Glossary."

62   Life Long Learning Hub, ibid, 12.

63   Luc Boltanski and Éve Chiapello, *The New Spirit of Capitalism*.

64   Boltanski and Chiapello, ibid, 419–83.

65   Maurizio Lazzarato, "The Misfortunes of the 'Artistic Critique' and of Cultural Employment," trans. Mary O'Neill, *Eipcp*, version 1 (2007). Online: www.eipcp.net/transversal/0207/lazzarato/en (Accessed June 7, 2018).

taken over by the student movements of the 1960s and 1970s, including, as I describe above, processes through which the demands have not only been incorporated in companies and enterprises, but also in institutions of higher education. The implementation of flat hierarchies and project-orientated ways of working has resulted (only) in staff members' desire for self-fulfillment, cooperation, and self-directed activities.

Against this backdrop, Boltanski and Chiapello's critique provides insight into artistic critique's mechanisms of appropriation by neoliberal forms of organization. They tie in with a long-standing discourse on art that has expanded a focus on aesthetic reception and consumption of high and popular culture to an interrogation of aesthetico-institutional production processes. Their separation of artistic from social critique instantiates a capitalist logic connected to the European policy papers. They assign struggles against oppression, the quest for social justice, and the redistribution of wealth outside the field of art and frame it as social critique. In contrast to this, their text reflects on how they frame a singular notion of artistic critique. Artistic critique seems to favor a particular cultural model or figure based on a modernist, avant-garde, male subject that finds its legitimization in autonomy, authenticity, and freedom. It is this figure and only this figure that brings Boltanski and Chiapello to their claim that artistic and social critique are incompatible. Through these generalizations they disregard the gendered and racialized histories of capitalism from the perspective of cultural production. The sociologist Maurizio Lazzarato and others (see also McRobbie above) have criticized Boltanski and Chiapello for lumping together a highly heterogeneous group of cultural producers to literally give body to their notion of artistic critique. Based on a survey with workers, artists, and technicians in the TV and radio sector in France, Lazzarato, Antonella Corsani, and Jean-Baptiste Olivo showed how divisions—"status, salaries, social cover, workload, job"[66]— cut across the so-called creative class, ranging from high to decent to poorly paid jobs, with and without any job security. One of the most convincing arguments against the biased division between artistic and social critique is in the slogan of cultural producers who protested in France at the beginning of

66   Lazzarato, ibid, 2.

92

the 2000s. "No Culture Without Social Rights."[67] Or to put it in Lazzarato's terms, "the neo-liberal logic can be thwarted: 'no freedom, autonomy, authenticity (culture), without solidarity, equality, security (social rights).'"[68]

As the feminist movement reminds us, the separation between artistic critique and social critique is furthermore based on a problematic understanding of autonomy as a practice that is always already infused and grounded in reproduction and maintenance, yet structurally "invisibilized" in order to keep its relationship to capital.[69] "The modern stakes for the autonomy of art had to do with severing itself from productive labour, conceivably to counter a world where the mental and manual labour brutalized some and idealised others."[70] The basis for this form of autonomy has been "the unfulfilled utopia of avant-garde as unalienated labour," while the labor of maintenance and reproductive work has remained alienated and invisible.[71] In this sense, Kerstin Stakemeier and Marina Vishmidt enrich Lazzarato's claim to "no autonomy without reproduction."

The legacies of these cultural practices and their demands can be found, according to Vishmidt, through the "artists and cultural workers assuming the organizational forms and demands of the labor movement such as fair pay and equitable working conditions [...] encapsulated in the history of Artists Unions in the UK and US in the 1970s, the Art Workers' Coalition in New York in the late '60s–mid-'70s, as well as current groups such as W.A.G.E. (Working Artists and the Greater Economy) and the PWB (Precarious Workers Brigade)." To this I add the feminist movement and the demand for the recognition of reproductive labor, and Graciela Carnevale's involvement in *Tucumán Arde* (1968), Mary Kelly with Margaret Harrison and Kay Hunt's *Women and Work* (1973–75), and Berwick Street Film Collective's *Nightcleaners* (1975).[72] Moreover, we can find anti-colonial, decolonial, and feminist demands by cultural

67 Slogan by "Coordination des Intermittents et Précaires," 2004, in France. See Maurizio Lazzarato, "The Misfortunes of the 'Artistic Critique' and of Cultural Employment."

68 Maurizio Lazzarato, "The Misfortunes of the 'Artistic Critique' and of Cultural Employment," 2.

69 See also Binna Choi and Annette Krauss' afterword, "Have You Had a Productive Day?" on page 165.

70 Kerstin Stakemeier and Marina Vishmidt, *Reproducing Autonomy* (London: Mute Publishing, 2016), 46.

71 Ibid, 46.

72 Marina Vishmidt, *Speculation as a Mode of Production in Art and Capital*, 124.

93

workers playing a role in the history of solidarity movements such as the Black Panthers, the Black Arts Movement, and the Guerrilla Girls, and also among Black feminist writers who continue to oppose the patriarchal, colonial conditions of Western late-capitalist society.

Where to go from here? This text unfolds broader sociopolitical conditions of education and learning, and the embeddedness of this writing in an academic and art instituitional context. My commitment articulated here is to consider how I can write (about) a more robust arts-based research on unlearning, when these practices are always already over-determined by capitalist market logics. However, to paint a regime of capitalist appropriation that is expansive and all-embracing is tricky, because the risk is that:

> Fears of co-optation become more powerful than desires for connection, and moralizing judgments are solicited in place of realistic assessments of successes and failures.[73]

Thus, there is neither a possibility of ignoring policy papers on lifelong learning, *nor* giving them a too powerful, thus overwhelming position. In the spirit of the collaborative efforts within *Site for Unlearning (Art Organization)*, I opt for what feminist economic geographers J. K. Gibson-Graham call a consideration of successes and failures instead of indulging in the fear of expansive capitalist appropriation. Departing from specific historical processes and contingencies, I ask: Which claims are not compatible with a capitalist market logic and therefore excluded?

Based on the study of lifelong learning and the discourses that surround it, I see the following aspects as tentative concretizations for further approaching practices of unlearning.

Who Is Excluded from the "Self"?

The current times are characterized by a rise in far-right political parties and policymaking in Europe and the US that express racist, xenophobic, and

---

73   J. K. Gibson-Graham, *A Postcapitalist Politics*
(Minneapolis: University of Minnesota Press,
2006), xxiii.

Islamophobic ideas with attempts to put them into practice. Wynter's "No Humans Involved" has been the writing on the wall since it was penned in 1994. Translated into the discourse around lifelong learning, her letter urges us to ask: Who is excluded in discourses of self-determination? And what concept of humanity is presupposed in models of learning? Wynter repeatedly reminds the reader that we cannot give up on tracing and working against the exclusions we produce on multiple levels, often to the disadvantage of marginalized groups. Recognizing that such an approach will always be threatened by the fear of co-optation, Wynter calls for a relentless analysis of exclusions in concepts (of un/learning), our (educational) institutions, and the way we relate to each other.

"No Culture Without Social Rights and Recognition of Reproductive Labor"

Questions on self-determination, autonomy, and freedom, as well as demands for equality, solidarity, recognition of reproductive labor and social rights, have been crucial to the modern-colonial project. However, as part of the rhetoric of modernity, their separation has inscribed itself in how institutions are organized, and how education and learning is conceptualized. The critical pedagogues of the 1970s and 1980s did not accept this separation. It is here that paths for other legacies of cultural practices are re-opened and intersect with practices of unlearning, namely unlearning the separation between coloniality and modernity, and the separation between artistic and social critique.

Practicing Collectivity Otherwise

The economization of learning is grounded in the human capital of the individual that drains itself for the phantasmal parameter of growth, wealth, and development. Institutions determine what needs to be learned in order to find out later on (through assessment) that learning took place. In the knowledge economy, this cycle is constitutive of quality assessment. Learning and knowledge need to be certified and simultaneously devalued in order to prolong educational careers that feed knowledge economies. Radical pedagogies propose a modest, seemingly irrelevant, shift in order to intervene in this logic. A group of people find out and determine together what is important

95

to learn and unlearn; and how. The sites for unlearning depart from there. This process not only places negotiation, disagreement, and difference as crucial aspects of education, but puts the question of collectivity at center stage. How do we think and practice collectivity otherwise? Who is the "we" in the shifting roles of the specific settings? And again, how does the modern-colonial matrix of power play into this? The collaborative practices are litmus tests for institutions and our own practices on the basis of the demands of "no freedom, autonomy, authenticity without solidarity, equality, recognition of reproductive labour and security of social rights."

An earlier version of this text is published in Krauss 2018.

THE IMPERATIVE FOR SELF-ATTAINMENT: FROM CRADLE TO GRAVE

Andrea Phillips

If what the worker desires is to be a poet, rather than to be on the barricade, in a sense that desire presupposes a dissolution of the whole social relations upon which the concept of the poet itself has become constructed.

— Adrian Rifkin[1]

Casco Art Institute's long-term engagement with *unlearning* produces important, if fragile and difficult, possibilities for a future reorientation of what the organization terms to be the "busyness" of art's conditioned labor. Learning to unlearn, as this publication enunciates, produces a systematic reshaping that is both personal and institutional, a process that refracts through the modes and scales of institutional organization and interpersonal relations. Casco Art Institute's broad project demands that we institute commons-based processes of working to create cultural events and affects, but such an approach demands forms of solidarity that are diametrically opposed—not simply by the socio-political framework in which Casco Art Institute sits, but on a much more pragmatic level—by the structures of employment, funding, reporting, and performing in public in which the workers of Casco Art Institute are enmeshed. Such a situation requires, therefore, a type of double-tracking, akin to that practiced by historical resistance movements for black, queer, and intersectional struggles. As the authors say in the afterword for this volume, "Unlearning institutional habits has a double trajectory: it involves ongoing

discursive and critical unlearning exercises that are coupled with bodily interventions, structural literacy, and imaginative jumps."[2]

Amongst the many trajectories of Casco Art Institute's long-term collaboration with Annette Krauss is a focus on the complex social and political history of the concept of "lifelong learning." Here I will pick up on Krauss' research in order to attempt to describe the complexity of the conjoined, or doubled, tactics of desire, empowerment, participation, and personal growth deployed by both contemporary European education policy and its deep institutionalization of capitalized life as well as those workers that attempt to resist such capture.[3] Lifelong learning, as Krauss points out and as has been practiced for a number of years at Casco Art Institute, is a complex site of "unlearning" precisely due to the fact that it both calls upon us to continue to reach for the stars within structures of meritocratic capitalism, and mimics and produces the emancipatory discourse we, in turn, often identify as our own.

Lifelong learning is a strategy that Krauss analyses in detail for its ambivalent aims—full of the promise of rich growth unrestricted by the prejudices of youth-focused education and at the same time a threat to non-productive and peaceable old age during which the shackles of consistent progress may be finally escaped. Krauss comes to the concept of lifelong learning through an artistic practice that has established itself as an intricate, understated, and thoughtful retort to the pressures and promises of (predominantly) Anglo-European arts and educational institutions as they co-opt, or are co-opted, into regimes of quantifiable knowledge production. Her focus is very often on the subjects of those productions—the learners, the users,

---

1   Adrian Rifkin, "Inventing Recollection," in
    *Interrogating Cultural Studies: Theory, Politics
    and Practice*, ed. Paul Bowman (London:
    Pluto, 2003), 114.

2   Binna Choi and Annette Krauss, "Have you
    had a Productive Day?" in *Unlearning Exercises:
    Art Organizations as Sites for Unlearning*,
    Binna Choi, Annette Krauss, Yolande Zola
    Zoli van der Heide eds. (Amsterdam: Casco
    Art Institute/Valiz, 2018), 165.

3   See Isabelle Stengers and Philippe Pignarre,
    Capitalist Sorcery: Breaking the Spell (New York:
    Palgrave Macmillan, 2011).

the participants—and the psycho-political impact of the regulations that bind their bodies into systematizations of education. Krauss demands that we understand the relationship between lifelong learning (progress-oriented and accumulative) and unlearning (one's privileges, to go against what one cannot not wish to inhabit). Having worked across a range of educational temporalities, such as with teenage kids reappropriating schooling spaces to arts education at tertiary level, Krauss draws attention to the continued psychic and economic oppression levelled at all natures of community through the concept of lifelong learning. Krauss says, for example:

> My aim is to outline connections between European policy making on lifelong learning as strategic implementation of knowledge-based economies in Europe since the 1990s, and the formation of a pedagogical subjectivity that are intertwined with the advancement of an artistic subject as a possible role model for the new economy. The reason why I take this specific perspective is two-fold. Firstly, lifelong learning functions, here, as an example of a progress-oriented, accumulative model of learning that pervades institutions and subjectivities today. Secondly, I situated my work within the field of arts, and the field of education and research, both inside and outside academic frameworks. Observing, as so many do, the detrimental effects of the commodification of art, education and research made it inevitable to better understand the discourse of lifelong learning that is promoted by European policies as one of the prevalent models for learning in the framework of European knowledge economies.[4]

Lifelong learning, understood by Krauss through the close reading of European policy documents and tracing the concept's development from the early 1970s, adheres and is produced by a conjunction of social, anthropological, and governmental ideas that would at a certain level seem contradictory. At once a concept that promises a transversalization and embodied idea of learning

---

[4]   See Annette Krauss, chap. 4 "Lifelong Learning and the Professionalized Learner," in *Sites for Unlearning: On the Material, Artistic and Political Dimensions of Processes of Unlearning*, (PhD diss., Vienna: Academy of Fine Arts, 2018).

(as opposed to education) seemingly influenced by such anti-authoritarian figures as Paolo Freire, bell hooks, and Ivan Illich, lifelong learning also inculcates the consistency of skills-acquisition, labor-advancement, employ-ability, and individualized responsibility for these things as the psycho-social domain of contemporary life. Structured to negate any consequences of organized protest (you can't demand better conditions for retirement through your union if the concept of retirement is annulled or infinitely extended), the soft power of lifelong learning has many equivalents within the growth of liberal government.[5] In her research and practice Krauss recognises what she calls the "entanglements" of once-radical forms of learning developed to oppose conventional authoritarian educational formats, open-ended offers of self-improvement through endless learning, and creative and/or artistic approaches to the learning environment in which new techniques and technologies of interaction establishing putative "freedoms" take the place of political solidarity and organized opposition:

> Lifelong learning, if successful, intends no disorganization or a dismantling of national educational systems. Softening institutional processes and valorizing non-formal learning get promoted as devices that render fixed and slow institutions more malleable and porous to outer institutional processes and the market. The processes of softening institutions are successfully obscured by policies on lifelong learning that seek to flexibilize

5   Joseph Nye traces the history of the in-corporation of knowledge as a political tool through, in the West, propaganda and media and communications growth and the concept of public diplomacy. Public diplomacy should not be confused with propaganda, he says, "Nor is public diplomacy merely public relations. Conveying information and selling a positive image is part of it, but public diplomacy also involves building long-term relationships that create an enabling environ-ment for government policies." See Joseph S. Nye Jr, "Wielding Soft Power," *Soft Power: The Means to Success in World Politics*. Harvard Kennedy School Belford Center. Pdf. Online: www.belfercenter.org/node/89707 (Accessed 12 September 2018), 8.

the given frameworks of education in order to bring non-formal learning, direct education and socio-economic developments closer into proximity. This indicates once more lifelong learning as a late-capitalist, neoliberal tool.[6]

Learning from the cradle to the grave has an Orwellian atmosphere. Yet, as Krauss identifies, it is a core policy in contemporary European government, intending to keep us busy, healthy, occupied, and laboring within increasingly precarious knowledge markets within a flexible and boundless concept of life and the self, implemented as a pan-European strategic advancement. In this essay I would like to take on Krauss' analysis of lifelong learning in the broader framework of her extensive engagement with the concept of education and attempt to link it to thoughts on meritocracy and the complex knot that is produced through the desire for intellectual and aesthetic engagement in and of the world and its concomitant capitalization.

I first encountered Krauss' interest in lifelong learning—and its connection to the broader concept of unlearning—whilst taking part in "Let's Mobilize: What is Feminist Pedagogy?" a collectively organized symposium held at Valand Academy, University of Gothenburg (where I am employed).[7] The tactics of the organizers of this symposium, held in 2016, were closely aligned to Krauss': to share methods for how to rewind processes of calibration in which structures of power—practical, conceptual, somatic, and psychically organized—could be stripped away to reveal a basis of ideological supposition. After an evening meal on one of the symposium days, in an elevated seminar room made messy through the rearrangement of furniture as well as by hours of joint thinking, talking, translating, acting, cooking, drinking, and eating, some of us gathered around Krauss as she introduced us to various legally-enfranchised documents produced by the European Union in which the goal

6   Annette Krauss, "Lifelong Learning and the Professionalized Learner," 144–45.
7   See the *Let's Mobilize: What is Feminist Pedagogy* tumblr, www.whatisfeminist-pedagogy.tumblr.com (Accessed July 5, 2017). and the *andpublishing* website, www.andpublishing.org/lets-mobilise-what-is-feminist-pedagogy. (Accessed July 5, 2017).

and doctrine of lifelong learning was described. The idea, like its sister, equality of education, is difficult for feminists to pursue. Our mothers and grandmothers argued for the right to learn, to be included in learning, and for the right to continue to access education until old age. Yet, as described above, the imperative to learn—to continue to be a productive unit within a systematically capitalized structure of education—seems far less enfranchising, particularly, as Krauss herself points out, when the "self"-ascribed task of learning by European bureaucrats is treated as though they are genderless, classless, and raceless.

Like Krauss, those that organized the "Let's Mobilize: What is Feminist Pedagogy?" event wanted to develop an alternative methodology for learning and experimenting with ideas and practices; alternative, in this particular instance, to the art school that they were variously employed at as doctoral students, administration, faculty staff, and amanuenses, etc. The three-day event, held in the autumn of 2016 at Valand Academy, was organized collectively by a group that ranged between three and fifteen people who worked together to develop a format that allowed access to people outside the academy, a free event with food included (we all cooked together) and an experimental format that encompassed reading, translating, performing, cleaning, sleeping, org-anizing, hosting, and skill-swapping, etc.. The process was transformative for many of us attending and contributing, but its event-based nature left us wondering how to implement some of the suggestions and questions at a more sustained level across our art school (and others). The basis of the question was a concern with the structural adjustments to concepts of education that had so evidently provided the language and methodology for lifelong learning and other franchises of creative practice within governmental frameworks. Krauss' reading group was thus uncomfortable as well as pedagogical—we sat and read through various EU documents—potentially rendering us subjects of a display of radicality, suggesting that equalities of educational opportunity and access to rich languages of critique might continue beyond the halcyon period we worked together.

Valand, like many art academies produced through a long history of conservatoire education in Anglo-European culture, struggles with producing spaces of egalitarian education within a system which is already loaded against those that do not have histories of educative access within their families and forums of sociality. A strong political ethic exists within the staff—across all

levels of staffing—and research produced by the institution reflects this. However, the infrastructural demand for individual attainment and autonomous excellence, in marking criteria, in teaching formations (the concept of studio practice, the solo critique versus the group critique, etc.), make the disparity between politics and outcomes seem, at times, impossible to surmount. The demand comes, and forgive the patrimonial metaphor, from above and below: if students demand different forms of education staff are obliged to show them the rule book, and if staff suggest different forms, students inquire as to why they are not getting, for example, individual attention. This bodily experience of segregation splits us from each other and ourselves. It is a form of what Foucault called biopower—the regulation of life in such a way that there is no need for the threat of death.[8]

The temptation of lifelong learning, then, is to continue to succumb to the being of this subject (in fact, in her analysis of European documents Krauss quotes from a UNESCO report that is called, astonishingly, *Learning to Be*). The assumption made is that every being attains or should be willing to attempt to attain such a subject. In a Europe riddled by the still-alive violence of its histories of colonialism, this subject is very much in question. Questions of difference—of the necessity to think alternatively about the context and circumstance of learning—are ridden over roughshod in the generalized capacity-building and endless attainment narratives of lifelong learning.

When I read Krauss' investigation of learning I am reminded of another Anglo-European political ambition related to education that comes close to, but also differs significantly from lifelong learning: this is the idea of meritocracy. Meritocracy is the idea that no matter what the social background of each person within a culture, if they have the natural capacity and the aspiration, they should be able to rise to the higher echelons of that society's social formation. The term was popularised by Michael Young, a major architect of the post-war Labour Party in the UK and a committed Socialist, in his fictional book *The Rise of Meritocracy*, published in 1958. The book, set in 2058 and narrated as the partial recordings of a dead historian called "Michael Young," charts the ascendance of a new form of social and educational organization in Britain, one

8   See Michel Foucault, *History of Sexuality*
     Volume 1 (New York: Random House, 1978).

not based on inherited birth right or riches, but on IQ; on "natural" talent. The schooling system in the book is reorganized so that rather than being based on class and gender (race is not tackled in the book, perhaps surprisingly given the influx of workers from Britain's ex-colonies at the time of its writing), it is based on natural talent which is nurtured where it is found. Part-satire and part-forewarning, *The Rise of Meritocracy* is a difficult and ambivalent book to read now, primarily due to the fact that, whilst depicted as a bad dream for Socialism by Young in the late 1950s, by the mid-1990s it had been taken up and espoused as a rhetorical and educational tool by Tony Blair's New Labour Party ideology to continued destructive effect.[9]

In "Meritocracy as Plutocracy: The Marketising of 'Equality' under Neoliberalism" Jo Littler explores the ascendance of the term in great detail. In particular, Littler is interested in what she calls "meritocratic feeling"[10] and its concomitant moral virtue that has taken hold in neoliberal culture, rendering palpable in both discourse and political action an understanding of equality of access related to people of divergent skills, experiences, and abilities replaced with an understanding of equality as "equality of opportunity."[11]

> Today, in many countries across the global North, the idea that we *should* live in a 'meritocracy' has become integral to contemporary structures of feeling: assumed by both right-wing and left-wing political parties, heavily promoted in educational discourse, and animating popular culture, meritocracy has become an idea as uncontroversial and as homely as 'motherhood and apple pie'. Why should issue be taken with such an apparently innocuous concept,

9   Whilst Young is often described as the inventor of the term meritocracy, Jo Littler points out that the term was first used by Alan Fox in 1956 in an article called "Class and Equality" in a way that was, "more extensively critical and politically radical" than the ways in which the term was deployed by Young. See Jo Littler, "Meritocracy as Plutocracy: The Marketising of Equality under Neoliberalism" in Jeremy Gilbert ed., *New Formations: Neoliberal Culture*, no. 80–1 (Autumn–Winter, 2013), 56.

10   Littler, ibid., 68.

11   Littler, ibid., 60.

one whose potency lies in its investment in the conception of social mobility, pitted against 'older' forms of inherited privilege? [...] I argue that we should pay close attention to meritocracy because it has become a key ideological means by which plutocracy—or government by a wealthy elite—perpetuates itself through neoliberal culture.[12]

In structures of education in the UK and other parts of Europe, in terms of resistance to comprehensive education (education offered to all on the basis of equal access), there is a gradual but apparent diminishing of political investment in the recognition of a broad range of abilities, some of which need more support due to social-contextual heritage and circumstance, in favor of competitive aspiration. In arts education this is especially so, where "raw talent" is spotted at an early age, where teenage aspiration within the arts at schools is modelled on individual success stories of blue-chip artists, where "blind" portfolio assessment is undertaken at degree entry level, where financial investment in artworks is based on hedonic indexing and where competitive marketization is the not-so-subtle mechanism of career development. This is also the language currently deployed by US President Donald Trump, coming as he does from a family whose pride in their "self-made" ascendency is well-documented and whose own rise in popularity comes in large part through TV talent show hosting.[13] As Littler says of the UK under David Cameron's leadership of the Conservative Party:

'Aspiration Nation' as a rhetorical strategy, and as an expression of meritocratic feeling, connects self-belief and aspiration with the trope of hard work. It is striking how, again and again, 'hard work' combined with self-belief is employed by an unprecedentedly privileged cadre of politicians and millionaire elites to justify their position and success and to prescribe this as a route for others.[14]

12   Littler, ibid., 53.
13   See Sidney Blumenthal, "A Short History of the Trump Family," *London Review of Books*, vol 39, no. 4 (February 16, 2017).
14   Littler, "Meritocracy as Plutocracy," 67.

But what if your circumstances do not allow for aspiration? What if, "there is far more talent, intelligence, hard work, and ability in the population than there are people lucky enough to find themselves in a position to exploit them"?[15] What if that intelligence takes time, space, confidence, cultural reformulation, cultural contextualization, shape-shifting, imagination, and alternative pedagogic approaches (ones that do not fit into a national curriculum) to develop? What if such development cannot or will not take place under the "equality of aspiration" rhetoric produced through meritocracy despite its putative basis in forms of classlessness, genderlessness, racelessness? What if we do not want to lose our class, race, or gender for the sake of meritocratic aspiration?

> Cultural location, especially in terms of shifts between patterns, is a much better model for explaining social mobility than is the mechanistic un-dialectical notion of 'intelligence'.[16]

In *Learning to Labour: How Working-Class Kids Get Working-Class Jobs* (1977), Paul Willis provides a now-seminal examination of school education in a Secondary Modern school in the Midlands, UK.[17] The social scientist

17   The post-war system of free universal education in the UK divided children at the age of eleven between Grammar Schools (to gain access to which a child had to pass an entrance exam), Secondary Modern Schools and Secondary Technical Schools. The medieval system of elite "Public" schooling (for which fees were paid) was retained and administered privately separately from the free system. In 1965—seven years after Young published the first edition of *The Rise of Meritocracy*—the British Labour government in power at the time sought to replace this tripartite system of free education with a general "Comprehensive" schooling system which sought in theory to eradicate the inequalities produced through the require-ment to take an entrance test to get into the "top" tier. This system was not, however, taken up cohesively across the country. Wallis' fieldwork took place in this context.

15   Stephen McNamee and Robert Miller, *The Myth of Meritocracy* (Lanham: Rowman & Littlefield, 2009), 16; as quoted in Littler, ibid., 65.

16   Paul Willis, *Learning to Labour: How Working-Class Kids Get Working-Class Jobs* (Farnham: Ashgate, 2000), 59.

conducts a close ethnographic study, in particular, on a group of between twelve and fifteen boys (self-appointed "The Lads") between 1972 and 1976 as they move through education, examination, recreation, and careers advice in the new context of the national raising of the school leaving age (from fifteen to sixteen years old in 1972) and during the initiation within education of governmental interest and accountancy of "social mobility." The Lads are all white (this despite the fact that the Midlands was rapidly becoming a racially diversified community within its cities and towns due to the expansion of the British workforce through the invitation to ex-colonial industrial workers after the war) and identify as working class, expecting to enter into manual labor, low skilled, and/or factory jobs as opposed to the "Ear'oles"; the boys who studied and were largely expected to enter into white collar jobs. In the analytic section of the book Willis makes continuous reference to the resistance to new, more experimental models of education being introduced into British schooling at the time (later to be dubbed by those who support meritocracy as a soft option for those over-provided for by the state without the individual capacity to develop themselves). "'The Lads,'" says Wallis, "are committing themselves to a future of generalized labour."[18] They are resistant to the new "permissive" models of education being introduced into schooling, in which they are asked to enter into dialogue, to participate in their own pedagogical shaping, to express what they are feeling. Wallis is sympathetic to this resistance and sees it in it a critical, if subsumed, understanding on the part of The Lads that educational experimentation was a continuation of the same hierarchical power structures already in place: "The crucial relationship [in such new educational models] is predicated on the consent of the pupils to reciprocate—willingly and from their own resources—in acts of educational exchange. Progressivism as it is usually practiced can be seen as a continuation of traditionalism in the sense that it attempts to preserve a version of the consent which has always been at the heart of the older method."[19] Educational experimentation, as stated, derided by the educational and conservative elite but, at the same time, working its way into the meritocratic system through the concept of self-attainment— had a bad smell. For what incentive is there for The Lads to enter a meritocratic

18   Wallis, *Learning to Labour*, 100.
19   Wallis, ibid., 87.

system within a labor system dominated by hegemonic stasis? In 1977 the "cumulative encrustment" of capitalism on offer within the rigidly class-bound structures of the Midlands' industrial landscapes is only beginning to be touched by the permissive society that is so feared by educational traditionalists—those opposed to "learning" instead of "education," Freire instead of examinations. Yet what Wallis, following Marx, diagnoses as "the permanent struggle" which keeps capital alive within such educational environs is precisely the same force that ushers in meritocracy. It is precisely why meritocracy—the continuous struggle with personal power within a culture of ascendant reward—is the technique of capitalism par excellence. Meritocracy embodies and performs struggle both personal and institutional, at the level of the home, the state, and the transnational.[20]

Jo Littler also picks up on permissiveness in education as both a fear haunting the plutocracy—she quotes David Cameron from *The Guardian* in 2012 suggesting that left-wing theorists "stand in the way of aspirational parents by excusing low expectations and blaming social disadvantage"[21]—and as an ushering in of aspirational culture, which was forcefully rejected by Wallis' Lads. This rejection was not to last much longer: following industrial decline and the destruction of trade unions by Margaret Thatcher's government in the 1980s, cities like Birmingham and areas of the Midlands had to turn to softer skills to maintain regional capitalization, and in the mid-1990s and early 2000s the region turned to heritage and culture as a major element of its rebranding. Such creative industrial enterprise necessitates aspirational workers; the Lads are left behind.

What happened in the warped logic of meritocracy to render social disadvantage a toxic asset and experimental, contextual schooling as ambivalently aspirational, when so evidently the increasing division between the working class poor and their rich neighbors was set to expand? Jo Littler would no doubt point out that this is exactly the point. The movement from collective creative collaboration within schooling—in which the pedagogues' right to

---

20 Wallis, ibid., 175. In *Learning to Labour* Wallis also pays a debt of influence to Stuart Hall and the Centre for Contemporary Cultural Studies set up in Birmingham in 1964, the principal industrial town of the Midlands.

21 Littler, "Meritocracy as Plutocracy," 66.

knowledge is challenged in processes of unlearning—to the privatization of creativity in the individual and their product is now tacitly accepted, as Littler says, like motherhood and apple pie. Or, as Adrian Rifkin, following Jacques Rancière would suggest, the very concept of the necessity to dissolve the social structure upon which in education the concept of the poet has been constructed, is further out of reach than ever.[22] What happens to those left on the heap of non-aspiration, in the eyes of the dominant regime, without talent and without merit but with lives that, thanks to almost eight decades of support from the National Health Service in the context of the UK, will live longer and cost more money due to divested pension funds? The answer is lifelong learning.

Those that can, rise to the top; those that cannot, continue to learn in a second tier and residualized version of aspiration produced through weak translations of experimental learning ideas half-imbided; a conveyor-belt of education until you die. It should be noted how, as Krauss points out, the idea of continuous education, adult education, etc., has also morphed, like meritocracy, from a concept of increased egalitarian provision to one of self-privatization.

Michael Young spent his life co-founding initiatives and institutions that, one by one, sought to produce epistemological change in the concepts of life and learning, always working within the structures of local and national government in the UK and internationally. Having established his political career with the Labour Party, in 1964 he established the Institute of Community Studies; in the late sixties and seventies he campaigned against grammar schools and for the abolition of entrance exams; he started the National Extension College in 1960 which provided a "dawn university" via television for people to be able to access around work hours (later to become established as The Open University); in 1982 he co-founded the University of the Third Age; and perhaps more mystifyingly, in 1997, the School for Social Entrepreneurs. In a career devoted to social change at a structural level, Young must have often found himself perplexed to find his ideas returned as an inverted version of their original intention, alongside Socialism's demise within mainstream politics. Meritocracy and lifelong learning seem to be evidence of such a shifting dynamic not simply heuristically but also in terms of the nebulous

22   Rifkin, "Inventing Recollection."

relation between accountability and the self. The problem is that what appears and "feels" (qua Littler) like progress, what accounts for equality of access and continued emancipation within the affective regimes of self-improvement so often turns out to be not simply governmentalized but turned back as a weapon against the establishment of real equality. The mantra of motivation keeps us going, whilst someone else runs to the bank.

TOILET (T)ISSUES #3

Against All Odds—Migrant Domestic Labor Struggle and Forms of Organizing

The following conversation below took place with migrant domestic workers in the Netherlands on the desire, difficulty, and necessity of organizing among themselves and others to improve the rights of undocumented migrant workers. Against all odds, these workers continue to fight for better living and working conditions through sharing knowledge and building solidarity, while also educating their fellow members to become future leaders. Despite today's hostile atmosphere towards migrants, the Indonesian Migrant Workers Union (IMWU) and Filipino Migrant Workers in Solidarity (FILMIS) constantly persuade public institutions to breathe life into the existing system and open up new spaces for their existence. Here, they share their diverse strategies and tactics for the self-organization and self-reproduction of their movement and communities, and envision the futures that are needed to bring (migrant) domestic work and

111

maintenance work to a rate of pay and social value that is equal to other waged work.

Participants include: Faisol Iskandar, Ismiatun, and Erminah Zaenah (with her seven-year-old son Luca) from IMWU; Jacob Apostol and Joy Melanie Escano from FILMIS; Binna Choi and Yolande Zola Zoli van der Heide from Casco Art Institute; Annette Krauss; and Sakiko Sugawa (*Center for Reproductive Labor*).* They were hosted by Eid Magdy in het Wereldhuis (the Worldhouse) in April 2018 in Amsterdam, a space frequently used by IMWU.

* Sakiko Sugawa initiated the project *Center for Reproductive Labor* in 2015, with the aim to resist worker exploitation and reconfigure the value of reproductive labor through prefigurative politics.

Sakiko Sugawa
Thank you so much for taking the time to talk with us about the activities and thoughts that let IMWU and FILMIS flourish and sustain themselves.

Annette Krauss
Our get-together takes place in the context of the collaborative project *Site for Unlearning (Art Organization)* and a subsequent publication that works through and imagines forms of organizing, and here we are attempting to relate with forms of organizing in the wider movement of migrant domestic labor struggles. We are particularly interested in how the organizational aspect of Casco Art Institute operates in the relationship between learning and unlearning, the role of art in this, and how to unlearn organizational habits that work against Casco's mandate to engage in the commons.

Jack Apostol
Why unlearning?

Annette
As artist, I'm working on the intersection of art and education to explore how, in schools and other educational settings and institutions, learning is mostly understood as acquiring and accumulating knowledge or skills. It is not a coincidence that this understanding of learning smoothly feeds the capitalist world, which tells me more and bigger is desirable. My privileges as a white woman with citizenship in a European country further feed into this, undermining quests for redistribution, equality, and justice. That's why I think that we need to experiment with other ways of learning and organizing. How could the work on unlearning intervene here? What do I need to get rid of, in order to do the work I am doing?

Yolande Zola Zoli van der Heide
As Annette mentioned we've been meeting with the team at Casco— it's been over three years actually! We worked on a set of exercises that range from "digital cleaning," struggling with Casco's wage system, to questions of temporality in the organization. The one that we are most successful at is cleaning together every Monday after our staff meeting. One of the things we wanted to unlearn was this feeling of busyness, and we realized that we always feel so busy because we're not actually valuing, or valorising, domestic work as part of our "real" or organizational work.

113

Annette

And we want to find out *how* we can continue to build solidarity with migrant domestic workers who are fighting for their rights here in the Netherlands. This started already during the *Grand Domestic Revolution* project initiated through Casco. And we asked Sakiko to be part of this conversation as her take on domestic work and her art practice is very compelling in these regards.

Sakiko

While I was running a small cultural center in Kyoto with my collaborators, we realized that in cultural institutions you always have to produce. But in order to produce there's lots of work that needs to be done in the back: you have to clean, organize spaces, and maintain relationships. People see the front side but not the work at the back, the type Annette and Yolande were mentioning, the type that is not appreciated, that no one wants to do, but that makes all other work possible. So, I started wondering why, that's how I started developing my interest in reproductive labor and domestic work. I think it's essential and fundamental labor. It can be amazing but the way it is valued in our society is opposite of its actual value. So, reconfiguring its value is my challenge. I know you guys all laugh at me when *I* talk about this dream!

Joy Escano

That's a big challenge!

Binna Choi

What I'd like to learn is how IMWU and FILMIS organize yourselves when you have so much work? Please share the secrets of your power!

Sakiko

... and the different aspects of organizing? It would be great if you specified different types of organizing tactics and strategies.

Faisol

Actually, it's pretty hard to organize. People are afraid and scared to talk with other people. For many years I learned how to connect people heart-by-heart. I learned how people would open up without them knowing. But it is a long process.

Yolande

Is it a question of gaining people's trust?

Faisol

Yes. I learned from Heri Slamet, one

of our IMWU founders before he passed away, that if you want to help people that are undocumented migrant domestic workers and build a movement then show that you are their servant not their leader or employer; if they ask you anything you should do it. Heri taught me, if people call me at two o'clock in the morning and need me then I'm coming!

Erminah Zaenah

You are really helping people twenty-four hours. Also, Heri would help people anytime, even when he was sick; anytime, and anywhere around the Netherlands.

Sakiko

Where does this drive and mission that you want to serve people come from?

Faisol

We needed first to think of a fast way to help people. In 2010 until 2012 when the police caught undocumented migrants, they would just get sent away from the country without asking why this happened: if you didn't have any documents then you had to go back to your country. And secondly, we needed to think of how to help people when they have a problem with their health, to try to teach each other how to connect with the hospital. The third very important thing is learning Dutch and English. So yeah, I grew up like this. We see what the problem is, how we can help, and we do it together, even without money. We let our weakness become our strength.

Ismiatun

We don't have money but we collect together. Everyone can do something and together we know a lot.

Erminah

The main point of IMWU is showing you're a servant for these people, and then people will know you and how important the organization is and more people come in and more people join. That's our secret weapon.

Sakiko

A beautiful one.

Annette

Is this also the reason why you try to organize from different locations in the Netherlands? How do you get members?

Erminah

We have a coordinator in Amsterdam, one in Den Haag and

also in Rotterdam. We're still looking for one in Maastricht or maybe another area where we can find Indonesian people who want to help people, and we ask them to join IMWU, so we can help each other.

Faisol
First things first, we make an info night about lawyers, police, and health. We spread the word via WhatsApp and people slowly get to know us. At the moment we are more than four hundred members.

Annette
How does it work with organizing in FILMIS?

Jack
Filipinos really love organizing. You'll know this if you're in Holland, there are lots of Filipino organizations, but not as big as IMWU.

Faisol
The funny thing I learnt from Filipinos is that when they don't like the leader they go and make a new organization.

Joy
In Holland, from what I heard, we have more or less fifty Filipino organizations with different objectives.

Jack
When I came here I joined one of them, because when I was in the Philippines I was also involved in organizing there, even during my student times.

Sakiko
You were a teacher back home, right?

Jack
Yes, job opportunities were very difficult to find in the Philippines and in 2000 there was an economic crisis so there was entrenchment in the schools and income was very low. Back then, I worked on basic human rights. When I came to the Netherlands, Migrante, an organization that focuses on the global alliance of overseas Filipinos, invited me and I joined. Migrante is also involved in political issues. I observed that in terms of organizing, there are a lot of challenges here. It's different from the Philippines of course. In the Philippines your actions are not limited because it's part of your rights, but it's not easy to organize here being undocumented. There are many constraints, for example, you cannot just hold an event as sometimes they ask you to pay through bank account. So, you need to find one who can use a bank account to pay for a venue.

Joy

I also left the Philippines in 2000, back then hundreds of companies were relocated to China, so there were millions left unemployed. For five years I was looking for a job but it was difficult and my kids were starting to go to school so that's when I decided to go somewhere. My first thought was of Saudi Arabia for domestic work, but my parents were so scared, so I decided to be an undocumented tourist in Europe because it's more safe in Europe than in the Middle East or Hong Kong.

When I came here it was difficult at first because I didn't know anything. People easily take advantage of you. I started as an au pair, an illegal au pair, and I worked from four o'clock in the morning until twelve o'clock at night, for 200–300 euros a month. I didn't have friends, so nobody was there to teach me my rights. I don't want other people to have the same experience. If people know that you are undocumented and ignorant of your rights, they tend to abuse you and treat you as second-class human beings. This is the main reason why I became involved in organizing. I wanted my fellow Filipino migrants to be aware of their rights.

Jack

As an undocumented migrant your mobility is very limited. You cannot just go, for example, to parties because if the music is loud and the neighbors call the police then there will be identity checks. So, we have to choose which friends to go with and whom to trust. I met Joy and other Filipinos who happen to be undocumented too; so, we are in the same situation.

Faisol

What's important now in the struggle is how we can save our money. Right now, we put our cash money in the house, but when the owner of the house kicks us out we cannot take our money and so we have a problem. Secondly, there are more and more places, for example, the buses, where we cannot pay cash anymore. This is a real struggle for us.

Joy

Yes, even some restaurants now don't accept cash. Being undocumented makes your rights so limited. But, somehow it makes you develop to be strong and patient in your struggle.

Jack

Yes, our world is getting smaller and smaller. We feel that the

government and private enterprises are deliberately making our space of mobility smaller and restricted. We are afraid that the time will come here in Holland when we can no longer act normally as human beings, because of these situations. How can we survive if we are not allowed to use cash in our transactions when buying food and paying our transportation instead of using public transport card? We can't have pin cards.

Joy
So sometimes if you want to go to a restaurant or buy a coffee at the big library in Den Haag, you have to look to see, does it take cash? And it makes us paranoid. I realize that the use of pin card is symbolic because it's a way to define what your migration status is.

Faisol
Right now, that's one of our biggest struggles. I hope maybe with Casco, we can make a story of the people who have lost their money because they've had to work but then the owner of the house has taken their money, and the owner says whose fault is that for putting your money in your room, why don't you put it in the bank? But, we don't have a bank account!

Binna
And IMWU cannot negotiate with a bank because they are ruled by the government?

Joy
The first thing they ask is for a BSN number. This is one of the challenges we are facing being undocumented. We work hard to save money so that we can have something for the future when we return to the Philippines. But how can we do it? All our income we send back ends up being spent by our families. But if we have a bank account, we can control it and save a lot.

Sakiko
So, it's the linking law, where the BSN number is linked to bank account, health care, and everything else. This really prevents people from running their day-to-day life. Joy, can you talk a bit more about how and why you and Jack decided to start FILMIS?

Joy
I think I had been with two organizations and FILMIS is the third one. With the two first ones I could not see the commitment of the leaders for undocumented workers. They were more for the

118

benefit of documented migrants, but the organization I want is one who can protect undocumented workers. That's why Jack and the three of us (Bing and Gee) decided to set up our own organization where it is actually us, the undocumented workers, who are the focus. FILMIS are composed mostly of undocumented and we know what we wanted. We learned from other organizations but we adapt it to our own.

Jack
We have to be clear about what is really the purpose of our organization. Of course, what we want is the protection of undocumented workers' human rights. That's why one of the main purposes of FILMIS is to protect human rights. Now, we want to involve as many Filipinos as possible but we know that the issue of human rights is something some Filipinos are reluctant about and don't want to get involved in politics.

Sakiko
So, people see human rights as politics?

Jack
Yes, politics. They think you're fighting the government or something like that. We decided

to involve culture and education so we can encourage Filipinos to join our organization and, in the process, maybe we inform them about human rights. So, when we interview our possible applicants or members, first we ask: Are you good in painting or other things?

Sakiko
You basically deceive them!!!

Joy
We ask, what are your interests!

Jack
That's why we also try to promote Filipino culture. We ask, do you dance traditional dance? Or are you good at painting or writing? Some of our members are au pairs because they like dancing. There are many young Filipino women here who work as au pairs. Au pairs are not really domestic workers, they come for cultural exchange, based on agreement, to expose themselves to Western, in particular Dutch, culture and learn their way of life. They should only work for their host families for a few hours. Unfortunately, they end up like domestic workers who are being abused. A few of these young people escaped and ended up as

119

undocumented. They enjoy sharing their knowledge with us and that's why we decided to form the FILMIS dance group. The cultural objective is very successful— and then some also get involved in human rights activities. We ask them to join FNV (Federation of Dutch Trade Unions) and we want them to develop their potential to be leaders too. The challenge is that most of our members are undocumented and afraid that they might be caught. We need to tell them what their human rights are, because being undocumented, they are vulnerable to abuses.

Joy
They want to join and campaign but they would not come to demonstrations, or only a few would come, because they are afraid to be caught.

Faisol
Same for us.

Jack
We understand that many domestic workers are not really politically-minded but still we continue to campaign for recognition of domestic workers' rights. We continue to encourage more Filipino domestic workers to join us for this campaign.

We explain their rights, and that if we ever succeed it is for the benefit, not only of you, but other Filipinos who come here as domestic workers. So those are part of our strategies in convincing Filipinos to join the struggle. Work permits or regularization are a part of the FILMIS struggle but we are committed to promoting human rights as workers.

Sakiko
How did you overcome this fear of being undocumented? You go to different organizations and demonstrations and show your face, and how do you do that?

Jack
Well actually now I don't feel any fear anymore. Especially in the campaign for recognition of domestic workers' rights. When we joined FNV you feel more secure because you see you're a member demonstrating with other members and are thinking the police won't arrest this number of people. Then you have on your side FNV—I think they are the biggest trade union in the Netherlands, so I don't feel any fear when it comes to campaigning. My FNV membership has provided me a feeling of security and confidence as an undocumented

migrant. This is what I wanted for our members to feel too. Once they feel it, I am sure, they become active in the campaign and human rights activities. This is the most important step in convincing them to be active—sense of security.

Sakiko
And you?

Joy
Overcoming fears came slowly. The first time of course you are afraid but in the long run when you campaign with the FNV, the confidence is building up: If you don't fight who will fight for you? That's also my principle that nobody can fight for me except me. I don't want people to face the struggles and experience that I experienced, so slowly I teach my other colleagues how to overcome their fears.

Jack
Actually, the campaign is led by a group of undocumented. That's the reality; the active members are undocumented. There are only very few that have papers and you see the difference of commitment. On the frontline it is actually the undocumented who spend their time, their resources, just to sustain the campaign.

So, with FILMIS, we wanted to make sure that when we campaign, all of us should benefit if we ratify. Not just those who have permits. I have learned many things about the differences between Filipino migrants who have papers and those who don't in terms of their commitments to the organization and attitude.

Joy
We look at who of our members has the potential to become leaders and slowly, slowly we're giving them tasks until the time comes when they don't know they're already leading! That's one of our strategies! We have this one that really likes dancing and we said, you're really good why don't you lead one of the performances? Then ok, you lead and we will help. Then it happened three or four performances and she was already the official choreographer! We believe that we are not permanent. People come and go in FILMIS, before we're gone somebody has to be already taking over our position. We should only be five years in a position and then somebody must take over. It's not really helpful that after five, seven, ten years we're still here, so we need to develop a successor. We believe that good leaders create leaders not

121

followers, so we have this kind of leadership and we give them tasks.

Annette
That is so strong! Can I ask about your experience working with other public institutions?

Faisol
We also work with the government to convince them that undocumented migrants are actually not criminals, we just want to work. If you allow us, we also want to pay tax. So, in 2014 or 2015 we worked together with Wereldhuis, Doctors of the World, and the government and made a booklet called *Amsterdam Passport*. This really, really had an effect for us. After that passport, the police acknowledged that we are not criminals. There's a big chance for us in there.

Sakiko
So, if the police scare undocumented people, then they won't come forward to report criminal activities that are committed against them, right? The idea was to ensure you can have safe entry to the police station and leave the police station safely without thinking you will be caught.

Binna
This *Amsterdam Passport* was made by IMWU?

Faisol
Yes, IMWU, het Wereldhuis, Doctors of the World, and Amsterdam municipality.

Annette
And it consisted of what exactly, this *Amsterdam Passport*?

Faisol
It consisted of knowing how you survive in Amsterdam. We also had connections with lawyers in Amsterdam. We made a book and a list for where to find things. How to deal with hospitals, health questions, where you can find food banks in Amsterdam, and shelters to sleep in. It still exists, but people start forgetting it. The *Amsterdam Passport* was a way for the police to know that these people aren't criminals. Amsterdam is a special place, it's very different to other places. That's why we try to make a different situation and a different law in Amsterdam.

Binna
Does it also exist in other cities, for example Den Haag?

Faisol

No, I think, there is too much government and embassies in Den Haag to apply the Amsterdam rule. In Amsterdam there are more tourists than government, it's a very different place. That's why we try to push again to activate and create shelter for people without documents. In 2010, we had a fight with our embassy that Indonesian people don't have documents here.

Erminah

Right now, it's easier because we offer the passport for five euros.

Binna

The *Amsterdam Passport*?

Erminah

No no, the Indonesian passport. Back then, we only get travel pass and we cannot use it in hospital.

Faisol

One time I brought someone to the hospital but they rejected him, he only had a travel pass. So, we fought with our embassy, and luckily at that time we had a new Ambassador called Retno Marsudi (now minister of foreign affairs) and I told her what our situation here was. So in 2014, we got the passport. I still remember

that time, February 25, eleven o'clock in the night, and Retno Marsudi the new minister calls me and said, "hey Faisol, good news! You gonna get passports!" I was really, really crying at that time. I just lay down and was crying because you can't imagine how precious that was.

Erminah

We try to push and push, again and again; for example, to create shelters for people without documents. We hope to make a cheque for payment so undocumented workers can get paid and we can pay tax. The idea is to make a voucher to give to our employers who pay maybe fifteen euros per cheque, and the cheque we bring to government and we get cash from that cheque. Not fifteen euros, less because they cut off the tax, so we get maybe ten euros and five goes to tax.

Jack

We are actually planning to propose that the Geneva model [of this voucher system] be implemented here. But first we want to experiment in Amsterdam and we are trying to establish contact with the politicians. Last month there was a debate in Amsterdam. We met two or three politicians from GroenLinks (GreenLeft) and the Socialistische Partij (Socialist Party)

and brought up this plan. They were receptive but wanted more information about the model.

Joy

I think Jack and Erminah are referring to our campaign, the ratification of C189 [see Glossary of Terms for details]. The first one was with a Belgian model, but because members of the Kalsbeek Commission saw a lot of flaws the Dutch parliament rejected it. Now we try again using the Geneva model of vouchers, because it works in Geneva for the undocumented, allowing them to be part of the social system and the undocumented domestic workers can also work normally as regular workers. This model doesn't oblige the government to subsidize the social benefits of the undocumented domestic workers.

Jack

But we need to study harder how this model really works in Geneva. Dan from Kabalaikat (another Filipino organization) is doing a lot to research on the complications. In fact, we are also planning to invite an expert to explain the model for us. We want to make sure this model is really effective for us and the government, and to provide concrete information to the politicians we ask assistance and support from.

Joy

When the Kalsbeek Commission rejected our proposal to adopt the Belgium model as a way to recognize our rights as domestic workers, the rejection demoralized the domestic workers. We worked hard for it and then all of a sudden it will not work. This time we really have to make double the strategy, double the information. We study different models as part of a new approach and adopt which model provides a win-win situation for both the Dutch society and us.

Sakiko

We didn't really talk about domestic work, the kind of work that you do, and the kind of reproductive work that is one of the focus of Annette and Casco's book: Why is it under-valued? Why is this type of labor or people who do this labor not recognized or respected? What needs to be done to bring domestic and maintenance work to the same wage level as other waged work? And as Annette asks: After the revolution who is going to pick up the garbage?

124

Annette

It's a quote from the artist Mierle Laderman Ukeles from the 1970s! Her quote attempts to question revolutionary social movements that do not seriously incorporate the challenges or grapple with the deprived status of maintenance and domestic work in movement building. She asks how we imagine societies and who is doing what kind of work under which conditions. Yes, I'd love to have a question about how to envision the future.

Sakiko

To be more specific, in the ideal scenario, who is doing this type of domestic and maintenance work and how is this work done? For example, in the future, people who work in the maintenance sector will tell companies what textiles to produce because those who wash clothes know what textile lasts or go bad after washing one time. The power is currently with the company, the ones who produce, and they make whatever clothes they like, using whatever fabric they can source cheaply. But in the society that I imagine, the power is with the domestic and maintenance workers. Those who reproduce decide and tell companies, because they maintain these clothes, and they know what works and what doesn't. That's the kind of society that I dream of.

Faisol

The important thing is why we, for example, make vouchers. Because we want to protect people without documents, so they can be more relaxed while working, and not be afraid to walk outside. That's very important. The first thing is the voucher and the second thing is to recognize that we are here. We want to ask to the Netherlands: Without us, the undocumented, hardworking people, what would happen to this country?

Erminah

It would be dirty! Also, the children: Who is taking care of them while both parents are working? We do! That is important too.

Faisol

So, first dirt, and second the economy. For example, with help from undocumented people every-one in a household can work, enjoy, and then when they go home to their house they can enjoy the house. Because when you come to your house it's clean and smells nice! We even take out the garbage. The

undocumented workers are also the garbage men and women.

Annette

A final question: How do you see the support from an art organization like Casco, or from the arts, or individual artists, like us?

Sakiko

Is there any particular support or certain skills that you expect to see? And how can we work together in the service of your struggle? You see a lot of interest, like this conversation.

Jack

The ratification of C189 is a very long struggle. Until we come up with this we should offer something else that convinces them. So, we have research done on the Geneva voucher model because it includes the undocumented so is something unique. It works for the undocumented domestic workers and the municipality. But before we proceed to that we wanted to make sure it really works. We have to know the details, so we're trying to do the research, and of course we need the support of different sectors. I believe that the support of arts organizations and artists is very important. We use this kind of strategy with FILMIS; at our events we have exhibitions, and encourage our members to explore their talents and their potential in drawing, painting, photography. I see that art is an effective tool to be used in outreach and improving awareness, and to express our demands for recognition of our rights as human beings. We need creative ways of expressing our demands. For example, with human rights in domestic work we exhibit some kind of reflection on the condition of human people, so we can campaign, we can ask the government through this form of arts, we can portray our conditions and the necessity of ratifying C189 through different forms of artistic expression. This is what we believe is important in collaborating with Casco.

Binna

What I would like to bring up is the use of uncommon language as our power. Before, we were restricted and criticized, and even a little bit undermined by "the unionists" for using different languages in our collaborative relationship. I think using different languages and trying to understand them actually could be our resource. In this light, may I

continue a little bit more? What has actually brought us to here is the capitalist economy. But that has been destructive in many ways, including on the earth. We need to pay attention to this connection between domestic work and environmental ecology. There are forces that are trying to change the current economic form, and what you are doing will influence that change. It may be useful to frame your politics in this change in terms of economic and political systems. Domestic work is fundamentally ecological.

Sakiko

It repairs the destruction made by labor under capitalism. It repairs people and our environment. It sustains all forms of life.

Binna

I have learnt so much from this conversation, I feel almost like I'm taking too much from you. It is important to bridge our gap and then see how we can support each other. Even if we are not directly working on your campaign we are changing the way art is working, how artists produce the work, how we make exhibition, and I think that helps to generate system changes which could help your struggle.

Faisol

It's like the same struggle but the other way.

Sakiko

So, it's like co-organizing, coordinating, and the things involved.

Faisol

We cannot just walk one way, we need to grow from here, here, here, and there. To have different strategies to support us.

Sakiko

And then sometimes I should ask you, for example, is what I'm working on actually serving your struggle? So there needs to be checks, right? There needs to be a conversation that happens once in a while.

Joy

And it's good for networking. You have a network that can help involve in the campaign. This network is very important for the campaign. I always maintain a belief that an organization is strong when it has networks. Our capacity to move and campaign will not succeed without allies in different sectors. That's why we try to

build an alliance of different
supporters from different sectors.
We become strong when we are
many. Our voice will be heard
by the government and the people
when it is loud.

SITES FOR UNLEARNING IN THE MUSEUM

Nancy Jouwe

As a writer committed to telling stories, I have endeavored to represent the lives of the nameless and the forgotten, to reckon with loss, and to respect the limits of what cannot be known.

—Saidiya Hartman[1]

Introduction

Can we find sites for unlearning in the arts sector? And if they were there, would we recognize them? In 2018, the year of the dog, we find ourselves in a new reality in terms of questions that Dutch museums ask themselves and actions that they take as they question themselves as institutions. Or, at least some of them do.[2] Not too long ago, at the beginning of the new millennium, things were looking quite stale. The fact that our rapidly globalizing world was impacting our local and daily lives more and more seemed to be passing museums by, especially the larger (art) museums. Els van der Plas, then director of the Prince Claus Fund (for progressive culture and development, established by the Dutch Parliament), said in 2007:

> Museums have for a very long time excluded a larger part of the world. Their knowledge and focus is on Euro-American developments in the arts. And because they are based on that Western tradition, they don't have the knowledge on offer and find it threatening if you open up the world; as a museum, you then cease to be an expert.[3]

129

This process of exclusion triggered another art fund, the Mondriaan Foundation (now Mondriaan Fund, the largest publicly-financed fund for visual art and cultural heritage in the Netherlands) to come up with their Diversity Prize in 2006 (more on that later).

The current dynamics are also being pushed from the outside into the realm of the museum. A case in point: Simone Zeefuik and Hodan Warsame, with others, started a critical conversation in 2015 under the heading "Decolonize The Museum," which has developed into a prime example of how decolonial interventions have literally entered museum spaces. Originally starting the conversation with ethnographic museums, as the following quote shows, they've now expanded the conversation into a wider range of art spaces:

Decolonize The Museum is an effort to confront the colonial ideas and practices present in ethnographic museums up until this day. We have worked throughout 2015 to stage a joint intervention in the Dutch National Museum of World Cultures. This intervention critiques the language, imagery and accessibility of its current exhibitions.

Our intent is firstly to expose the violence perpetuated by ethnographic museums by critiquing its Eurocentrism, white supremacy, its assumed neutrality and its excuses of "only having so much time/space". We base this critique on the museum experience of ourselves and our friends whose heritage is studied and analyzed, but who, ourselves, are seldom the target group of ethnographic museums. Simultaneously, we push a conversation about how—if at all—the ethnographic museum can contribute to

1   Saidiya Hartman, "Venus in Two Acts," *Small Axe*, Indiana University Press, no. 26 (2008): 4.

2   I'm thinking of the Rijksmuseum and their push for changing the terms used in their collection descriptions; the Tropenmuseum for stepping into a process of becoming a postcolonial institute in the twenty-first century and what that entails; art center Witte de With announcing their name will be changed; Centraal Museum and their revamping of the collections display; and the Van Abbemuseum who revisited their *Be(com)ing Dutch* exhibit ten years later with the project *Becoming More*, to name a few.

3   Els van der Plas quoted in Fenneken Veldkamp, "Wat de Boer Niet Kent" (what the farmer does not know), *ZAM Africa Magazine*, vol 11, no. 2 (2007): 18. (Translation by the author.) Online: www.archive.niza.nl/docs/200706-211117213985.pdf?&username=guest@niza.nl&password=9999&groups=NIZA&work-group= (Accessed June 8, 2018).

reinstating the agency and histories of colonized peoples, life and territories. Last but not least, Decolonize The Museum is about educating and challenging the organization so that neo-liberal conceptions of 'diversity' do not become the limit of change for these institutions.[4]

Utrecht-based art hub Casco Art Institute and collaborator Annette Krauss asked me to write about unlearning practices within Dutch art institutions as expressions of decolonial thinking since not much has been written on this. I thought it was a great question, although I wasn't sure I could address it properly. In the end, I can only offer some of my experiences and, within the confines of this article, I will mostly draw on examples from Dutch museums.

In this article, I want to centralize the following questions: How can we engage in practices of unlearning in the arts sector? How can we read or understand these practices as decolonial processes? What factors helped or hindered these practices?

I will do so by sharing vignettes of my experiences in the arts sector over twenty years and what they have taught me. Secondly, I will use the case of the Diversity Prize, issued in 2006, and focus on one of the contenders, the Centraal Museum (for art and culture, Utrecht's main municipal museum). I won't necessarily provide sufficient answers to the above questions, but hopefully the examples offer food for thought.

To Decolonize

Decolonial thinking is not widely exercised within today's Dutch academic institutions, quite the contrary, and this is even more the case within the arts sector. Yet we have seen, in the past three years or so, decolonial thinking and practices become more and more prominent for a relatively small but vocal group of activists, writers, and thinkers—who are unsurprisingly often people of color—in places such as Middelburg, Eindhoven, Arnhem, Utrecht, and Amsterdam. I already mentioned the Decolonize The Museum initiative;

4   "Decolonize The Museum Conference April 16th 2016," *AFRO Magazine*. Online: www. afromagazine.nl/agenda/decolonize-museum-conference-april-16th-2016 (Accessed June 8, 2018).

blogger/researcher Egbert Martina, researcher Patricia Schor, and visual artist Patricia Kaersenhout are just a few examples. Academic Rolando Vázquez co-organizes a successful annual decolonial summer school in Middelburg that has been running since 2010, and recently two more summer schools were started in Amsterdam. Similarly, initiatives such as the Black Archives and University of Colour (respectively, an archive containing the legacy of black writers and scientists, and a working group that aims to decolonize the university; both founded in Amsterdam in 2015), and the Black Heritage Tours in Amsterdam (a guided tour of African legacies of the past and diverse Dutch culture, since 2013) adhere to decolonial thinking.

To decolonize has become a leading notion in efforts to expose and explore "global" politics (how global geopolitical issues have consequences on a local level and vice versa), to push for transgressive choices and voices (in the sense that it pushes through hegemonic canonical Western boundaries), and to inspire other ways to look at and transform the world. Hence, because decolonial practices are many different things to different people, they are ultimately both a source of inspiration and sometimes also pose a danger to themselves, in that the term decolonial is also being used as a buzzword without content.

For clarity, I will briefly touch upon some key concepts. Central to decolonial thinking is the conflation of coloniality and modernity as a matrix of power.[5] Coloniality/modernity are purposefully paired as concepts that inhabit two sides of the same coin and continue to influence our present-day lives. The beginning of modernity is connected to 1492 and Columbus' so-called discovery of the Americas, that time when Europe started to see itself as Europe and a Western civilization deeply interconnected with the violence of colonialism was being developed. Coloniality/modernity means that racism, colonialism, and the consumption of lives are not aberrations of but constitutive to modernity; there is no progress without violence and no development without poverty.

Within this constellation, Europe produces and needs an alterity (Europe vs other) in order to reaffirm itself and claim a superior position. This const-

---

5   Aníbal Quijano, "Coloniality and Moderni-
     ty/Rationality," *Cultural Studies* vol. 21, no.
     2–3 (2007): 168–78.

ellation of coloniality/modernity works on a material/institutional and symbolic level. A system of appropriation is established through the (continued) appropriation of land (for example, indigenous peoples' lands), and of bodies (for example, slavery and forced labor, including sexual labor). This is accompanied by a system of representation in which ideas about reality, visibility, and world history are (re)produced. This system of representation can be found in the museum and the university; they both function as pillars of Western knowledge and subjectivity.

As a member of diaspora communities from the Asia-Pacific region, I recognize this. Our Papuan-Dutch community shares collective living memories of being uprooted, disconnected, forgotten, and traumatized, as if nothing but postcolonial waste. Our (grand)parents' lives were far removed from important notions of belonging, recognition, and cultural and political citizenship. Meanwhile, human remains of Papuans gathered during colonial times still lie in storage at the Tropenmuseum (museum of the tropics; an ethnographic museum in Amsterdam). This is a real and yet painful expression of the same logic.

Coloniality is different from colonialism in that coloniality does not need colonialism to function, its logic exists by way of continuing the "hidden process of expropriation, exploitation, pollution, and corruption that underlies the narrative of modernity, as promoted by institutions and actors belonging to corporations, industrialized nation-states, museums, and research institutions."[6] In other words, coloniality is the underlying logic of colonialism that continues beyond it.

Decolonial thinking functions as a critique of the hegemony of Western imperialist thinking and its continuation in our current-day institutionalized lives. It proposes epistemic disobedience[7] by denouncing modernity/coloniality, which has informed and organized our lives, and by opening up a space of thinking and being that reaches beyond this closed matrix of power.

6   As explained by Rolando Vázquez, during the Decolonial Summer School, Middelburg, June 17, 2015.

7   Alvina Hoffman, "Interview—Walter Mignolo/ Part 2: Key Concepts," *E-INTERNATIONAL RELATIONS*, (January 21, 2017). Online: www.e-ir.info/2017/01/21/interview-walter-mignolopart-2-key-concepts/ (Accessed June 8, 2018).

Decoloniality then, appears in between modernity/coloniality as an opening, as a possibility of overcoming their completeness. It means that there is an alternative to modernity, which starts by revealing and showing modernity as a locality posing as a global design with universal pretenses.

How can we move beyond a singular notion of the truth? How can we unveil the erasures and negations that modernity/coloniality has produced? How can we have other conversations and realities? How can that which is suppressed re-emerge? These are decolonial questions, they propose an existence that has a different relationship with time and space, a different temporality from the one that modernity offers. Instead, a decoloniality of aesthetics, knowledge, and being is proposed.

Decolonizing a museum, then, starts by looking at the museum as a site where European culture, the nation state, and national memory are consolidated and function as an expression of the Western self. Art museums, like all museums, display modernity through representations of the Western self or the memory of the West. Similarly, coloniality is at work by offering an idea of whiteness while othering sub/dehumanized/racialized/colonized others, like in ethnological museums.[8] This can, but does not necessarily, work in the same way for art spaces and galleries at large, so for the purpose of this article and steering clear of oversimplification, I will stick with the museum sector (i.e. art, ethnographic, and cultural-historical). Thus, to decolonize is to think about how museums have institutionalized representations of modernity/coloniality through controlling narrative, having the power to name and mute, and steering notions of how to relate to the past.

To Unlearn

The practice and process of unlearning are at the core of both decolonial and postcolonial thinking processes.[9] Following the current interest of the arts

[9] Sara Danius, Stefan Jonsson, and Gayatri Chakravorty Spivak, "An Interview with Gayatri Chakravorty Spivak," *boundary 2*, vol 20, no. 2 (Summer, 1993), 24–50; Madina Vladimirovna Tlostanova and Walter Mignolo, *Learning to Unlearn: Decolonial Reflections from Eurasia and the Americas* (Columbus, OH: Ohio State University Press, 2012).

[8] See footnote 6.

sector in Europe's colonial history and the necessity to unveil hidden stories, deconstruct dominant paradigms, and centralize the work of artists searching for alternative futures, it becomes even more relevant to connect unlearning to the arts sector.[10] This is not necessarily a new development but the current developments, as this volume shows, are quite exciting. Casco Art Institute has dedicated itself to becoming an exemplary site for unlearning, focusing on how organizational bodies can unlearn systemic modes of oppression and make new, healthier habits, thus denouncing the devaluation of reproductive labor for economic gain, as described in more depth in other articles in this volume.

Coloniality at Work

Let's start with how this can play out on a personal level. I love roaming through large and small art spaces. My private conversations with the art pieces I encounter invoke strong affective responses that inspire me. It feeds the senses. Similarly, having played in several music groups, I cherish the feelings of joy I've felt when creating and performing together.

I've had the opportunity to organize art prizes for women and exhibits of women artists since 1997 through the feminist fund Mama Cash (a public-private international fund for feminist activism based in Amsterdam). In 2006, I started at Kosmopolis Utrecht (an intercultural, multimedia platform for art and culture), working with visual and performative artists like Michael McMillan, Marcel Pinas, Raj Mohan, Denise Jannah, Quinsy Gario, and others. We mostly worked outside of museum spaces, in galleries, churches, or public spaces such as schools, and open air in the streets, alongside roads or railway stations. This was done for several reasons: we wanted to make the work of artists more accessible to audiences who would not typically step into museums and we also did not want to bother with restrictions to do with time, space, and dominant notions of quality (more on quality later). But maybe,

---

10   Nora Sternfeld. "Shaking the Status Quo*:
      Notes on Unlearning," Mezosfera.org. *Inside
      the Mozosfera*, no. 2 (September 2016); Annette
      Krauss, *Sites for Unlearning: On the Material,
      Artistic and Political Dimensions of Processes
      of Unlearning*, PhD diss. (Vienna: Vienna
      Academy of Fine Arts, 2017).

most importantly, we wanted to create spaces of representation that were not seen as temples of Western culture, as museums are often perceived, although many museums are trying to get rid of this perception. As such, Kosmopolis was proposing a decolonial option, without necessarily wording it that way.

In working with artists, we also worked within a larger context of communities who had a vested interest in the narratives that these artists would convey. This meant creating a space of co-creation with (members of) the community, evolving into a space of co-ownership.

These experiences helped me in understanding the importance of non-institutional spaces, unheard voices and stories, the importance of critical interventions by artists, and the need for non-hegemonic communal artistic practices. These experiences taught me valuable lessons on the interconnectedness of the personal and the political (within the arts) and harnessed me against the more depressing aspects of the arts domain and academia.

I'll share a vignette. As a student at Utrecht University, around 1990, I took some classes in art history. For class, we had to read *The Story of Art* by E.H. Gombrich, a classic. But we were told to skip the section on non-Western art. This was done without much disclosure on why, as if it were self-evident. Meta Knol, the director of Museum de Lakenhal (Leiden's municipal museum of history and fine art), had the exact same experience at the same university.[11] In another class, we watched a film clip in which a building of flats crashed to the ground in a neighborhood where predominantly black folks lived. I can't remember the exact location but let's say the Bronx, NYC. The effortless way in which some of my fellow students starting joking about how they hoped its inhabitants were still in the building, thus displaying utter disrespect for the human dignity of black people, made my nappy hair stand on end. As the single black person in the room I looked at the teacher, urging her non-verbally to speak. I remember saying something myself—or wanting to. I can't really remember anymore. But I stopped taking art history classes as a result. The violence drained me. In hindsight, this experience must have been traumatic

11   Quoted in: Meta Knol, *Beyond the Dutch: Indonesië, Nederland en de beeldende kunsten van 1900 tot nu* (Indonesia, the Netherlands and the visual arts from 1900. to now), (Amsterdam: KIT Publishers, 2009): 18.

136

since I have forgotten how it really went down.

A second vignette refers to the infinite whiteness of Dutch art spaces, on how white presence and thinking is the unspoken norm. In April 2014 I was graciously invited by curator Mirjam Westen to open an art show called *Don't Support the Greedy* by Esiri Erheriene-Essi, a black female award-winning visual artist. It was her first big show in the Netherlands, taking place in the Arnhem Museum (a municipal museum of modern, contemporary, and applied art and design). This was a celebratory moment for her of course, but I felt jubilant as well, as it was a rare occasion to have someone like her and her artistic vision be the central focus in a Dutch museum space.

Within minutes of meeting each other (for the first time) we sort of laughed hysterically together because of the whiteness of the space. We had both noticed instantly that she and I were (at that moment) the only two black people in the room. We laughed because we immediately understood what the other was thinking and feeling, we laughed because it released tension and this was how we dealt. After this invigorating intermezzo, we pulled ourselves up and mingled in this white space, as we were used to doing.

In my speech, I referred to race a couple of times and spoke about its absence and the myth of a post-racial society, I also referred to Edward Said and Gloria Wekker's concept of the cultural archive since I was reminded of how, in her work, Esiri Essi tries to shoot holes into this archive. The audience looked at me in bewilderment, some not knowing how to react. Afterwards, the proverbial elderly white woman came up to me to ask why I spoke such good Dutch. She demanded an explanation. Usually this is supposed to be a "compliment" ("wat spreek je goed Nederlands!")—there is always someone who goes there. In this case, the person was better informed: she knew who I was, and that I was partly Papuan. This time, her subtext meant that I was betraying "my people" with my "flawless" Dutch. I gathered this while interacting convivially with her.

Her comments showed that she had a depressingly singular, primitive notion of the Papuan. My presence or representation of a Papuan confused and disturbed her; I did not act in the way I was supposed to. She wasn't capable of looking at me as a fully-blown human being with all its layers and contradictions, the label Papuan had prevented that. She could not fathom that I was born and raised in the Netherlands and that, considering the topics I covered in my

talk while speaking flawless Dutch, I had probably had some form of higher education.

To Delink

These examples show how the museum, despite great curators and artists, can still function as a violent contact zone for people like me. These are not isolated incidents and it's not just about me; for this is coloniality in practice, the everyday utterings of a system. To become aware of this is part of the process of unlearning. I detached myself from this dreadful personal encounter by realizing we are both caught in this Western system, bearing in mind that the proverbial elderly white woman and I have different work to do because we inhabit different temporalities and speak from different levels of knowledge (of course, I cannot be sure what her learning moment consisted of). By detaching I was delinking, a conscious decolonial act where I denounce this Western knowledge structure to look for a space that acknowledges and engages with my reality. Delinking involves not just changing the content of (sometimes literal) conversation but also the terms. On what terms are we having this conversation?

Similarly, in my earlier example of Kosmopolis Utrecht's work on co-creation, a space was provided for voices and ideas that traditionally are not offered any form of curatorial agency in a museum space. This too, can be seen as an act of delinking. It enables us to engage actively in practices of unlearning.

Come On. We're Beyond the Dutch

In 2006 a Diversity Prize for the Dutch art sector was issued, officially called *Stimuleringsprijs voor Culturele Diversiteit* (incentive prize for cultural diversity). An initiative of the Mondriaan Foundation (as it was then known), the prize consisted of half a million euros. The underlying mission for a diversity prize was triggered by the fact that art museums in the Netherlands did not relate well enough with the current multicultural reality of the Netherlands and current twenty-first century global art dynamics. The Netherlands was lagging, in comparison to other European countries. Gitta Luiten, then director of the Mondriaan Foundation, said during the delivery of the prize in 2006 that museums have to adjust to the fact that the Western world isn't white anymore.

The combination of a diversity prize combined with a large sum of money brought about an enormous wave of criticism. Journalists, politicians, and the art sector itself saw it as a threat to artistic autonomy, too much meddling from an art fund, and fueling needless competition between museums.

The winner of the prize was the Van Abbemuseum (a museum for contemporary and modern art in Eindhoven) who could then execute their ambitious project *Be(com)ing Dutch*, which consisted of an exhibition, a caucus, gatherings, and an extensive website. The central question to their project was: What does it mean to be Dutch in a globalizing world? Is it a process of becoming or a static affair of being? Hence the wordplay of be(com)ing. The prize was issued only once and, although the Mondriaan Foundation wanted to continue it some four years later, the then State Secretary of Culture Halbe Zijlstra was keen on severe budget cuts and bestowed a bleak political wind upon our cultural landscape.

The Centraal Museum was tipped within the sector as a serious contender for the prize, and due to financial support from the Mondriaan Foundation they were able to develop their plan into the exhibition *Beyond the Dutch: Indonesia, the Netherlands and Visual Arts From 1900 Until Now*, which ran from October 2009 until January 2010. It consisted of an exhibition, a publication (KIT Publishers, 2011), and a side program called *Beyond Java*, which Museum Maluku (a museum in Utrecht—closed in 2012—dedicated to the story of the Moluccans in and outside the Netherlands) and Kosmopolis Utrecht co-developed. The exhibition was hailed in most media and brought in new audiences. More on some criticism of that, later.

The original plan, developed by the late Michael Zeeman, focused on Edward Said's book *Orientalism* (1978). Curator Meta Knol was assigned to develop it into a curatorial concept and wanted to include contemporary art. She decided to focus on Indonesia, invited Indonesian artists, and co-curated the exhibit with Indonesian curator Enin Supriyanto. During her research visits to Indonesia she spoke with Ade Darmawan, director of art collective ruangrupa (an artists' initiative with a focus on urban issues and collaborative projects in Jakarta), and asked him if he saw Dutch influences in current Indonesian visual art, to which he answered, "Oh no. Come on, we're beyond the Dutch!" Hence, the title of the exhibition was born. The starting point for *Beyond the Dutch* was to look at the cultural heritage of colonialism, cultural

influences, and the dramatic changes that the process of decolonization produced over a timespan of one hundred years. The aim was to disconnect the art pieces from an ethnographic discourse and instead show them as autonomous works, from an art history perspective.

Three chronological periods were covered: the colonial time (1900), the consequences of decolonization and independence (circa 1950), and the current period of post-colonialism (circa 2000). Over forty artists were on show, including FX Harsono, Tintin Wulia, Tiong Ang, Heri Dono, Raden Saleh, Jan Toorop, Isaac Israels, Affandi, Hendra Gunawan, Sudjojono, Indieguerillas, Fiona Tan, Agus Suwage, Roy Villevoye, Hadassah Emmerich, Mirjam Bürer, and others.

Starting a Conversation

Some of Meta Knol's colleagues had doubts about the focus on Indonesia because they were concerned about the lack of quality it would bring. They had associations with copy art, ethnography, furniture, and room screens: "Alle stereotypen kwamen langs" (every stereotype was mentioned), according to Knol.[12] Similarly, artists and colleagues expressed a fear Indonesian art would be second-rate derivatives from "Western high art."

Here we see a deeply embedded cultural archive at work, where ideas of Western superiority are translated into canonical hierarchical notions of what is considered high and low art.

It shows the pressing necessity to not just focus on content and curatorial choices but unpack the deeper implications of the museum as an institution. What does it take to unlearn old Western thought patterns? And are we, in 2018, better equipped to tackle this?

Knol's aim for the exhibition was to show the art pieces as autonomous works, and for ethnographic discourse to be kept out of the way. This is consistent with how Knol had positioned herself as an actor in the Dutch art discourse at the time.[13] Knol was trying to flip the script. Although admirable, these efforts do not necessarily problematize the binary opposition of ethnographic art versus autonomous art (as the highest form of art). Instead, a danger

12   Interview with Meta Knol by Nancy Jouwe,
      Museum De Lakenhal, Leiden, August 20,
      2010 (unpublished).

140

lurks; that of reproducing this binary and locking the Indonesian artists into a Eurocentric framework.[14]

Another aspect to consider is that as an institution the Centraal Museum hardly, if at all, considered the uneven power relations that were at work, leaving their institution untouched, as if it was not implicated. It is an unfair burden to put on Knol alone as it implies so much more and everyone in the institution is implicated in this process. If institutional power dynamics remain untouched, a process of unlearning is hard to make and will probably not succeed.

In relation to the exhibition, professor Susan Legêne was keen on a more self-reflexive and critical reading of the Netherlands as a former colonial empire, driven by expansion and a memory of an expansive past, wherein inequalities and hierarchical differences are reproduced.[15] She emphasized that art and museums are sections or parts of these mechanisms, and the role or implicit authority of the museum as an institution was not problematized.[16] A relevant commentary, especially since the focus was on Indonesia and the Dutch East Indies.

The Centraal Museum example shows that a conversation was started, but the question remains of whether it was developed into a necessary practice of unlearning. One thing is for sure: the main players during that time, directors Pauline Terreehorst and Edwin Jacobs, and curator Meta Knol, have all left the

13   "Het onderscheid tussen westerse en niet-westerse kunst is achterhaald," (The distinction between Western and non-Western art is outdated) NRC, Meta Knol and Lejo Schenk, January 2, 2010. Online: www.nrc.nl/nieuws/2010/01/02/het-onderscheid-tussen-westerse-en-niet-westerse-kunst-11832313-a176574 (Accessed June 8, 2018); see also Edwin Jacobs, Meta Knol and Stijn Huijts, "Naar een mondig museum" (towards an empowered museum), NRC, December 2006. Online: www.nrc.nl/nieuws/2006/12/01/naar-een-mondig-museum-11237877-a236037 (Accessed June 8, 2018).

14   Charles Esche, interviewed by Koen Kleijn and Stefan Kuiper, "Musea lopen verschrikkelijk achter" (museums are horribly behind), *De Groene Amsterdammer*, May 14, 2008. Online: www.groene.nl/artikel/musea-lopen-verschrikkelijk-achter (Accessed June 8, 2018).

15   During the Framer Framed debate "De koloniale blik" (the colonial gaze), December 13, 2009, Centraal Museum, Utrecht.

16   See Legêne's points in the report of the symposium "Omstreden geschiedenis. Een symposium over de (re)presentatie van de Nederlands-Indonesische geschiedenis in musea" (concerned history: a symposium on the (re)presentation of Dutch-Indonesian history in museums). Held at the Indo-European Memory Foundation, Arnhem, February 2012. Online: www.indischherinneringscentrum.nl/files/afbeeldingen/Verslag_Symposium_Omstreden_Geschiedenis-lowres.pdf (Accessed June 8, 2018).

Centraal Museum. What has happened since within the institution? Interestingly, new developments seem to indicate they want to reconnect with questions posed during the *Beyond the Dutch* period.

To Conclude

To engage in practices of unlearning in the arts sector involves becoming aware that we come from different contexts as people in a museum or art space, and these different contexts matter, thus a single narrative will not suffice. A mere (re)production of a singular white Western gaze simply won't cut it anymore in the twenty-first century.

As an institution which canonizes and represents ideas of nationhood and belonging, museums have immense representational power. They can invoke feelings of pride but also exclusion, even becoming spaces of symbolic violence. These processes of exclusion occur on different levels: via language, the architecture (including accessibility), the people who visit, and the collections on display, including how they are narrated and visualized.

Museums are part of a certain space and time, where living memories become discourses or objects in the museum. Being aware of this might start a decolonial conversation and can open up ways to unlearn as a museum. Thus, internal processes are key for museum staff. A single visionary curator/director/producer will be frustrated in her or his accomplishments if others stay detached. This could mean becoming aware of how binary oppositions work in the arts sector (as mentioned earlier) or looking at key factors like autonomy and quality (for example, the prejudice that Indonesian artists are unable to bring artistic quality).

Decolonial examples exist through the wonderful work of artists, activists, and cultural entrepreneurs who offer alternative ideas, teach us through the senses, bring unknown herstories to the fore, and invite us to expand. Artists (often literally) lend their bodies and perspectives, using their own realities instead of those from Western modern civilization they are capable of moving beyond it, thus showing us paths to delink and unlearn.

What does this mean for Dutch citizens? The hindrances referred to in this article point to a lack of knowledge and sheer ignorance, to the point that one is ignorant of their own ignorance. And it also involves not wanting to give up power.

142

When a process of rising awareness does take place, let's not get stuck in feelings of guilt. I know that for many people it is an obvious step towards becoming more aware but ultimately it is an unproductive position. Instead, we can use accountability as a more productive strategy or starting point which involves positioning yourself (including your relation to power). A concept which the Dutch arts sector is still quite unfamiliar with, but which is nonetheless useful, is intersectionality. This concept makes us aware on both personal and institutional levels how we are all positioned in a place of power or lack thereof due to interacting axes of difference. Intersectionality helps us in starting a conversation that does not shy away from our lived realities, for instance by looking at ways to unlearn privilege. It helps us all to tackle aspects of discrimination and empowerment: in ourselves, in our institutions, in our representations.

DECOLONIZING ART INSTITUTES FROM A LABOR POINT OF VIEW

Binna Choi and Yolande Zola Zoli van der Heide

"Knowing who is cleaning your Kunsthalle has no bearing on their conditions."
— Kerstin Stakemeier and Marina Vishmidt[1]

A Dutch landlady corrects her Indonesian domestic worker's flower arranging and scolds her for coming back late from an errand. This colonial scene is recounted in a compilation of film clips ironically entitled *Van de Kolonie Niets dan Goeds: Nederlands-Indië in Beeld, 1912–1942* (nothing but goodness in the colony: the Dutch Indies in pictures), made available to us by the Tropenmuseum (museum of the tropics; an ethnographic museum) in Amsterdam in 2003. As historic as this scene is, it also rings true for contemporary art institutions. The presentation of postcolonial critical works in these often-Western institutions means the conditions in which they are shown, how they are contextualized, and which taste or style they are presented in falls into a negotiation with the structures of power that allow—often through funding—for the museum, gallery, or non-profit art center to exist in the first place.

Let's return to "Nothing but Goodness in the Colony," where a grocery-shopping scene soon follows the flower arranging. The scene becomes a metaphor for the contentious funder-fundee relations in art institutions, where the white Dutch female landowner living on Indonesian soil represents the contemporary funder whose role it is to oversee the Indonesian laborer in reproducing Dutch cultural values. The film goes on to show the Dutch woman measuring time and irritated over an errand delayed yet again. A later scene

144

reveals the domestic worker reproducing the very same oppressive conditions for her co-worker. As she makes him carry groceries solo in spite of their overbearing load, we witness an act steeped in classism, determined and perpetuated by the systemic racism implemented by their shared oppressor. While it's not clear from the film why the domestic worker held a higher position in the social strata than her co-worker, we might discern from common colonial practice that complex class and racialized distinctions have been made.[2] As constructions of the oppressor, these markers and classifiers must be dismantled by all of us. The scenes go on in a rather humorous manner, accompanied by a variation of a lullaby popular in the Dutch Indies. Regardless of whether the actions are fictional or, as suggested by the documentary form, representational, this short film serves as a disturbing reminder that coloniality is a well-entrenched structure that infects all of our minds irrespective of race, class, sex, or intentions. Hence, we wonder, is there a way to break from this mode of colonial activity by cultivating new labor relations while concurrently engaging with the politics of identity and cultural heritage? Decoloniality has long focused on the latter but, in our view, it is the former that strikes a nerve; especially at a time when labor power is dispersed, where union efforts and ethics don't meet, and where artists from (former) colonies are exposed to superficial modes of representation as the art market propels them into superstardom.

Another cinematic moment depicting an imbalance of labor acutely captures the riddled nature of colonialism in a different context. Ousmane

1   Kerstin Stakemeier and Marina Vishmidt, *Reproducing Autonomy: Work, Money, Crisis and Contemporary Art* (London/Berlin: Mute, 2016), 77.

2   For example, historian Bart Luttikhuis challenges the established notion in colonial studies that the colonial population was essentially subdivided into binary opposites—ruler and ruled, colonizer and colonized, "European" and "Native," and argues instead that social positioning of individuals and groups was determined by a complex set of markers: in his dissertation *Negotiating Modernity: Europeanness in Late Colonial Indonesia, 1910–1942* (Florence: European University Institute, 2014).

Sembene's 1988 film *Camp de Thiaroye* is based on the little-known Thiaroye massacre on November 30, 1944, when French commanding officers turned their guns on their *tirailleurs* (colonial infantry) and up to three-hundred African soldiers were killed.[3] The soldiers were former prisoners of war that had been freed from Nazi German camps, repatriated to West Africa, and placed in a holding camp in Thiaroye, on the outskirts of Dakar, where they awaited discharge. In a call for justice, they successfully negotiated equal wages with their white colleagues, an agreement that was eventually dishonored, denounced as a mutiny and met with brutality. In Sembene's two-and-a-half-hour film rendition of historical fiction we slowly follow the daily routines of the black soldiers in the camp along with a young Senegalese intellectual named Diatta. Diatta speaks both French and English and serves as a sergeant, even though the French army raided his village and killed much of his family years earlier. He is the embodiment of dilemmas faced by African nations in the 1945–60 independence period and thus offers us a complex perspective for examining how soldiers coped with the unjust treatment of French powers. While the soldiers negotiated equal pay and went on to celebrate their seeming success, ultimately, they got fooled by it. The painful point being that colonialism has continued to reign well past 1965 up until this day, albeit through more invisibilized forms like arts funding structures.

What is significant for us as reflective viewers is that Sembene's film puts the issue of labor and wage at the center of its narrative in the relation between the colonizer and the colonized. Furthermore, it complicates this relation by revealing an internal inability amongst the colonized to communicate and organize. A mute soldier, ironically named Pays (meaning "country" in French), was the only one who sensed something awry in the negotiation with the French army and also the one who saw French troops approaching to attack the camp where his fellow soldiers lay resting after celebrating their supposed

3   "The French admit that thirty-five died, but
       war veterans say 300 black African soldiers
       were killed in the evening of November 30,
       1944." Nazanine Moshiri, "A Little-Known
       Massacre in Senegal," *Aljazeera.com*,
       November 22, 2013. Online: www.aljazeera.
       com/blogs/africa/2013/11/97751.html
       (Accessed September 12, 2018).

146

triumph. No one even tried to understand Pays' desperate murmuring as he attempted to inform his colleagues and organize an escape to prevent their eventual downfall. In the original story, the soldiers were from all parts of the French West African empire—from Guinea, Mali, Senegal, Burkina Faso, Chad, Benin, Gabon, Ivory Coast, Central African Republic, and Togo. With no language in common, they communicated in pidgin French but didn't manage to find enough common ground to organize against their colonizer, whose power was what was fundamentally at stake. Here, we are confronted with an agonistic pairing: the necessity to demand decent pay within existing hegemonic structures and the, perhaps more urgent, necessity to conjure counter-hegemonic structures and practices beyond capitalism.

These cinematic scenes of our wide colonial heritage rang especially true to the authors of this text as we exchanged and discussed them with each other during the 2017 annual Arts Collaboratory (AC) assembly held in Costa Rica. AC is a trans-local network of arts organizations predominantly located in the so-called "Global South" and funded by the Dutch-funded DOEN Foundation (that redistributes lottery money to cultural initiatives). This network of similarly-minded arts initiatives, to which we at Casco Art Institute belong, focuses on collective governance, social change, and sustainable practices in their respective contexts with the aim of being effective in and beyond the field of art. Following the rotational hosting structure for the assembly, we were received by San José-located TEOR/éTica (an independent project space for contemporary art from Central America and the Caribbean) for ten days. Alongside our regular program, we were shown around by our hosts and offered a view of Costa Rica more complex than its reputation as a land of coffee and Chiquita bananas. In fact, at the root of this agricultural stereotype lies the exploitation of labor of people of color, dating back to the first arrival of Afro-Costa Ricans who were brought by the Spanish conquistadors as part of the slave trade in the nineteenth century.

With these particular histories of colonial heritage in mind, there are two practices at Casco Art Institute that engage with different modalities of labor relations in the context of art. The first is the above-mentioned Arts Collaboratory network, where the possibility of collectivizing labor and self-governance in a trans-local dimension is sought out by the members to wrestle with the funder-fundee relationship as illustrated above. The second practice is

the project *Site for Unlearning (Art Organization)* that the Casco Art Institute team has been developing with artist Annette Krauss in our long-term and feminist engagement with the commons. It deals with the usual trap of invisibilizing reproductive labor.

Site for Unlearning began in 2014 alongside our move to a new building and the inaugural exhibition *New Habits*. As part of this relocation and as prompted by artist Annette Krauss, the shifting team at Casco Art Institute took on the challenge of unlearning institutional habits embedded in the many facets of our work. Unlearning is an active critical investigation of normative structures and practices in order to become aware and get rid of taken-for-granted "truths" of theory and practice. The process of unlearning is directed towards embodied forms of knowledge and (un)conscious operations and ways of thinking and doing, while integrating processes of de-instituting. One (un)learns in order to de-institute or dismantle the oppressive parts of an institution.

The unlearning process proceeded with ongoing bi-weekly team meetings with Annette. In the beginning, we focused on identifying what we wanted to unlearn together. The outcome of our discussion lay in a common desire to unlearn the "busyness" of art's conditioned labor, elsewhere summed up by Krauss as: "the habitual, psycho-somatic state of busyness"—whereby accelerationism and the denial of singular and differential rhythms are identified and necessitated by the neoliberal condition. In short, we joke that we are unlearning the business of busyness in that we came to understand and associate the term *business* with the abstracted economic framework in which we are implicated, and understand *busyness* to speak to the inescapable bodily-emotional consequence of performing within this unnatural rhythm of *business*.

This entire collective process of engagement of those subjected to wage labor in an art institution could be considered as part of the task of unlearning. Over the past two or three years we have developed fourteen exercises for unlearning this psycho-somatic state of busyness, some that we continue to practice and others that were one-time trials. One of the most structural exercises is a collective cleaning of our office every Monday, which has become a new institutional habit. This came about after two colleagues sent an email to communicate their frustrations over being the only ones that were cleaning the office, which they signed off with a poignant and ironic remark, "from your lovely housewives." This instance became a subject at one of the subsequent

148

unlearning meetings, and an idea was put forward that we treat it as a regular collective unlearning exercise. We now all clean together at the same time every Monday in a "minor" effort to resist the capitalist conditioning that separates production from reproduction and devalues the latter, thus also discarding the bodies of color that often take up this work, in order to sustain its mechanisms of influence and oppression. This tendency is astutely articulated by Marina Vishmidt and Kerstin Stakemeier, who remind us via Adorno that:

> Art 'conceals' labour like other commodities in capital, but that, due to its absence of use value, it does so to an even greater extent, and thus figures as the 'absolute commodity[...]. Concretely, this can mean outsourcing; gender, racialized, migration-related invisibility of workers; or degraded working conditions as they stand in a determined non-relation to art-world academicism, i.e. ideal 'radicality', or criticality, without relation to its conditions of reproduction. Importantly, just as fair trade doesn't subvert production for value, knowing who is cleaning your Kunsthalle has no bearing on their conditions.[4]

Our list of Unlearning Exercises also asks what a reconsideration of our wage system might look like beyond monetary remuneration and when taking the notion of well-being into account. The time diary helps us begin to articulate and give value to the time of reproductive labor and imagine through practice what consequences such a recognition might have in our immediate surroundings and field of work.

While we have been grappling with the notion of the commons in our program, *Site for Unlearning* has been interfering with our organization, especially our internal relations, asking what an art for the commons might look like and ultimately questioning: *How can art and art institutions contribute to the commons?* Along with the unlearning process, this question led us to take on the challenge of applying the commons to the back side of our institute

---

4   Kerstin Stakemeier and Marina Vishmidt,
     *Reproducing Autonomy: Work, Money, Crisis
     and Contemporary Art*, 77.

in order to embody and define a set of ethical principles with the commons in mind in all facets of our internal work matters, while further investigating and engaging with the commons in our public programming as well. This year (2018), we officially take on a new institutional name, Casco Art Institute: Working for the Commons, binding us pre-figuratively to our commitment to practice the commons. Oftentimes, an art institution is identified with and through the art it shows, because the art it shows is considered to be the institution's primary focus, and/or the art represents the institution. As common as this identification is, we have also witnessed that art institutions do not operate according to the ethics of the art they present. For instance, showing art that critiques capitalism does not mean that an art institution operates in non-capitalistic ways; showing art that is anti-racist does not ensure that art organizations consist of practitioners from varied backgrounds and heritages. This contradiction is near-impossible to avoid, but it's our conviction that we need to work on lessening it if we want to more effectively prove the power of art and prevent "art washing." For this reason, we continue the "art" of unlearning and art as commoning, however slow its processes may be, as it is important that we demonstrate commitment to processes beyond the usual time frame of project-based "productivity."

The Arts Collaboratory network extends this effort in a broader collective dimension in search of modes of solidarity to practice. Since 2013, Arts Collaboratory has been undergoing an experimental process of transforming itself from an artificially-constructed network brought together by funders into an interdependent and trans-local cooperative ecosystem operating in solidarity with each other and each other's networks. Such experimentation is slowly garnered through mutual trust, shared resources, and responsibilities in order to achieve a common wealth and to become practically and actively engaged in "paradigm shifts" concerning the way successes of member organizations have been judged in the funder-fundee relation. This relation is especially important given that most of the AC member organizations work under the legacy of colonial heritage and its persistence. Most organizations also get their funding resources from the West, in particular the Netherlands, which consciously and unconsciously embody the exploitative, judgmental, controlling mechanisms rooted in the colonizer (as illustrated in the films above). And so the colonizer-colonized relation continues, keeping the

organization's production and presentation machinery running without space for questioning its fundamental structures or for radically imagining[5] an alternative reality of relations through which to produce and present.

To transform it is thus to collectively reimagine a future vision complete with a set of ethical principles for guidance in the process of self-governance. AC's co-written future plan, for example, was used to convince our primary funders to relinquish their control, in practical terms, of the system of judgment, selection, and progress and evaluation reports, allowing instead for AC to report to one another without dressing it up, and to also be transparent when it comes to struggles and failures, and all in the spirit of self-governance. The annual assembly, where rotating representatives from each organization come together to work and live with one another for ten days, is the backbone of this way of operating. Our joint major task in the coming years lies in the cultivating, managing, and sharing of these common material and immaterial resources and collective financial pot. In other words, Arts Collaboratory is about to further activate the process of commoning the network/ecosystem; at its best this is but one response to the questions of what if the domestic worker had shared the load with her co-worker in "Nothing but Goodness in the Colony" or, what if the soldiers had heeded and organized around the murmured warnings of Pays?

An earlier version of this text was produced for *oncurating 35: Decolonizing Art Institutions*, edited by Ronald Kolb and Dorothee Richter, and presented during an accompanying forum with the same title.

5   For more on radical imagination see the Glossary of Terms on page 183.

TOILET (T)ISSUES #2

The Elephant in the Room (and Different Ways of Dealing with It)

The conversation below follows "Toilet Tissue and Other Formless Organizational Matters," but took place a year later with new interlocutors and in a more intimate, closed setting. The former conversation (pages 57–73) focuses on how commons-orientated organizations work in the field of art, culture, and social practices across Indonesia, the Netherlands, and the United Kingdom and went on to address the unrecognized reproductive work found in practical organizational matters, such as who purchases the toilet paper. This discussion centers on "the elephant in the room," a metaphorical idiom for the obvious problem that no one wants to discuss. The group acknowledges, both directly and indirectly, how proverbial elephants come in different forms and degrees of opacity within collective work. Together, they address common problems across collective organizations and discuss organizational methodologies that negotiate between

individual desire and collective vision. Speaking of collectivity in this intimate setting brought up relational questions of loneliness and belonging, what makes one stay or leave an organization of this kind, and how it might be possible to be part of multiple "gangs" in order to traverse intersecting struggles. This conversation demonstrates a revealing moment in time for the participants, as structural shifts have taken place and some do not retain the same position or status within their respective organizations. Subsequently, and as a matter of course, the feelings and thoughts expressed here may have changed.

Participants include: Binna Choi, Ying Que, and Yolande Zola Zoli van der Heide (at the time of the conversation respectively director, community and projects, and head of publishing, at Casco Art Institute, Utrecht, Netherlands); Brigitta Isabella and Ferdiansyah Thajib (members of KUNCI Study Forum & Collective, Yogyakarta, Indonesia); and Yollotl Alvarado and Andrés García (members of Cooperativa Cráter Invertido, a México City based artists' collective, México). The conversation was held on June 17, 2016 at Marco Polo Pension, Issyk-Kul, Kyrgyzstan during the Arts Collaboratory Assembly.

Binna

Ferdi expressed so much excitement to do this "Toilet (T)issue" conversation. I wondered why. He said that he could finally know more about internal matters at Casco. Indeed, through the "Toilet (T)issue" conversation we had at KUNCI during the "Formless Organization Matters" conversation last year we heard of internal conflicts in a very subtle way.

Ferdiansyah (Ferdi)

I don't mean to sound like a culturalist, but there is a culture of not speaking about the elephant in the room. Instead, attempts are made to find a way to acknowledge the tension, but indirectly and without being sharp.

Brigitta (Gita)

But I think that's good, because you are not talking about the elephant *physically*. Meaning that you don't expose the elephant's existence by pointing to one personality. I would prefer to concede that there is something wrong indeed, but not explicitly say that a specific person causes it. Because, if it is explicit, the group's dynamic can be consumed by the aversion to a person and from what I feel in KUNCI, there's high tolerance towards personalities that we think cannot be changed. Everyone knows that there is an elephant in the room, but the focus is not about how to make it visible but how to deal with it, together.

Yollotl

This year I have been doing interviews with cooperatives and collective organizations (who are not working in the art field) to ask them about their problems for a publication in a resource called *Common Tools*. And I've been interviewing inhabitants of Amilcingo, an indigenous community southeast of the Morelos state in México. The community is struggling against the Proyecto Integral Morelos (PIM), a megaproject consisting of a pipeline that crosses underground through the communal territory. These interviews focus on the communal autonomous institutions created by the community as a way of showing that people are organizing outside governmental infrastructure for the reconstruction of their territory and identity. By taking a look at the problems others are facing, I hoped to find some kind of mirroring that could allow us to face our struggles as an organization. I was inspired to do this because dealing with internal issues is difficult. It was really surprising how psycho-

historical trauma emerged really fast in all the organizations that I interviewed. All of us are sharing the same problems, whether we are an art organization or not.

Binna
Can you say what the common problems are? I wonder if there was any form, cooperative, or communal type of organization that has no— or at least less—tension and conflict among those organizations, groups, or collectives?

Yollotl
No, they all have the same problem.

Ferdi
And do they all have the same format?

Yollotl
Very similar. The main issues were that there is no way of respecting the natural rhythms of assembly, and how the rhythm is imposed and not natural. With external agendas— like fundraising, and dealing with government support, curators, and politicians asking for something that requires a quick response—you lose your own way of making decisions. The other issue is the idea of respecting members' temporality, like punctuality for example. It's a really

important issue. When you have this really strong program and the meeting starts at four but you are not on time and it's delayed by two hours then the meeting starts with feelings of frustration.

Yollotl
Yeah, we have a similar problem. We call it "self-goal," like in soccer. We always talk about it, as we're really good self-goal players.

Ferdi
Do you mean self-sabotage?

Yollotl
The metaphor comes from when you're playing soccer and you make a goal on your own side. I think it's related to the distinction between collective vision and individual desire. This not only happens in-house, but also when outside invitations take you away. So really, in an informal way, an organizational task or project might be addressed two months after it was brought up by someone, because this person has this desire to do it and waits and waits and waits for the others to make a decision, and then tries to arrange it with them. We have this problem and it's not clear how best to deal with it. It's a kind of

155

administration of energy where you start pushing in a way that is not verbal, like instead of making suggestions to, "Let's do this" and "Let's do that," you show your commitment in a practical way by taking the first step. Then everything starts to happen and everyone gets engaged in this issue. So, it's like you take the initiative to score the goal for yourself. Did I explain myself well?

Yolande

So, someone always has to tailor an idea or task and pull people in according to what they get excited by?

Yollotl

Another way to deal with this problem is to make decisions by yourself. For example, I will do an application for project funding and when the funding is granted and the project can happen then everyone gets involved by asking questions, understanding the methodology, and providing their ideas to the collective discussion.

Gita

Do you think it is better for people to start first with practical actions or with ideas? Which is more ideal? To

do research, put it in a drawer, and wait for everyone to give thoughts, or to do the application first?

Yollotl

I think it's best to begin with methodologies. The big scare is that we have a lot of ideas, but there are no clear tools for how we work with ideas.

Ying

It's also a way to build with time. If you have an idea, you can bring the idea to a brainstorm session as a first step. To form the idea and methodology first means you can formulate it according to what you had in mind initially, as opposed to adding labor for those who did not have the idea. Otherwise, if you make it a collective process all the time, it is so exhausting, demotivating, and very hard to make something happen. If someone brings a well-thought-out proposal based on a collective discussion, then people are much more inclined to get involved because there is a line of action.

Ferdi

Actually, that example takes a different direction to my question. But in that sense, what usually

happens with us is that someone comes up with an idea and possible tools but because we are always working remotely, there is a big chance for misunderstanding. The ideas are often quite clear, but the tools are not always clear. There is also a kind of willingness to let go. Once you present the ideas and the tools, people either understand, don't understand, or try to interpret it but in a different direction from the first person who conceived it, then they work on it and it grows in a different direction. I think it is interesting that the first person that initiates the idea will then follow the dynamics. So, at first the direction is A, but because of miscommunication or misunderstanding, it becomes B. Then the one who initiated it realizes, "oh, okay, that could also work, so let's just go with B." Sometimes the process gets stuck, but then the initiator tries to find a solution for B, instead of going back to A. They try to work with the existing context.

Binna

So, this is what happens when it is understood that the direction has shifted, so then can the plan go through?

Ferdi

It is a slower process, but at least it's taking in more voices for consideration. It's not about being democratic, it's more about building up ideas slowly so that everyone can follow through, and then if something goes wrong, all those involved will share the responsibility. Sometimes the group can even decide, "No, we take the other way around." Or maybe it is not even a conscious decision to go in the other direction. The main thing is it doesn't feel as lonely anymore. Because if things don't go well, then it would become a shared failure and if it is a success, it is a shared success. I think it is tied to a selfish reason also, not just to self-limitation.

Binna

That is also what I was about to ask, whether what we are dealing with is necessarily about everyone participating in decision making. This also brings me to the question that I wanted to raise in the beginning: Why are we really interested in talking about this? And why are we so attached to working in an organization in this manner? By working on Gwangju Biennale, a larger organizational structure, I realized how aggressive these kinds

of organizational machines are. So, further, I wonder how to deal with the aggressive machine on a macro level without losing faith in the value of the micropolitics, which we're spending a great deal of time on.

Ferdi
I think it is interesting that you make the division between external and micro-politics. I think they're totally related. They feed off each other. How you deal with external pressures also affects how you are dealing with micropolitics, and vice versa. To me, they mirror each other.

Binna
Here we are dealing with quite an intricate matter of how our affect works in relation to our value of a certain horizontality because we do care about things. You know, there exists a perfectly functioning organizational form in terms of achieving goals and that form has a totally totalitarian structure.

Gita
Do you think you are forced to be together in Casco?

Binna
No, I think we are constantly confronted with moments in which we question whether we should l eave or quit, or even whether Casco should stop existing. Then, there is something that makes us continue, which could be money, ideology, or philosophy and related possibilities.

Ying
I think what makes me stay at Casco fluctuates. Because when I am feeling I want to leave the only reason I stay is because it provides a steady income. When I want to stop and I ask, "Why do I stay?" it's because I feel working at Casco is the only way I can do what I want to do. And I have a desire to make it better, too. Usually, when I have this crisis there is a moment where the things which make me go into it are resolved.

Yolande
How are they resolved?

Ying
In various ways. Sometimes it's affection, the team, group dynamics, sometimes it's the type of work and the people I meet through work, sometimes it's the possibilities of the space, the radical imagination, or the challenge for myself. It's always different. But if crises don't get resolved, well, that's a problem.

Yollotl
KUNCI, have you experienced
the desire to step out?

Gita
I think we discussed it and someone
said that KUNCI might disappear,
but I don't think someone could
step out of KUNCI.

Ferdi
That's not true, there are people
that have.

Gita
Yeah, in the past. But in our program
now, I just can't imagine it. Maybe
I'm too sentimental about whether
someone would quit because it's my
life. I can't imagine KUNCI not
existing.

Ferdi
What if I tell you I'm thinking of—
well, not quitting—but retiring?

Gita
Yes, but I can still access you.

Ferdi
Of course! It's not about breaking
up. But I think I want to move
on, especially after seeing that the
collective has been doing well.
On the other hand, I'm not satisfied
with what I have now, I don't think
that what I want to do can actually
happen if I stayed. It doesn't fit
with KUNCI's desire. It's not out of
emotion, it's based on doing the next
thing for myself. But not only that,
I want to try different struggles.

Gita
The reason why I said that I cannot
imagine someone quitting is because
you can stay a member of KUNCI
without doing anything. For
example, when I did my studies
I did nothing, but I still felt I
belonged to KUNCI as a member.
When you have to do your thing,
we don't ask you for anything.

Ying
Is it true that you really don't do
anything? Are you not helping clean?

Gita
Not when I have to go abroad. And
everyone is abroad; Ferdi is in Berlin
so he can only respond by email. He
cannot buy the dish towels.

Ying
But, maybe he communicates with
KUNCI members to deal with issues
they have. Maybe Ferdi's doing some
affective labor.

159

Ferdi
All the time.

Yollotl
Is being a member about the idea
of belonging to something you
think is important, or is it more like
you are really interested in what is
happening? Because they are different.

Yolande
You also talked about it before in
terms of addressing yourselves as
"family" versus "gang."

Ferdi
That's the thing for me, I should be
able to leave my family if I want.

Binna
Maybe with a gang, you cannot.

Yollotl
They will kill you.

Binna
There is a belonging, but a
belonging that supports a certain
idea and practice. It's not that you
belong anywhere. Anyhow, I am
convinced it is really powerful to
have semi-autonomous collective
efforts as a way to counter larger
violence, because it is a support
structure. It's evidence that there

is a different struggle and value, and
so you have the courage to fight, too.

Yollotl
There is an issue about loneliness.
Collectiveness as a way of dealing
with loneliness.

Yolande
I was thinking about that in a kind
of existential way. Like, what if your
"gang" fails to support you in an area
that you particularly need? Can you
belong to several gangs and approach
it that way?

Ying
Have you had a case in which that
happened?

Yolande
I've been thinking about it in
terms of race. And then in the
particular comparison between
Arts Collaboratory, let's call that
a "gang," versus or in parallel with
the Casco gang, and what I can get
out of one gang and not the other.

Ferdi
Can you be more specific?

Yolande
I am talking in terms of race politics.

160

Binna
That we are a diaspora?

Yolande
No, specifically me, in terms of blackness.

Binna
That at Casco you are the only black person? And here?

Yolande
Yeah. I was talking to Teesa [Bahana, the director] from 32 Degrees East [Ugandan Arts Trust] in Kampala, for instance, and how whilst she has lived in several places she has decidedly chosen to be based in Kampala, to reside amongst people that look like her and who are culturally alike. And while she's talking about studying in Goldsmiths [University of London] she is affirmed that she would go and then return to Kampala afterwards, and this is related to blackness and to the idea of "belonging." And then we came to talk about race together. She was asking me about how it is to grow up black in Europe, particularly in the Dutch context, and how I deal with this and that. This type of conversation in this very articulated way—reproductive as well—is only possible with her, or with the universal black

Teesa. I often have these exchanges concerning strategies for survival as a black subject with other black people, be they diasporic or otherwise. So, I wonder about this. I was coming at her from the point view of culling ways for coping, whilst trying to remain open about how I manage within my "gang."

When I say the "black subject" I also mean blackness in the widest sense, that is perhaps in the way that Fred Moten and Stefano Harney put "black studies" at the center of their Undercommons project. That is also including brownness, yellowness, queerness, what-have-you-ness but also insisting on valuing the differences within these communities. Ferdi also once pointed out the limitations to that. And the older I get the more I think about the limitations because of a feeling of disappointment I have in my primary "gang." I don't know if an extension or ecosystem of this "gang" is possible. I can also extend this to my nuclear family with all its racial difference, if we touch upon that.

Binna
But would there be another gang that could alleviate this?

Yolande

Having several gangs is one way that I've come to think about it. This maneuvering amongst your several gangs becomes a question: How are we best to go about that? How to contribute fully in a committed way to several and is it important to do so?

Ying

Do you think that it's something that you cannot escape?

Yolande

How do you mean?

Ying

Because I cannot relate to you in the sense of blackness, but I can relate to being in white spaces. At Casco I have become more aware and politicized about race and have also felt affirmed because Casco is a diverse—I hate the word—but a diverse space. And I've learned a lot from speaking specifically with you and have come to think a lot about my position in the leftist scene, and to look very actively for colored activism. But, at the same time I am accepting of the white spaces in which I also move, in which I also see value and importance. I see how I can contribute to these spaces by

being a killjoy, although mostly a feminist killjoy, actually, because it's a less confrontational approach than bringing race into a white space.

Yolande

Yeah, and I'm trying to address a limitation in that kind of feminist approach. For instance, even when we think about the so-called first and second waves of feminism we can see that this is a white feminist canon that didn't include class or race at a point in time, which is what the intersectional approach to feminism is wrestling with today.

Ying

But then, I feel that I'm accepting these different attitudes I have in different spaces, whilst I try to find different gangs so that I can have different ways of speaking and mediating between them. That it is what I have to accept if I want to continue to be in a mediational role. You know what I mean?

Yolande

What is it you have to accept?

Ying

This whiteness, basically, and the inability to address it in the way I would like to address it.

162

Yolande

I think it's interesting in your specific case because (while I am bearing in mind Gita's warning against making tensions personal) I want to repeat your anecdote from the Teesa-style conversation that we had together, when you spoke about how you grew up, and pointed to the fact that maybe you had a late realization that the white kids on the playground didn't want to play with you because of your "yellowness." And that you had never registered that for your entire life until now, I find really interesting. That kind of late registration was not an option for me.

Ying

Yeah, exactly.

Yolande

While our conversation may have been generative for you, maybe, I have had countless examples of these types of talks throughout my life. Even back in South Africa growing up as the token black person due to class. Ying, we talk about tokenism often, it's exhausting too! My discussions with Teesa, well the "universal her," have a different departure point. We share that sense of exhaustion and can address the insecurities that come with that

because we're growing parallel and figuring that shit out. Yet, is that approach—whereby we are exhausted and have to unpack each time—the right one? When does one just get to be, without relating to or undoing whiteness as the primary thing?

Ferdi

This is also my question. I don't think there is any right strategy for containing struggles, or from collapsing them. That's why one struggle is also interconnected with others, and so it's why it's not a challenge, by the way. That is actually why it is hard for me to give up KUNCI because I thought—to be honest—I want more struggles concerning queer issues, for instance, and I don't feel that KUNCI necessarily accommodates me in that context. While they would love the idea of engaging with the issue, I don't really have partners to talk with in that sense. So, it's not that I feel left out, it's more that there is a part of my struggle that is not real to other members. So then should I do both KUNCI and queer theory/activism at the same time? How am I to connect them? Sometimes it is not possible. It also doesn't work when you start to compartmentalize these struggles. It's going to haunt you.

When I am at KUNCI I'll have all these voices telling me, "Hey, this is more important." And then when I go to the other space they'll say, "Hey, you have actually already dealt with this." And then, how do I choose? I'm not specifically addressing your issue, but I do not think there is any right strategy.

Binna
Well, we are not NGOs. That's also why we have these kinds of problems in concrete matters.

Ferdi
And I'm not speaking about LGBT rights and the like, but of queerness and thinking about queerness. Because I am also not so happy with how LGBT issues are being talked about nowadays, it's overtly liberal.

Gita
I think what makes us different is that KUNCI cannot accommodate you and your struggle in exploring the discourse of queerness. I also have to struggle in my situation and there are things I like that KUNCI cannot accommodate. But the things that I like I can do by myself. In the meantime, I need other people to do other things. You know what

I mean? So, I have my solo project [*Yolande misheard Gita to say "sorrow project"*], and I have KUNCI to keep me sane, and to feel that I have support.

Andrés
Sorrow show, we can end with the sorrow show.

Afterword:
HAVE YOU HAD
A PRODUCTIVE DAY?

Binna Choi and
Annette Krauss

Instead of doing art, art history, art criticism, and curating in the ways we usually understand and practice them, with *Site for Unlearning (Art Organization)*, the Casco Art Institute team and the artist Annette Krauss have been "busy" with the different structures of Casco Art Institute and how they work on a daily basis. These often invisible and unquestioned organizational structures became the subject of our collective focus while we also experimented with different ways of working together. During this time, Casco Art Institute has continued to organize exhibitions, discursive and performative public events, and support artists to produce new works, and Annette has continued her artistic practice. At a certain point, this seeming "double track" met, and as a result Casco reframed itself as "Casco Art Institute: Working for the Commons," adopting the logic of the commons not only as the object of study but also in its work as an art institution. The words that follow will be a reflection on this pathway. Before beginning, we would like to inform the reader that "we," Binna Choi and Annette Krauss, will be recasting the net of our plural pronoun to include the shifting Casco Art Institute team who have co-constituted this process of "unlearning" institutional habits—we hope that in doing so we do justice to the collective.[1]

Focusing on the invisible, organizational practices of Casco Art Institute, some skeptics found the unlearning practice to be a form of navel gazing or hyper reflexivity, and doubts were constantly raised on whether its aims could actually be achieved. Others claimed that the risks of failure, which could

influence the public funding Casco Art Institute gets, were too high and that it was better, therefore, to leave things as they were. The broader and lingering question has been: Wouldn't it be better just to focus on art as we know it? The current and expanding #MeToo movement and those decolonizing institutions would answer this question with a resounding no. Starting with the fields of art and culture across the world women—often BPOC—artists, producers, researchers, and administrators alike are speaking out about the sexist, racist, patriarchal, and capitalist-colonialist conditions of their work. These self-same conditions have been the subject of critical art works, but rarely have they "betrayed" the contradiction between what they (re)present and the reality of (re)producing such representational works. Is this what we call systemic? **As artistic and cultural producers we ask: If art and cultural productions express a desire for social change, then doesn't what we show need to be reconnected to the conditions in which our artworks and shows are made possible, so that this process might become leverage for the change itself?** To embark on this process, we believe, is exactly how *institutional critique* as an artistic genre and the ensuing *new institutionalism* as a key artistic discourse of the last decades could move forward; namely to activate the front and the back of an institution, the visible and the invisible, to operate *in tandem*. Institute as you (re)present, and even blur such divisions!

Institutional Critique—Revisited

As an artistic genre, institutional critique comprises of artistic investigations into, and responses to, *both* the art institution and the institution of art itself by exposing the institutional apparatus on which the category of art relies. Critique takes place via investigations into the art market, galleries, collectors, sponsors, local and national government museums, art spaces, self-organized groups, and artistic practices, among others. A red thread crosses this two-fold understanding of institution—whether it's an art institution or an institution of art—that that implies **the institution is in fact inside of us and shapes the embodied and habitual ways we work and relate to each other.** Artist Andrea Fraser, a seminal protagonist of institutional critique, described this dynamic: "So if there is no outside for us, it is not because the institution is perfectly closed, or exists as an apparatus in a 'totally administered society,' or has grown all-encompassing in size and scope. It is because the institution is

166

inside of us, and we can't get outside of ourselves."[2]

With this immanent notion of institution in mind, our approach in *Sites for Unlearning* has been to study and (if necessary) intervene into the art organization Casco as an exemplary "body." This approach takes a tangential or critical measure to so-called new institutionalism, the art institution's own take on institutional critique. The practice of new institutionalism carried on the legacy of institutional critique in self-reflexive yet only discursive forms,[3] making discursivity the medium of presentation. Instead, *Sites for Unlearning* has taken a performative form—as an expanded form of performance—in looking at the institution and working with the team as a site of group coordination (including human and non-human actors) in different spaces (also globally) and across different times, including habits and working routines as the embodiment of the institution. Consequently, the practice of "institutional critique" enacted by *Sites for Unlearning* has been negotiated, in the first instance, amongst those who work at Casco Art Institute and embody the institution in interaction with Casco Art Institute's wider community, while it has also been shared with a wider public. We, the whole team of Casco Art Institute, including one or two interns and Annette Krauss, have carved out this site for unlearning within our working hours in the form of bi-monthly collective meetings.[4] During those hours, we collaboratively examined the

3   As a series of curatorial, art educational, as well as administrative practices (from the mid 1990s to the early 2000s), "new institutionalism" consisted of attempts to establish alternative forms of institutional activity of mostly medium-sized, publicly funded contemporary art institutions. It mainly resulted in a shift on a discursive level "away from the institutional framing of an art object as practiced since the 1920s with elements such as the white cube, top-down organization and insider audiences" which at the same time opened the institutions up to new forms of managerialism and corporatization. See: Lucie Kolb and Gabriel Flückiger, "New Institionalism Revisited." Online: www.on-curating.org/issue-21-reader/new-institutionalism-revisited.html#.WwkNwqNh2Hp (Accessed June 2, 2018).

1   For more on the demand for an ethics of speaking as "we," see the unlearning exercise 6.2 "(Collective) Authorship" on page 48–49.

2   Andrea Fraser, "An Artist's Statement (1992)," *Museum Highlights: The Writings of Andrea Fraser*, ed. Alexander Alberro (MIT Press, Cambridge, 2005), 104.

4   For an elaborate list of the shifting team at Casco Art Institute see the colophon, pages 211–30.

spatio-temporal, embodied, and material relationalities inherent in the institution of Casco Art Institute.

Commoning Institution

In the background of this performative collective practice is Casco Art
Institute's 2013–16 program "Composing the Commons," which was named in
reflection of and as a continuing guideline from the past program, which
involved participatory and collective forms of artistic production in tandem
with a broader social movement.[5] The necessity to reflect on collectivity on all
levels, including political, economic, and psychological ones was sensed and
charged with an urgency to resist the expanding privatization and financialization of space, time, and subjectivities entangled with ongoing conditions
of coloniality; and not least, increasing forms of precarization and competition
that underlie all of our relations. The term "the commons" seems to allow this
multiplex of concerns. In simplistic terms, the commons are established
through a collective management of common resources which can be found in
different historical and cultural contexts. To translate its meaning and operations to a viable present day understanding and practice means to complicate
it. For instance, one of Casco Art Institute's central approaches to the commons
is a feminist perspective that, after Silvia Federici, seeks to collectivize domestic
and reproductive labor that has been made invisible or devalorized, as manifest
in gendered and racialized forms of no payment or low wages. Federici's
research on women's legacies of the commons beyond Europe and the Western
idea of land enclosure are a crucial part of our "complication" of the commons.[6]
The concept of "the undercommons," as elaborated by Fred Moten and Stefano
Harney, underlies the poetics and agency of collective resistance and struggle
that takes place *beneath and within* the existing system, pointing to anti-slavery
struggles, hence differentiating itself from the institutionalized commons with

5   The first long-term project at Casco Art
     Institute, *The Grand Domestic Revolution*
     (2010–12), was a central work in this direction.
6   Silvia Federici, "Feminism and the Politics of
     the Commons," *The Commoner*, 2012. Online:
     www.commoner.org.uk/?p=113 (Accessed
     June 2, 2018).

168

its potential to be trapped into a logic of management and control. Instead, as a form of collective struggle and mutual learning, "study" is a way of commoning "under the existing institutional radar" that resonated strongly with a collective desire felt within the Casco Art Institute team and in its wider networks, most notably Arts Collaboratory, in the name of a "desire for deep understanding."

This approach to the commons has been accompanied by a number of artistic and other collective experimental inquiries over several years, and has entailed the question of how Casco Art Institute, as an art institution, relates to the commons. A few marking points plot out the answer to this question. One is our exhibition titled *New Habits* (2014), which was special as it inaugurated Casco Art Institute's new location and building. Alluding to Casco Art Institute's new "body," the exhibition took a cue from Giorgio Agamben's recent research into Franciscan communities[7] while responding to the artists who we were working with at that time.[8] Agamben's main thesis describes how the Franciscans evaded authoritarian institutions like the church by focusing on common rules and ethics of "use" against those of "property," and "poverty" against "wealth." These rules are loose in comparison to laws and involve "forms" including what to wear, whereby "habits" are named in a double sense. At the same time, artists like Aimée Zito Lema, Christian Nyampeta, Ayreen Anastasa, Rene Gabri, and Sung Hwan Kim brought certain demands within the team and Casco Art Institute's surrounding communities to exercise their daily practices, from what and how to eat, to how to deal with daily rhythms as part of their artistic projects. It is also in the context of dealing with "habits" that Annette Krauss, Casco Art Institute's long-term collaborating artist, and the whole team of Casco Art Institute agreed to start the *Site for Unlearning* venture. This journey has proceeded as much as interwoven with the wider collective working process of the Arts Collaboratory network, which Casco Art Institute is part of. For most of its

---

7   Giorgio Agamben, *The Highest Poverty: Monastic Rules and Form-of-Life* (Stanford, CA: Stanford University Press, 2013).

8   The new premises of Casco Art Institute, we found out, used to be a convent that lived according to the Third Order of Saint Francis, a history that connected us more closely to our research than we had anticipated.

members—comprised of twenty-three art organizations based in the so-called Global South—and the only and main funder from the Netherlands, Stichting DOEN, it did not take long to realize that unless the underlying and invisible structure for their program was changed they could not further their respective local artistic-social engagement as well as their trans-local collaborations. By structure, we mean those hierarchical colonial-era labor and financial relations that most of the member organizations inherited. We need to "do commoning" in our institutions. In order to do so, we also need to unlearn our old habits. These twin concepts echo back and forth, again and again.

Unlearning Institution

What do we mean by unlearning? It's also our habit to attribute positive value to those learning and art institutions in general that have been busy with positioning themselves as a place for learning. Then, why *un*learn? To approach these questions requires us to look through the relationship between learning and unlearning to explore the connecting tissue between unlearning, learning, lifelong learning, and institution. Here (and in this book as a whole), lifelong learning—as learning from cradle to grave—is examined as a specific derivative of European knowledge economies since 1990s, and one of the dominant conceptions of learning that is accumulative, progress-oriented, and insti-tutionally driven for economic profit. Many scholars[9] agree meanwhile, that lifelong learning's economic focus pervades institutions and subjectivities today. As an art institution and artistic practice with research and experi-mentation as key modalities—for instance, the programming of artistic research projects around the commons—*Sites for Unlearning* might be actually reinforcing this kind of "lifelong learning" agenda.

"Unlearning," in the terms set out by Annette, juxtaposes this agenda and instead echoes an expression coined by postcolonial feminist thinker Gayatri

9   For further details on the discourse on lifelong learning and the economization of learning, see Annette Krauss, "Lifelong Learning and the Professionalized Learner," in *Unlearning Exercises: Art Organizations as Sites for Unlearning,* Binna Choi, Annette Krauss, Yolande Zola Zoli van der Heide eds (Amsterdam: Casco Art Institute/Valiz, 2018), 74–96.

170

Spivak: "unlearning one's privileges."[10] Spivak urges us to find ways of questioning and reworking one's assumptions, prejudices, and histories in order to tackle injustices in a globalized world. In other words, unlearning is less about acquiring new skills and knowledge and more about taking on an active critical investigation of normative structures and practices in order to become aware and get rid of taken-for-granted "truths" of theory and practice with the aim to think and work through inequalities in everyday life. **This notion of unlearning, hence, directs our attention to habits again.** Habits are those practices of thinking and doing through which we engage bodily with our daily environment, practices that have always already slipped our rational analysis. They constitute learned gestures, rhythms, or postures of our bodies that are incorporated in a particular space and time. Therefore, habits form the political identity of our bodies and are inseparably linked to the world views and knowledge that we consciously and unconsciously perform. **We know how difficult it is to become aware of a habit, let alone to get rid of it, and therein lies the complication.** Have you ever successfully rid yourself of your stress-induced hair pulling habit? Or attempted to banish the habit of thinking, after Spivak, "that I am necessarily better, I am necessarily indispensable, I am necessarily the one to right wrongs" in encountering each other?[11] It needs extra work, energy, and imagination—mental and bodily—in order to get rid of a specific working and thinking "direction" and engage in a different one.

So, in this light, and while the art institution itself is fed by the capitalist economy and its logic of accumulative learning, advancement, and growth we could reasonably question whether it is even possible to unlearn something like an art institution. While attempting to confront what we have internalized to be impossibilities, **unlearning marks both an engagement with institutional processes that has the potential to break with the promise of limitless economic advancement and growth, and an attempt to intervene in the institution of learning itself.** Not surprisingly, one of the recurring

10   Susan Harasym, ed., *Spivak, G. The Post-colonial Critic* (Routledge, London, 1990), vii.
11   Gayatri Spivak, "Righting Wrongs," *The South Atlantic Quarterly* vol 103 (2004): 523–81, 532.

discussions in our collective meetings revolved around the sheer impossibility of unlearning, and whether we should return to more pragmatic, "possible" organizational business as we know it.

We didn't. Instead the experiments we conceived of (see more on them below) also have to be seen as collective research into the politics of (im)possibilities that play a crucial part in approaching processes of unlearning within an organizational structure. They build a support structure for this research with and into an institution when the collective encounters dominant forms of thinking and behaving, (affective) structures of impossibilities, and their entanglement with embodied knowledges.

Thus, *Site for Unlearning* is both an attempt to thicken these practices of unlearning and a means of feeding the embodied imagination towards unlearning capitalism within the institutional structures of an art organization. This resonates with learning the commons in the formation of new habits.

Being Busy as an Institutional Habit

Should there be any preexisting methods for unlearning, one might be to set the terms of collaboration. The whole team of Casco Art Institute and Annette[12] agreed on having two-hour-long bi-weekly or monthly meetings at the Casco Art Institute office, during which we approached the questions of what we wanted to unlearn, how to approach unlearning, what we were struggling with, and what we agreed upon, to integrate these meeting hours into their general working hours rather than claim them as extra, while freelancing work was reimbursed. Our identification of institutional habits for collective unlearning was intertwined with a vision for the commons that is enacted, visualized, and formulated in exhibitions, public discussions, pub-

12   The team has varied in size from four to nine people. Over the period of the collaboration the team at Casco Art Institute has consisted of six to eight regular staff members and two paid interns. Additionally, two to three freelancers (including Annette), have been connected to specific project phases. This includes the continuous transcriptions and comment on each meeting by Whitney Stark and the designer Rosen Eveleigh.

lications, community work, and the way Casco Art Institute as an organization is run on a management level, including its administrative ethos and its methods of production and communication. After a few meetings, a common priority to unlearn **our problematic relation with a sense of busyness arose. "Feeling busy" is a psychosomatic state that causes anxiety and frustration.**

Ying Que, who by then worked as the Community and Project coordinator at Casco Art Institute, expressed this sense of busyness at Casco Art Institute in the following:

> Yes, it is like when you ask someone here, "how are you doing?" and they reply, "Very busy, very busy. I am so busy." A couple of years ago, I read an article called "Stop the Glorification of Being Busy" and from researching that further, I came upon this collection of essays by Bertrand Russell entitled, *In Praise of Idleness*, which campaigned for a twenty-one-hour work week. This could be quite interesting for us, as we seem to always be so very busy and quite stressed. It is just part of our rhythm to try and deal with our workload, balancing our work ethic with work and life together. [...] I thought it might be interesting for us to look at unlearning the internalized processes of having to produce results, measurable results, of being productive in that sense: to be in the office for eight hours and present Excel sheets, project plans, schedules, and e-mailing. There is this opposition of having to be productive versus doing nothing, in which doing nothing is just considered unproductive, while it could actually be quite elevating for the spirits and inspiring. You can be quite tired and so not really think things over because you have to produce all the time.[13]

13   This quotation is an early articulation from one of our initial conversations in 2014, then audio-recorded and transcribed as part of the meetings of *Sites for Unlearning (Art Organization)*. It is taken from one of from *Business/Busyness* one of four transcription booklets that we produced for the *New Habits* exhibition (2013).

In subsequent meetings and conversations, we—the team and Annette—discussed and accounted for different problems of being busy and the relations to our working environments that have concerned all of us. The conversations gained a certain momentum on the occasion of a mis-hearing of the word busyness as business. Closer study assured us that feeling busy is not just a banal sense of pressure we happen to share. Busyness is the constant demand for productivity in terms of commodification, including production and reproduction, and brings about an increasingly unpleasant and oftentimes unhealthy state. Our study of institutional habits of busyness and its relationship to business revealed that we were interested in those moments of busyness that are in fact materializations of what we understood as business—as the neoliberal condition of profit orientation and economization, with its driving force of optimization. **"Busyness in the neoliberal sense comes from larger societal processes that celebrate being busy and equate its effects to signs of being a productive citizen with a successful career and vibrant social life**. Artists are busy. CEOs of big companies are busy. Students are busy. Bankers are busy. Activists are busy. Professors are busy. Mothers are busy. Even our children and grandparents are busy. The Casco Art Institute team is also always busy. How can we ever unlearn this habit of busyness, or as we call it, busyness/business?"[14]

Let's come back to Spivak. Habits, she claims, cannot be disabled through the classic philosophical re-examination of an argument and its premise. Instead, she argues for the **"training of the imagination,"** which could result in an aesthetic that *"short-circuits* the task of shaking up the habit of not examining [the premises]."[15] This aesthetic short-circuit comes from weaving together literature, literacy, and political intervention as a way of "training the imagination for epistemological performance and [...] intervention."[16] For Spivak, this involves a "productive undoing" that must be carried out along the "fault lines of the doing, without accusation, without excuse, with a view to

---

14   Excerpt from collective writing: Team at
      Casco Art Institute, and Annette Krauss,
      "Site for Unlearning (Art Organization),"
      The Public School for Architecture, ed. Lars
      Fischer, Rachel Himmelfarb (Brussels:
      Common Books, 2015), 101–23.

15   Gayatri Spivak, *An Aesthetic Education in
      the Era of Globalization* (Cambridge: Harvard
      University Press, 2012), 6.

16   Ibid, 122.

174

use."[17] Hence, in her spirit we entwine our performative approach and the study of the affective structures of (im)possibilities. In this sense, unlearning institutional habits has a double trajectory involving ongoing discursive and critical investigations coupled with bodily interventions, structural literacy,[18] and imaginative jumps.

The potential of this double trajectory lies in the very linking of aesthetic and social forms made possible through the activation of a performative register; an understanding of form that speaks beyond the discourse of aesthetics to connect aesthetic, social, and historical contexts. This aesthetic-social form resonates with the compelling work of literary critic Caroline Levine who ties form to politics, as in her view form not only organizes works of art but also political life.[19] In a similar way to *Site for Unlearning*, Levine articulates an expanded idea of form as being the "work of form to make order"[20] through specific arrangements, configurations, and distributions. Thus, if form organizes not only art but political life, it equally organizes the *ways* we know art, politics, and institutions. Against this backdrop, we propose to look at our collaboration, the work at Casco Art Institute, and the unlearning project from another perspective, namely as **forms of organizing**. *Site for Unlearning* is both deeply embedded in an understanding of the institutional that is embodied, performative, and process-orientated and it attempts to push, reconsider, and in the best case unlearn the very limits of what form is and does in this particular institutional context. In this sense, it is a study of organizational forms to understand how aesthetic form functions in overlapping and colliding in arrangements with other social or political forms in order to thicken processes of unlearning.

17   Ibid, 1.
18   In the sense of becoming able to read structural
       trajectories entangled with our daily everyday
       practices.
19   Gayatri Spivak, *An Aesthetic Education in the
       Era of Globalization*, 3.
20   Caroline Levine, *Forms: Whole, Rhythm,
       Hierarchy, Network* (New Jersey: Princeton
       University Press, 2015), 4.

Unlearning Busyness/Business

The aims of our two-hour-long bi-weekly or monthly team get-togethers at the Casco Art Institute office raised certain questions: How did we attempt to train the imagination? Were we able to produce an aesthetic short-circuit? Have we unlearned busyness/business? We were constantly in search of what and how to unlearn together. With no pre-given solution or methods available we sometimes got tired of this process. But as we continued to meet and study together, this constant searching and questioning eventually led us to fourteen exercises,[21] which we named *unlearning exercises.*[22] To a certain degree, these Unlearning Exercises first instituted what we now do on a regular basis and have begun a body of (art) work. Among the fourteen, some have remained one-off trials, having nevertheless been important for our unlearning investigations, their development, and connected experiences. For example, "Care Network," as inspired by the *Nanopolitics Handbook*,[23] revealed professional and emotional relationalities of interdependency within the team. This led us to "Mood Color," through which we hoped to address and take care of some affective interactions occurring in our team. Affect hugely affects relationships but is hard to articulate and express—even more so than emotion. "Time Diary" aimed to track our use of time over a week. While this process may resemble a managerialist time management method, in our case we hoped to use it to examine how our management of time(s) causes busyness in the hope of finding other modalities of time and rhythm towards allowing value in so-called "really unproductive" time. Other Unlearning Exercises have become long-term engagements including organizing "Collective Reading" time for sharing relevant reading materials and ensuring a regular team

---

21   The etymological origin of the term "exercise" in Latin is *"exercere,"* meaning "keeping busy," connoting its use in hierarchical disciplinary contexts such as existing educational institutions, (professional) sports training facilities, military training facilities, and so on. We aim to grapple with the double bind of the term exercise, hence proposing the term "unlearning exercise."

22   Please see pages 17–56 in this book for the comprehensive overview of the unlearning exercises.

23   *Nanopolitics Handbook: The Nanopolitics Group,* Paolo Plotegher, Manuela Zechner, and Bue Rübner Hansen eds. (New York, NY: Minor Compositions, 2013). Online: www.minorcompositions.info/wp-content/uploads/2013/09/nanopolitics-web.pdf (Accessed April 4, 2017).

"Meeting" to allow sufficient time for face-to-face conversations. More challenging, ongoing Unlearning Exercises include "(Collective) Authorship" through which we address the politics of citation and authorship, including within *Site for Unlearning*. "Property Relations" is the one that caused the most resistance and discomfort within the group, including the question of how it related to unlearning busyness. Other questions included: What do each of us own? What do we own collectively? What does the art organization own of us? Is there a different way of sharing? Bifurcating from this is "Well-being and Wage," the ongoing, unresolved exercise of reconsidering our wage systems.[24] The process of unlearning busyness is indeed the process of unlearning the capitalist logics of relations in all facets towards the commons. The "impossibility" of unlearning is an acknowledged possibility given that Casco Art Institute's economy is heavily dependent on a public funding system whose measures and expectations are not so different from "busyness" in other areas; in the case of art, product and profit are audience numbers and visibility. Yet, what if this very impossibility is what capitalism teaches us; what if the mechanism of learning, as an accumulation of knowledge and skills, lets us learn that unlearning is impossible? Could we make the impossible possible?

Cleaning as a New Habit

Weekly collective cleaning is the exercise that has become the most established as a new institutional habit. Every Monday after the weekly team meeting the whole team cleans the office together. As office cleaning was always a team task it has never been outsourced, however it was mostly being done by just a few people in the team. One day, two of those who often did the cleaning sent an e-mail out to the rest of the team with a plea to pay attention to this problem. The email was signed off with the poignant remark "from your lovely housewives." This instance happened during the early period of our collaboration and it became the subject of one of the unlearning meetings. An

---

24 Inspired by Chapter 5, "Take Back Property: Commoning," J. K. Gibson-Graham, Jenny Cameron, and Stephen Healy, *Take Back the Economy: An Ethical Guide for Transforming Our Communities* (Minneapolis, MN: University of Minnesota Press, 2013), 125–58.

idea was put forward to try to make cleaning together every Monday at the same time a regular collective Unlearning Exercise. Which we did and still do.

And, a reader might ask, are you no longer busy? Our answer is "No." We feel less busy, but we certainly have even more work to do. The habit of collective working processes in the spirit of the commons does take much more time than a hierarchical decision making and labor process, even though we don't follow the logic of consensus-based decision making. Neither does it guarantee that the decision is right. Although some of the institutions that fund us do support our engagement with the commons and unlearning process, there are others that do not understand our efforts and would rather undermine our work-practice by relegating it into the realm of invisibility. Or, to tell the story from a different angle, regular cleaning at Casco Art Institute as a micro habit, act, and gesture implies much more than its scale proposes and perhaps even more, as we still clean even when we encounter the desire to postpone the work because we feel busy. The implication of this ongoing practice embraces not only the whole organization but also the notion of art as our primary focus. What do we mean by this?

The Art and Politics of Cleaning

Here we return to reproductive labor, or domestic labor and maintenance, a familiar subject of Casco Art Institute's program. The long-term research project *Grand Domestic Revolution* (GDR 2012–15, including the touring *GDR Goes On* iterations) has focused on domestic labor as gendered, racialized, invisibilized, isolated, and devalorized labor. GDR brought works like *Women and Work* (1973–75) by Mary Kelly with Margaret Harrison and Kay Hunt, and *Nightcleaners* (1972–75) by Berwick Street Film Collective to the program. It presented *Manifesto for Maintenance Art! 1969* by Mierle Laderman Ukeles, who radically questioned what is subsumed under avant-garde and conceptual art and contested the separation between the artwork and housework as being artificial. Working along these borders, her manifesto interrogates forms of domination and exclusion perpetuated by the hierarchical relationships between maintenance and art, and maintenance and development. Above all, a group of cultural workers, including the shifting team at Casco Art Institute and Annette formed ASK!,[25] in an attempt to align with the cleaners' movement in the Netherlands and the struggle against the international

178

division of labor. At that time the cleaners' movement included the Dutch Labor Union (FNV) and the Indonesian Migrant Workers Union (IMWU); most members of IMWU work as domestic workers yet are also undocumented migrants.[26] With the support of artist Andreas Siekmann we created a series of isotypes that represented domestic workers as militant workers to be stenciled on the street along with the domestic workers' movement mottoes: "Domestic Work is Work" or "Recognition and Respect for Domestic Work."

After now some years since the beginning of the domestic workers' movement in the Netherlands around 2011, there has been no legal improvement for those migrant domestic workers and so their working—and living—conditions remain extremely precarious. The GDR exhibition and performative actions of stenciling have stopped, yet cleaning has become a habit of ours that remains a constant reminder for the status of (migrant) domestic labor not only in our organization but in a broader social context. This is a reminder that the pervasive social inequalities that perpetuate the colonial-capitalist structure are still increasingly racialized and gendered. In the face of these constant, sticky reminders, how can we continue to "produce art" in the way we used to know, especially if we desire to bring art for the society of the commons? Speaking of "we" again, with this question we are not alone. Feminist theorists Kerstin Stakemeier and Marina Vishmidt claim that the tension between art's presumed autonomy and the underlying material condition is acute. Autonomy, they say, is a practice that is always already infused and grounded in re-production, yet structurally "invisibilized" in order to retain its relationship to capital: "The modern stakes for the autonomy of art had to do with severing itself from productive labour, conceivably to counter a world where the mental and manual labour brutalized some and idealised others."[27] The basis for this

25   The members of ASK! experimented with making visible the conditions and demands of "invisible work" of domestic workers in the Netherlands while reflecting on our own "domestic conditions" in the cultural sector. See Sven Lütticken, "Social Media: Practices of (In)Visibility in Contemporary Art," *Afterall* vol 40 (Autumn/Winter 2015). Online: www.afterall. org/journal/issue.40/ social_media (Accessed June 3, 2018).

26   For more details see "Toilet (T)issue #3: Against All Odds—Migrant Domestic Labor Struggle and Forms of Organizing," *Unlearning Exercises: Art Organizations as Sites for Unlearning*, Binna Choi, Annette Krauss, Yolande Zola Zoli van der Heide eds. (Amsterdam: Casco Art Institute/Valiz, 2018), 111.

27   Kerstin Stakemeier and Marina Vishmidt, *Reproducing Autonomy* (London: Mute Publishing, 2016), 46.

form of autonomy has been "the unfulfilled utopia of avant-garde as unalienated labour," while the labor of maintenance and reproductive work has remained alienated, resulting in its ongoing difficult existence within the realm of art.[28]

For an Art Institution That is Not Busy, as ...

The unlearning exercise "Rewriting Maintenance Manifesto" is an enactment of rewriting Ukeles' manifesto. Both manifestos engage with the fact that while reproductive labor is often symbolized by cleaning it is not about cleaning alone. In the case of art institutions reproductive labor also includes, for instance, maintaining the work space, archives, and library, personally welcoming visitors with a cup of tea, and taking care of oneself when sick or feeling down, and many other relations, including those with artists and migrant domestic workers. These tasks are now acknowledged as part of our workload alongside fundraising, negotiating commissions, managing budgets, traveling, preparing, learning, teaching, making, and collaborating. Here, the commons are not only the subject, but our guide for ways of working and instituting. Hence, we have even more work and it's hard to not be overwhelmed by busyness. Perhaps it's even harder since the more explicit we became with our intention and engagement with new practices of the commons, the greater the number of skeptical eyes came to focus on the mistakes and contradictions that might prove our vision to be an *impossibility*.

... Other Forms of Governance and Expertise Unfold

In January 2016 we had the opportunity to discuss some of the Unlearning Exercises with feminist geographer and economist Kathrine Gibson in the context of the forum "Commoning Economy" at Casco Art Institute. We had been struggling with the way "Time Diary" and "Wage and Well-Being" were resembling a managerialist method to optimize time management after intending instead to examine how our management of time(s) causes busyness in the hope of finding other modalities of time. Gibson linked time and

28   Ibid.

180

busyness to the notion of expertise and, in this case, the shifting nature of the team at Casco Art Institute, proposing "cross-training time" as a new modality where organizations allow time to their staff members to "skill other people up in one's own skills. [...] It is about a certain spare capacity, so when it's needed, that capacity can be used."[29] Gibson noted that this time, particularly absent in the cultural sector, could be a sort of "resilience measure for organizational work"[30] in case people get sick or leave the job. "Cross-training time" can also be understood more radically, as a thorough structural implementation of this time modality poses a challenge to the habit of hanging on to competencies and expertise needed to uphold a regime of productivity and its time patterns. In a more expanded form, it could be further seen as a step towards articulating and practicing another form of governance and sharing of power—a form of governance particularly interesting with regards to commoning. This responds to a question that we are frequently asked: Why would it be important to meet in person, spend time together, and study our working conditions together when instead, we could individually read analysis of neoliberal working conditions? The collaborative study of busyness/business—in all its impossibilities—sets out to intervene in the economy of time in order to thwart the interpellation by the business modalities of an art institution and one's own artistic practice. This desire for intervention addresses questions of governance and expertise, and puts forward the attempt to break open hierarchies of (knowledge) production. It is on these grounds that **a collaborative study and practice is crucial for the project of unlearning.**

Ultimately, questions of governance and expertise ask for a different sharing of power and conjure again the debates on the commons and forms of collectivity. Following a conversation between Mara Verlič and Stavros Stavrides on the commons and governance, the claim to regulate power collectively is a pivotal one in commoning processes. Relating to the rotation of duties in the Zapatista movement in which people build forms or organizations to govern themselves, Stavrides argues that the accumulation of

29   From transcriptions of the audio-recorded "Wage and Well-Being Workshop," January 18, 2016, Casco Art Institute archives.

30   Ibid.

power is **"not only a question of personal ethics; we need to have concrete social mechanisms that prevent the accumulation of power."**[31] In a somewhat surprising turn, Stavrides grants institutions a role in this, seeing them not only as normalizing technologies in the accumulation of power but emphasizing their potential as so-called **"threshold institutions"**[32] to come. These counter-institutions are based on the sharing of power, on equality and solidarity, and therefore necessarily prefigure a future differently. Their processes cannot be implanted top down, but emerge through experiments in practice, which, as Stavrides stresses, are and will be contradictory, ambiguous, and messy. Against this background, the *Site for Unlearning* works towards a mechanism that could regulate power (in the institution of Casco Art Institute) collectively. Concomitantly, if unlearning and the commons are dedicated to other forms of collectivity and organizing, the question of governance (and expertise) is crucial and needs to be confronted. This is what we would see in the coming, determined paths of Casco as "Casco Art Institute: Working for the Commons"— however contradictory, ambiguous, and messy they might be.

31   Stavros Stavrides and Mara Verlič, in
      "Crisis and Commoning: Periods of Despair,
      Periods of Hope," *Spaces of Commoning:
      Artistic Research and The Utopia of the
      Everyday*, ed. Anette Baldauf et al. (Berlin,
      Vienna: Sternberg Press, 2017), 56.
32   Stavrides and Verlič, *Spaces of Commoning: Art-
      istic Research and The Utopia of the Everyday*, 54.

Parts of this text appear in *How Institutions
Think: Between Contemporary Art and
Curatorial Discourse*, edited by Paul O'Neill,
Lucy Steeds, Mick Wilson (2017), and in
Unlearning Routines of the Impossible,
Janine Armin, and Annette Krauss (2025).

GLOSSARY OF TERMS

Administration of energy

An effort to acknowledge and find ways to deal with the energies of a group or collective. For example, when a group member takes the first step to form the idea, research, or methodology for a project they demonstrate their commitment in a practical way and attempt to free up collective processes and energies to do other work. The expression, used to illustrate leadership and governance in self-organization, comes to us via México City-based artists' collective Cooperativa Cráter Invertido. See page: 156.

Amsterdam Passport

The *Amsterdam Passport* is the result of an initiative by the Indonesian Migrant Domestic Workers, Wereldhuis, Doctors of the World, and the Amsterdam municipality. The passport provides information for undocumented migrant workers on how to survive in Amsterdam. The passport contains a list of where one can find foodbanks in Amsterdam, shelters to sleep in, answers to health questions, and tips on how to deal with hospitals. See pages: 122–23.

Bologna Process

The Bologna Process has introduced a far-reaching transformation within European higher education since 1999. European member states have agreed on the instalment of standards regarding degrees at bachelor, master, and doctorate levels in order to ensure comparability of higher-education qualifications in Europe. See pages: 76, 88, 90, 196.

Busyness and business

While the team at Casco Art Institute and Annette Krauss understand *business* as the operations of the economic framework we live in, they see *busyness* as a bodily-emotional condition produced by the constant need to perform within the rhythm of business. During *Site for Unlearning (Art Organization)*, they collectively identify the habitual, psycho-somatic state of busyness as an undesirable trait of institutional work to be un-learnt. To put it in a nutshell; they attempt to unlearn the business of busyness. See pages: 18–19, 51, 97, 113, 148, 173–82, 199, 218.

Care

Researcher, facilitator, and cultural worker Manuela Zechner approaches politics through embodied experience. She describes care as follows: "Care can be understood as the practice through which we hold together our everyday, pay attention to others, our environment and ourselves, and value life as worth sustaining. It's that absolutely vital practice mostly engaged [in] by women and subaltern people, undervalued and invisibilized not only in patriarchal and capitalist spaces but often also considered secondary in political organizing.

[...] Care consists of many kinds of interactions and relations which often overlap, for instance, mutual dependency, conviviality, cohabitation, friendship, intimacy, love, eroticism, bodily care, learning together, sharing resources, lending each other money, collaborating." See: Manuela Zechner, *Nanopolitics Handbook*, 183 and 194; see also pages: 34, 38–39, 43, 49, 63, 72, 126, 158, 176, 180.

Commoning

Commons are not yet made but always in the making; they are a product of continuous negotiations and reclaiming—thus, of commoning. Commoning means "working for the commons," and is the constant practice of reclaiming the ethics of the commons from the privatized or abstracted commons. Common-ing preserves the commons as a resource, practice, and community that is dedicated to difference. At the prefigurative stages of Casco Art Institute's engagement with commoning, "Casco Art Institute: Working for the Commons" aims to embody commoning by applying these ethics to the back side of the institution while further investigat-ing the commons on the front side. See pages: 6, 8, 9–10, 15, 27, 151, 168–70, 180–82, 186, 194, 199, 210–11, 222–25.

Commons

Historical European definitions of the commons mainly refer to the commons as a piece of land but also include other material resources that are collectively managed and shared to challenge neoliberal politics of accumulation and exclusion. Collectives, cooperatives, communes, and even communities and any collaboration are concepts and practices associated with the commons. The commons can be distinguished from land or resources managed by a landlord or an individually owned company, and from pseudo collectives like the gated community, who collectively manage their own common properties yet lack the ethics of being-in-common with one another on a broader scale. For the same reason, a private company or public institution who emphasises collaboration and community for the sake of productivity yet distributes their outcomes and governance processes unequally cannot be said to be a commons, and rather contributes to community capitalism.

Most importantly, the European legacy of the commons forces commoners to continuously work on the significant absences within Western accounts of the commons, while, as Indigenous scholar Eve Tuck poignantly demands, "attending to what is irreconcilable within settler colonial relations and what is incommensurable between de-colonizing projects." See: E. Tuck and K.W. Yang, *Decolonization, Indigeneity, Education and Society*, 1; see also pages: 7, 10, 16, 19, 37, 43–44, 57, 62, 97, 113, 148–50, 152, 165–72, 177–82, 192, 198, 199, 210–11, 222.

Cleaning to unlearn

Every Monday after the Casco Art Institute team meeting the team was meant to clean the office together. Cleaning had been a team task for some time, however, it was often left to just a few. One day, two of those who frequently cleaned the office sent an e-mail out to the rest of the team with a plea that attention be paid to this problem. The e-mail, which included an acknowledgement of how busy everyone was, was signed off with a poignant and ironic remark: "from your lovely house-wives." This instance became a subject at one of the subsequent unlearning meetings and an idea was put forward that the team at Casco Art Institute and Annette Krauss treat it as a regular collective unlearning exercise—resulting in the whole team cleaning together every Monday. See pages: 15, 18, 28–33, 39, 52, 63–64,

102, 113, 144, 148, 177–80, 190, 193, 197, 199, 212, 214, 220.

Cross-training

Feminist economic geographer Katherine Gibson proposes "cross-training time" as time for organizational upskilling, where staff members, "skill other people up in one's own skills. [...] It is about a certain spare capacity, so when it's needed, that capacity can be used [...]. However, mostly in this [Casco Art Institute's] kind of cultural sector you never have that [time]." When thoroughly implemented, "cross-training" challenges the individual retention of skills and expertise that uphold a productivist regime and its time patterns. See: Katherine Gibson, "Forum I: Commoning Economy, with (Un)usual Business, Katherine Gibson, Martijn Jeroen van der Linden, and Philippe Van Parijs." See also pages: 45, 181.

Double-track approach

Akin to the practices of historical resistance movements for black, queer, and intersectional struggles, a double-track approach protests what is being opposed whilst building an alternative. A double-track approach is prefigurative in nature. Unlearning institutional habits at Casco Art Institute involves ongoing discussion and critical thinking through Unlearning Exercises, coupled with bodily interventions, commoning literacy, and imaginative jumps. See pages: 7, 97–98, 165, 175.

Elephant in the room

A metaphorical idiom for an all-too-obvious problem that no one wants to discuss. The idiom of the "elephant in the room" also indicates the broader theme of this book, which addresses how proverbial elephants come in different forms and degrees of opacity within collective work, collective organizations, and unlearning processes. See pages: 152–64.

Geneva voucher system

An employment voucher system for undocumented migrant workers known as "Chèque Service." It has existed in the canton of Geneva since 2004. It aims to make things simpler for employers by declaring, on their behalf, their domestic workers' wages to compulsory social insurance schemes. It also promotes the social protection of domestic workers and transparent employment relationships.

As no tax deductions are available to the users and the authorities do not provide any subsidies, this

employment voucher scheme does not cost the Geneva cantonal authorities anything. On the other hand, the social insurance payments from the employers and employees, collected by the PRO (a private social enterprise that manages Chèque Service) are a plus for the social insurance funds. Domestic workers without papers are entitled to all social services except unemployment benefits once they join the Chèque Service. PRO is under a duty of confidentiality concerning the data provided by its members, meaning that people in irregular situations who are employed under the Chèque Service scheme are not at risk of being denounced to the authorities, who could deport them. See pages: 124, 126.

Habits

Habits are those practices of thinking and doing through which we bodily engage with our daily environment, practices that have always already slipped our rational analysis. They constitute learned gestures, rhythms, or postures of our bodies that are incorporated in a particular space and time. Therefore, habits form the political identity of our bodies and are inseparably linked to the worldviews and knowledge that we consciously and unconsciously perform.

When attempting to understand habits, the team at Casco Art Institute and Annette Krauss often return to the definitions of Gayatri Spivak and Sarah Ahmed. According to Spivak, habitual behavior often goes unnoticed because the person does not need to engage in self-analysis when following particular routines. Thus, for Spivak, what is crucial in habit formation is exactly what is missing in it: "a habit does not question." This lack of questioning complicates attempts to learn new habits. In a similar vein, Ahmed connects institutions with unconscious routines in her observation that "when things become institutional they recede from consciousness. To institutionalize [is] to become routine or ordinary." This indicates that institutional habits are both the structural perspective of fixed, regular, and stable institutions and the personal, embodied involvement that allows institutions to institute over time. See: Gayatri Spivak, *An Aesthetic Education in the Era of Globalization*, 8; and Sara Ahmed, *On Being Included: Racism and Diversity in Institutional Life*, 12; see also pages: 6–7, 14, 18, 51, 97, 113, 135, 148, 165, 167, 169–75, 187, 197, 199, 218.

Intersectionality

Intersectionality is a concept for understanding the complex, cumulative way in which the effects of multiple forms of discrimination (such as racism, sexism, ablism, and classism) combine, overlap, or intersect; especially in the experiences of marginalized individuals or groups. It came out of black feminist scholarship and was introduced by Kimberlé Crenshaw to help people understand that inequalities are "overlapping and mutually constitutive rather than isolated and distinct." See: Adia Harvey Wingfield, "About those 79 Cents," The Atlantic (October 2016). In speaking of the potential of intersectional awareness on both personal and institutional levels, Nancy Jouwe states: "Intersectionality helps us in starting a conversation that does not shy away from our lived realities, for instance by looking at ways to unlearn privilege. It helps us to tackle aspects of discrimination and empowerment: in ourselves, in our institutions, in our representations." See: Nancy Jouwe, "Sites for Unlearning in the Museum," 129–43; see also pages: 97, 113, 143, 162, 186.

Knowledge economy

The term "knowledge economy" is used in this publication to refer to a concept of growth that is dependent on the effective acquisition, dissemination, and use of information. In a knowledge economy, the accumulation of knowledge plays a major role in value production, income distribution, and economic expansion. An accumulative understanding of learning and the European knowledge economy are intertwined. An integral part of the European knowledge economy entails an increased focus on educational projects and learner-centered context. Therefore it can be specified as a learning economy. See pages: 6, 13, 82, 88, 95, 188, 190.

Labor; affective

Feminist writer, teacher, and activist Silvia Federici critiques the concept of affective labor on the grounds that it undoes a feminist analysis of reproductive labor: "'affective labor' [...] brings reproductive work back into the world of mystification, suggesting that reproducing people is just a matter of making producing [sic] 'emotions,' 'feelings.' It used to be called a 'labor of love;' Negri and Hardt instead have discovered 'affection.' The feminist analysis of the function of the sexual division

of labor, the function of gender hierarchies, the analysis of the way capitalism has used the wage to mobilize women's work in the reproduction of the labor force— all of this is lost under the label of 'affective labor.'" See: Silvia Federici, "Precarious Labor: A Feminist Viewpoint." See also pages: 38, 40, 43, 52, 60–61, 110, 135, 172, 175–76, 197.

Labor; production, reproduction, and consumption

Clear-cut divisions between these spheres seem to be increasingly dissolving. Authors Ekaterina Chertkovskaya and Bernadette Loacker note that in Fordist-capitalist societies production "took place within 'the factory' and 'the office' and, thus, within enclosed organizational boundaries," whereas consumption was traditionally understood as the realm where goods and services were bought and sold. Silvia Federici describes how reproduction and reproductive labor clearly belonged in the private-domestic sphere, where it has typically been carried out by women and enabled paid, "productive" labor. Chertkovskaya and Loacker also remind us that within post-Fordism the governing principles of market

and economization permeate all three spheres, and consequently the schema of productivity emerges across different social spheres. The blurring of boundaries between production, reproduction, and consumption becomes particularly relevant in regards to the symbolic value of cultural production. Work in the cultural field emerges as a self-signifying activity that can hardly be thought of without the mobilization of personal potential. As a consequence, cultural workers become entrepreneurs of their human capital in a form of labor that ties work and consumption together, while at the same time invisiblizes other forms of labor that seemingly no longer play a role. See: Ekaterina Chertkovskaya and Bernadette Loacker, "Work and Consumption: Entangled," 6; Silvia Federici, *Caliban and the Witch.*

In questioning how the conditions of art's production are so often disconnected from the criticality of art institutions we turn to the observations of Kerstin Stakemeier and Marina Vishmidt who explain that: "Art 'conceals' labour like other commodities in capital, but that, due to its absence of use value, it does so to an even greater extent, and thus figures as the 'absolute

commodity [...]. Concretely, this can mean outsourcing; gender, racialized, migration-related invisibility of workers; or degraded working conditions as they stand in a determined non-relation to art-world academicism, i.e. ideal 'radicality', or criticality, without relation to its conditions of reproduction. Importantly, just as fair trade doesn't subvert production for value, knowing who is cleaning your Kunsthalle has no bearing on their conditions." See: Kerstin Stakemeier and Marina Vishmidt, *Reproducing Autonomy: Work, Money, Crisis and Contemporary Art*, 77; see also pages: 6–8, 9, 19, 26, 52, 63, 92–93, 98, 111, 132, 149, 151, 166, 168, 173–78, 179, 181, 188, 195, 196.

Learning
Learning is commonly understood as the accumulation of knowledge, skills, and behaviours. Accumulative concepts of learning are intertwined with the knowledge economy, a system that fosters capitalist ideas of accumulation and growth dependent on the effective acquisition, dissemination, and use of information. These concepts of learning are very often institutionally driven, and legitimate concepts of progress that emerged at a moment when Europe

declared itself superior to other people and cultures. *Site for Unlearning (Art Organization)* sets out to tackle this understanding of learning by challenging it through the practice of unlearning. See pages: 5–8, 10, 13–14, 76–96, 97–110, 113, 169, 184, 188.

Lifelong learning
In 2001, the Commission of the European Communities defined lifelong learning as, "learning from pre-school to post-retirement, lifelong learning should encompass the whole spectrum of formal, non-formal and informal learning," and in 2000 proclaimed it to be: "All learning as a seamless continuum from 'cradle to grave.'" The concept of lifelong learning has seen a renaissance in European policy papers since the late 1990s. As a specific derivative of European knowledge economies, the solely economic focus of processes of lifelong learning are pertinent. Page two of a 2001 Communication from the Commission details, "Lifelong learning [is seen] as a key element of the strategy, [...] to make Europe the most competitive and dynamic knowledge-based society in the world." Annette Krauss' research looks into the relationship between lifelong learning (progress-oriented and accumulative) and

unlearning (of one's privileges, to go against what one cannot not wish to inhabit). See: Commission of the European Communities Brussels, *Commission Staff Working Paper: A Memorandum on Lifelong Learning*, and *Communication from the Commission: Making a European Area of Lifelong Learning a Reality*; and Annette Krauss, *Sites for Unlearning: On the Material, Artistic and Political Dimensions of Processes of Unlearning*; see also pages: 6, 12–13, 74–96, 99, 103, 109–10, 170.

Maintenance art

The attentiveness to Maintenance art has to be seen within Casco Art Institute and Annette Krauss' concern for reproductive labor, or domestic labor and maintenance work.

Recurrently, *Manifesto for Maintenance Art!* by Mierle Laderman Ukeles has been an important reference. In it, Ukeles radically questioned what is subsumed under avant-garde and conceptual art and contested the separation between artwork and housework as being artificial. Ukeles' manifesto remains a touchstone for discussions about labor and feminism today. Moreover, it protests the conditions that ensure maintenance workers remain without adequate pay and endure sustained low cultural value: "Maintenance is a drag; it takes all the fucking time (lit.) / The mind boggles and chafes at the boredom / The culture confers lousy status on maintenance jobs = minimum wages, housewives = no pay." See Mierle Laderman Ukeles, *Manifesto for Maintenance Art!*, 1969.

Furthermore, and perhaps building on Ukeles' critique, the Casco team and Krauss have worked over the years to recognise, address, and honor the fact that invisible maintenance work is widely performed by precarious and invisibilized people of colour. One of their various attempts has been a series of inverse graffiti actions using stencils of a domestic worker army, designed by artist Andreas Siekmann and appropriated by ASK! (*Actie Schonen Kunsten*, or Action Clean Arts), a migrant domestic workers' solidarity group that some Casco team members and Krauss were part of. See pages: 37, 64, 178.

Meritocracy

Meritocracy is a system based on the idea that a person's natural capacity and aspiration, not their social or cultural background, determines whether they are able to rise to the top of society.

Scholar Andrea Phillips problematizes meritocracy for assuming equal footing at the expense of difference and therefore not considering the race, class, and gender differences that may affect one's "fair-shot" at capitalist success. Phillips further criticises meritocracy for its inability to acknowledge how undesirable this kind of capitalistic success may be. See: Andrea Phillips, "The Imperative for Self-Attainment: From Cradle to Grave," 97–110; see also page: 13.

Mirroring organizations

A comparative practice to help organizations recognize and address the problems they are facing by looking into an affinity organization and studying together. See pages: 154.

Modern-colonial matrix of power

Anibal Quijano, and Walter Mignolo and Madina V. Tlostanova describe the modern-colonial matrix of power as a system that determines the management, institutionalization, and dissemination of epistemic, material, and aesthetic resources in ways that reproduce modernity's imperial project. A study of modern institutions needs to take into account the modes of control of social life, economic, and political organization that have been engineered in the colonies and the entanglements between capitalism and colonialism. These technologies have shaped Western institutions, our ways of learning, and relating to each other. See: Anibal Quijano, "Coloniality of Power, Eurocentrism and Latin America," 533–80; and Madina V. Tlostanova and Walter D Mignolo, *Learning to Unlearn*, 1–60; see also pages: 12, 77, 95–96, 99.

New habits

A concept connected to new rhythms, cooperative modes of working, and ways of living that are based on the commons and which involve differing forms of working with other groups and participants. *New Habits* was an exhibition at Casco Art Institute in May 2014, where *Site for Unlearning (Art Organization)* first featured as a project and practice. See pages: 148, 169, 172, 187, 193, 218–19.

Nina bell Federici

The figure of Nina bell Federici (Nina bell F.) arises from the Casco team and Annette Krauss' admiration for Nina Simone, bell hooks,

192

and Silvia Federici and their artistic, black, feminist, and political engagements. Her/their collective persona inspires *Site for Unlearning (Art Organization)* to move beyond the (institutional) frameworks of Casco Art Institute and artist Annette Krauss. Nina bell F. articulate(s) a proposition to be taken up in future experiments. See pages: 15–16, 48–50, 197.

Radical imagination

The thorough rethinking of things that are otherwise not thought of. This notion is taken from scholar-activists Max Haiven and Alex Khasnabish who lay claim to the radical imagination as "the ability to imagine the world, life and social institutions not as they are but as they might otherwise be. [...] It's about bringing those possible futures 'back' to *work* on the present, to inspire action and new forms of solidarity today." By connecting differently to the past, the radical imagination imagines the present differently, representing "our capacity to imagine and make common cause with the experiences of other people; it undergirds our capacity to build solidarity across boundaries and borders, real or imagined. Without radical imagin-

ation, we are left only with the residual dreams of the powerful, and for the vast majority they are not experienced as dreams but as nightmares of insecurity, precarity, violence and hopelessness." This concept has been important for the development of the Arts Collabratory (AC) network/eco-system, which seeks social change vis-á-vis the imagining of a different world through artistic practice that does not fit any existing box of doing and thinking. For the AC the practice of radical imagination has primarily meant analysing, studying, cultivating, and transforming the persisting colonial-capitalist systems that have influenced its member organizations. See: Max Haiven and Alex Khasnabish, *The Radical Imagination: Social Movement Research in the Age of Austerity*, 3–4; see also pages: 5, 158, 198.

Ratification of C189

The "Convention on Domestic Workers," formally the "Convention Concerning Decent Work for Domestic Workers," is a UN convention attempting to set labor standards for domestic workers internationally. It is the 189th ILO (International Labour Conventions) convention and was adopted during

the 100th session of the International Labour Organization. It entered into force in 2013. See pages: 124, 126.

Reproductive labor

By valuing reproductive labor and studying its entanglement with unpaid labor as the backbone of capitalist societies, we attempt to unlearn the habit of priviledging a productivist mentality. Architect and researcher Julia Wieger tracks how the term reproductive labor developed through Western feminist economics: "Our struggle to re-evaluate and restructure tasks like cooking and cleaning isn't new. In the 1970s feminist Marxist thinkers and activists like Mariarosa Dalla Costa, Selma James, and Silvia Federici introduced the term reproductive labor to describe the unpaid domestic labor typically carried out by women in private homes. In their 'Wages for House-work' campaign, they criticized traditional Marxist concepts for ignoring the significance of domestic labor, and therefore papering over a gendered division of the working class between those who get paid for their work and those who do not. This was possible, they argued, because women's labor in the private home had been made invisible by the ideology of the family, which framed domestic labor as being in the nature of women. Feminist economists like J. K. Gibson-Graham later showed that such argumentation still adhered to a rather capital-centric imaginary and missed out on alternative forms within a diverse range of economies not covered by the dichotomies of waged/unwaged, productive/repro-ductive labor. Still, the campaign powerfully revealed and helped to understand the mechanisms of cap-italism's devaluation of reproductive labor—which is still worth keeping in mind today." See: Julia Wieger, *Spaces of Commoning*, 156; see pages: 9–12, 15, 18–19, 28–30, 34, 52, 93, 95, 112, 114, 135, 148–49, 168, 178, 180, 188–89, 194, 196–98.

Revolution

Could commoning be a revolutionary practice? According to architect and activist Stavros Stavrides, the answer is: "yes, if we mean by revolution the explosive ruptures inflicted upon existing forms of domination due to the confluence of commoning initiatives and political struggles that create forms of social organization based on the sharing of power. I'm not sharing the old anarchist dream of

the abolition of power. There is no outside of power because power is inherent in all human relations. The important question is: How can we share power and how can we always be able to prevent any form of accumulation of power? Power in its molecular manifestation is expressed in the act of someone who imposes his or her will on someone else, either through knowledge, through economy, through mere brutality, through fantasy, and so forth. The problem is how to regulate power collectively. It's not only a question of personal ethics; we need to have concrete social mechanisms that prevent the accumulation of power. [...] Like the rotation of duties in the Zapatista movement in which the people learn how to govern themselves. They believe that governing is not a privilege but a burden, a duty. [...] This is a form of revolution." See: Stavros Stavrides and Mara Verlič, *Spaces of Commoning*, 55–6; see also pages: 64, 81, 88, 114, 125, 178.

Self-goal

A metaphor that comes from a move in soccer whereby you score a goal on your own side. Coopertiva Cráter Invertido uses it to refer to the contentious situation in their collective when one is caught between collective vision and individual desire. The self-goal can also take place when outside invitations take one away from existing collective tasks or duties. See page: 160.

Sites for Unlearning

Facilitated by Annette Krauss, "Sites for Unlearning" consists of different experimental and collaborative settings where concrete efforts to unlearn specific tasks are initiated, explored, discussed, and conceptualized over different durations. The third and longest-term instalment of the project *Site for Unlearning (Art Organization)* is made in collaboration with Casco Art Institute. Research for this project is based on a process of "unlearning by doing," where collaborators deal with, identify, and reorder dominant forms of thinking and behaving. Unlearning projects with other groups have focused on "unlearning to ride a bike" and "unlearning my library." At the core of all these experiments is an investigation of art's potential to engage with the seemingly "impossible" and to imagine things otherwise.

It is important to note that the

word "site" is derived from the term "situation" and "being situated," and is not limited to a simply spatial understanding. In this regard, site ties in the legacy of (artistic) situationist practices—the so-called Situationists—and the feminist approach of "situated knowledges" theorized by feminist philosopher of science Donna Haraway. *Site for Unlearning* attempts to bring together three elements: the practice-oriented artistic approach of the Situationists, a feminist under-standing of situated knowledge production, and the challenges of postcolonial and decolonial scholarship. See: Donna Haraway, "Situated Knowledges: The Science Question in Feminism and the Privilege of Partial Perspective." See also pages: 5, 7–9, 96, 129–43, 167, 170, 182, 188, 209–28.

Soft law politics

The term "soft law" refers to a quasi-legal instrument in the EU. It was established around 1993 as a form of governance to both regulate and encourage the cooperation between the EU member states on a voluntary basis. Soft law politics is a mechanism to distribute policies among the EU states without direct regulation. In return, member states draft their own proposals for meeting EU objectives. The imple-mentation of the Bologna Process is an example of soft law politics. |Local adaptations can "include differences in tuition fees, the level of cooperation with the private sector, or the level of austerity measures imposed, the financial role of the individual state or the number of students accepted per term." See: Nafsika Alexiadou and Bettina Lange, "New Forms of European Union Governance in the Education Sector?," 322; and Lina Dokuzović, *Struggles for Living Learning*, 78; see also page 86.

Speculation

Writer, editor, and critic Marina Vishmidt reminds us that specula-tions are not solely practices of art and philosophy, but also and crucially "mediated by financial rather than welfare state institutions and in the subjective parameters of 'human capital' ideology." See: Marina Vishmidt, "Speculation as a Mode of Production in Art and Capital," 119.

In her upcoming book *Speculation as a Mode of Production*, Vishmidt examines the role of specu-lation in the shaping of subjectivity by value relations. There she de-

scribes the role of speculation as: "1. The demand that you learn to be yourself by upgrading to human capital; and 2. A social system built upon those premises, held in dark-enlightenment grip of money, brutality, and resentment as much as by automated reproduction. Speculation moves across scales and can work transversally across and within bodies as they cohere at various scales. It goes past critical and clinical to the projective but doesn't constitute another commodity abstraction of thought because it only makes sense as a grammar of felt history, human, natural and otherwise." See Marina Vishmidt, *Speculation as a Mode of Production* (forthcoming–2018); see also pages: 91, 94, 211.

Spillover

Spillover is an affirmative term to describe the reciprocal effects that activities in Casco Art Institute's regular unlearning meetings begin to have on other situations, activities, or groups of people. Spillovers are a practice of empowerment that acknowledge indirect outcomes, they work against the invisibilization of labor since the processes and situations in the meetings tend to be ephemeral and overshadowed by the urgencies of institutional deadlines, workloads, and affective politics. In their attempts to detect subtle mechanisms that lead to authorship the team at Casco and Annette Krauss acknowledge spillovers by asking the question: At what point does reproductive labor turn into authorial labor? The discussion and activities around Nina bell F., the formulation of ethical principles by the Arts Collaboratory assemblies, and the inspirational activities around unlearning within organizations in the close network of Casco Art Institute are a few examples of spillovers. See page: 49.

Study

The concept of "study" that has informed the Casco team and Annette Krauss' work is inspired by Stefano Harney and Fred Moten's book *The Undercommons*, in which the authors propose an engagement in *study* as a mode of thinking and doing with others, aiming to transgress what sociologist Stevphen Shukaitis has called "the limits of the conception of collectivity." See: Class War University, "Studying Through the Undercommons." The team at Casco Art Institute have translated Harney and Moten's proposition into

studying the patterns and habits of how they perceive their being and coming together in the institutional framework of Casco Art Institute, in order to examine, and if necessary shape differently the forms that this particular sociality takes. See: Stefano Harney and Fred Moten, *The Undercommons: Fugitive Planning and Black Studies*.

Study has been crucial for unlearning, and "[w]hen we first started unlearning we wanted to unlearn the feeling of being busy at the expense of deep time, deep understanding, or study. This came with the realization that, by valuing study over cleaning or maintenance, we too had fallen into the tendency of devaluing reproductive labor." See: "Introduction" on page 9. Thus, our question since then has been: How do we study as, for, through, and alongside reproductive labor? See pages: 5, 10, 14, 18, 22, 36, 45, 48, 50, 77, 94, 124–29, 167, 169, 173, 174–81, 193, 198, 220–21.

Toilet (t)issues
A term that speaks to a developing series of conversations dealing with invalidated domestic work or reproductive labor that the team at Casco Art Institute and Annette Krauss have have engaged in with sister institutions. More specifically, the term "Toilet (T)issues" is taken from taken from a public conversation in January 2015 between members of KUNCI Study Forum & Collective, Yogyakarta; The Showroom, London; and Casco Art Institute, Utrecht on how commons-orientated organizations work in the field of art, culture, and social practice. It came to light during a discussion that one comrade was buying all the toilet paper, an issue which points to an imbalance in the distribution of domestic tasks in the organization, and which also indicates a systemic tendency to undervalue this kind of work. See pages: 13, 57–75, 114–33, 157–70.

Tooling
The Tooling Working Group in Arts Collaboratory (AC) provides the following definition: "Tooling is a process of generating tools that have been (consciously or unconsciously) used in our practices. / Tooling is a way of practicing our radical imagination not only for making artworks but also for supporting the way we organize our daily life resistance. / Tooling is a method for reflecting and or making sense of the way we do our (im)material

labour. / Tooling is a strategy for sharing knowledge inside and outside AC ecosystem, as well as building a solidarity/interdependent relations based on our open ethical principles beyond AC ecosystem. / Tooling is a mechanism to sustain openness." From unpublished material from Arts Collaboratory workshops, 2016. See pages: 10, 89, 126, 154, 157–57, 222–25.

Undercommons

The concept of "the undercommons," as elaborated by Fred Moten and Stefano Harney, underlies the poetics and agency of collective resistance and struggle that takes place beneath and within the existing system, pointing to anti-slavery struggles, differentiating itself from the institutionalized commons with its potential to be trapped into a logic of management and control. Instead, Harney and Moten propose "study" as a form of collective struggle and mutual learning as a way of commoning "under the existing institutional radar." See: Stefano Harney and Fred Moten, *The Undercommons*.

FTC Manning sets the relation between the commons and under-commmons in terms of form: "Fighting for the commons is a dead-end, the commons itself is an untouchable underground reservoir of revolt.

This reservoir is the undercommons, best described as a frequency or form of energy. It is arguably completely unavailable to representation." See E.C. Feiss quoting FTC Manning's "The Commons, the Undercommons and Communization," in "Whiteness as Property: Reform as Material." In *White Paper*, 147; see also pages 80, 161, 168, 197.

Unlearning

Taking cues from Gayatri Spivak's "unlearning one privileges," unlearning denotes an active critical investigation of normative structures and practices in order to become aware and get rid of taken-for-granted "truths" of theory and practice in order to tackle inequalities in everyday life. For the last several years the team at Casco Art Institute and Annette Krauss have taken on the challenge of unlearning institutional habits embedded in many facets of their work. Thus, unlearning has become a process of de-instituting and is directed towards embodied forms of knowledge and the (un)conscious operation of ways of thinking and doing. See pages: 5–8, 9, 14, 17– 56, 76–99, 100–02, 113, 119, 131, 134–35, 138, 141–42, 148–50, 165–82, 176–88, 211–30.

Unlearning exercises

The Latin origin of the word exercise, *excere*, means "keep busy." It connotes hierarchical disciplinary contexts such as educational institutions, professional sports training facilities, and military training facilities. Casco Art Institute and Annette Krauss' unlearning proposal opposes this mode of discipline and their aim is to unlearn this sense of busyness, hence they propose the term "unlearning exercise." Efforts to unlearn the dynamics of busyness/business have led to ideas for and trials of fourteen Unlearning Exercises that were developed collaboratively by Annette Krauss and the team at Casco Art Institute at ongoing bi-weekly or monthly meetings. So far, the exercises include: Meeting, Off-balancing Chairs, Assembly, Cleaning Together, Digital Cleaning, Reading Together, Rewriting Maintenance Manifesto, Care Network, Mood Color, Property Relations, (Collective) Authorship, Time Diary, Passion and Obstacle, and Work and Well-being. See pages: 9–10, 17–56, 98, 149, 176–77, 180, 211–30.

Well-being

J. K. Gibson-Graham describe well-being as a consideration that surpasses material security (surviving well) in the constitution of human happiness, as material security is but a single factor among many others. Well-being, as they describe it—and vis-à-vis Tom Rath and Jim Harter's *Wellbeing: The Five Essential Elements*—"Is about the combination of our love for what we do each day, the quality of our relationships, the security of our finances, the vibrancy of our physical health, and the pride we take in what we have contributed to our communities. Most importantly, it's about how these five elements interact." These elements are: material well-being, occupational well-being, social well-being, community well-being, and physical well-being. See: Chapter two "Take Back Work: Surviving Well," in J. K. Gibson-Graham et al., eds., *Take Back the Economy: An Ethical Guide for Transforming our Communities*. See pages: 45–47, 149, 180.

BIBLIOGRAPHY

Foreword: Unlearning to Unlearn

Bourdieu, Pierre. *Outline of a Theory of Practice.* Cambridge: Cambridge University Press, 1977.

Elson, Diane, ed. *Value: The Representation of Labour in Capitalism.* London, Atlantic Highlands, N.J: CSE Books Humanities Press, 1979.

Dalla Costa, Mariarosa, and Selma James. *The Power of Women and the Subversion of Community* (1971), 3rd ed., Bristol: Falling Wall Press, 1975.

Grant, Paul Douglas. *Cinéma Militante: Political Filmmaking and May 1968.* New York: Wallflower Press, 2016.

Guattari, Félix. *Psychoanalysis and Transversality: Texts and Interviews 1955–1971.* Translated by Ames Hodges. Cambridge, MA: semiotext(e) and MIT Press, 2015.

Ford, Simon. *Wreckers of Civilization.* London: Black Dog Publishing, 1999.

Nesbit, Molly. "What Was an Author?" (1987/2017). In *Yale French Studies,* no. 73 (Fall 1987). Re-edit (2017). In: Molly Nesbit, *Midnight the Tempest.* New York: Inventory Press, 2017, S.9-41.

Phillips, Andrea. "The Imperative for Self-Attainment: From Cradle to Grave." In *Unlearning Exercises: Art Organizations as Sites for Unlearning.* Edited by Binna Choi, Annette Krauss, and Yolande Zola Zoli van der Heide. Amsterdam: Casco Art Institute/Valiz, 2018.

Rifkin, Adrian. "Inventing Recollection." In *Interrogating Cultural Studies: Theory, Politics and Practice.* Edited by Paul Bowman, 101–124. London: Pluto, 2003.

Que, Ying. Transcription (26 February 2016) for "6. Property Relations." In *Unlearning Exercises: Art Institutions as Sites for Unlearning.* Edited by Binna Choi, Annette Krauss, and Yolande Zola Zoli van der Heide. Amsterdam: Casco Art Institute/Valiz, 2018.

Unlearning Exercises

Danius, Sara and Stefan Jonsson. "An Interview with Gayatri Chakravorty Spivak." In *Boundary 2,* vol 20, no. 2 (1993): 24–50.

Gibson-Graham, J. K., Jenny Cameron and Stephen Healy "Take Back Work: Surviving Well." In *Take Back the Economy: An Ethical Guide for Transforming our Communities,* 17–48. Minneapolis, MN: University of Minnesota Press, 2013.

Haraway, Donna. "Situated Knowledges: The Science Question in Feminism and the Privilege of Partial Perspective." *Feminist Studies* 14, no. 3 (1988): 575–99.

Ukeles, Mierle Laderman. "Manifesto for Maintenance Art, 1969!" In *Grand Domestic Revolution Handbook*. Edited by Binna Choi and Maiko Tanaka. Amsterdam: Casco Art Institute/Valiz, 2014.

Vishmidt, Marina. "All Shall Be Unicorns: About Commons, Aesthetics and Time." *Open! Platform for Art, Culture and the Public Domain*, September 3, 2014. Online: www.onlineopen.org/all-shall-be-unicorns (Accessed September 25, 2018).

Zechner, Manuela. "A Politics of Network-Families? Precarity, Crisis and Careful Experimenta-tions," and "Mapping Your Care Network Exercise." In *Nanopolitics Handbook: The Nanopolitics Group*. Edited by Paolo Plotegher et al., 183–98. New York: Minor Compositions, 2013. Online: www.minor-compositions.info/wp-content/uploads/2013/09/nanopolitics-web.pdf (Accessed April 4, 2017).

———"Barcelona en Comú: the city as horizon for radical democracy" *ROAR Magazine*, March 4, 2015.

Lifelong Learning and the Professionalized Learner

Burke, Penny Jane, and Sue Jackson. *Reconceptualising Lifelong Learning: Feminist Interventions*. New York: Routledge, 2007.

Commission of the European Communities. *Commission Staff Working Paper: A Memorandum on Lifelong Learning*. Brussels, 30.10.2000 SEC(2000)1832: Luxembourg Publication Office, 2000. Online: www.arhiv.acs.si/dokumenti/Memorandum_on_Lifelong_Learning.pdf (Accessed December 3, 2016).

——— *Communication from the Commission: Making a European Area of Lifelong Learning a Reality*, Brussels, 21.11.01 COM (2001) 678 final. Directorate-General for Education and Culture; Directorate-General for Employment and Social Affairs, Brussels, 2001. Online: www.viaa.gov.lv/files/free/48/748/pol_10_com_en.pdf (Accessed September 29, 2016).

Caffentzis, George, and Silvia Federici. "Notes on the Edu-factory and Cognitive Capitalism." In *Toward a Global Autonomous University*. Edited by The Edufactory Collective, 125–31. New York: Autonomedia, 2009.

Daffron, Sandra, and Iris Metzgen-Ohlswager, Shari Skinner, Loretta Saarinen. "Acquiring Knowledge, Skills, and Abilities Across a Lifetime by Transferring to One's Own Practice." In *Second International Handbook of Lifelong Learning*. Edited by David N. Aspin, Judith Chapman, Karen Evans, Richard Bagnall, 613–29. Dordrecht: Springer, 2012.

Dokuzović, Lina. *Struggles for Living Learning: Within Emergent Knowledge Economies and the Cognitivization of Capital and Movement*. Vienna: Transversal Texts, 2016. Online: www.transversal.at/media/pdf/livinglearning.pdf (Accessed September 10, 2018).

European Higher Education Area (EHEA) and Bologna Process (website), accessed February 2 2017, www.ehea.info/pid34247/how-does-the-bologna-process-work.html

European Civil Society Platform on Lifelong Learning (EUCIS-LLL). *Twelve Years After: A Call for a Renewed Memorandum on Lifelong Learning*. Brussels: EUCIS-LLL, 3 September 2012. Online: www.lllplatform.eu/lll/wp-content/uploads/2015/10/A-call-for-a-renewed-Memorandum-on-Life-long-Learning-EUCIS-LLL1.pdf (Accessed October 15, 2016).

European Commission. "Erasmus+. EU Programme for Education, Training, Youth and Sports." Online: www.ec.europa.eu/programmes/erasmus-plus/node_en. (Accessed December 15, 2016).

——— "Horizon2020. The EU Framework Programme for Research and Innovation." Online: www.ec.europa.eu/programmes/horizon2020. (Accessed December 15, 2016).

Fejes, Andreas. "Lifelong Learning and Employability." In *Challenging the 'European Area of Lifelong Learning.'* Edited by George K. Zarifis and Maria N. Gravani, 99–109. Dordrecht: Springer, 2014.

Foucault, Michel. "What is Critique?" In *The Politics of Truth*. Edited by Sylvère Lotringer and Lysa Hochroth, 23–82. New York: Semiotext(e), 1997.

Andreotti, Vanessa de Oliveira, Sharon Stein, Cash Ahenakew, and Dallas Hunt. "Mapping

interpretations of decolonization in the context of higher education." *Decolonization: Indigeneity, Education & Society* 4, no. 1 (2015): 21–40.

Freire, Paulo. *Pedagogy of the Oppressed*. New York: Continuum, [1968] 2000.

Gibson-Graham, J. K. *Introduction to A Postcapitalist Politics*. Minneapolis: University of Minnesota Press, 2006.

Harney, Stefano, and Fred Moten. *The Undercommons: Fugitive Planning and Black Studies*. Wivenhoe: Minor Compositions, 2013.

hooks, bell. *Teaching to Transgress: Education as the Practice of Freedom*. Routledge: London, 1994.

— — — *Yearning: Race, Gender and Cultural Politics*. Boston: South End Press, 1990.

Illich, Ivan. *Deschooling Society*. Hardmondsworth: Penguin Books, [1971] 1978.

Lazzarato, Maurizio. "The Misfortunes of the 'Artistic Critique' and of Cultural Employment." *Eipcp*, January 2007. Online: www.eipcp.net/transversal/0207/lazzarato/en (Accessed June 7, 2018).

European Higher Education Area, "Lifelong Learning in European Higher Education Area and Bologna Process." Online: www.ehea.info/pid34787/lifelong-learning-2007-2009.html (Accessed September 10, 2016).

Life Long Learning Hub: Creating a Space for Lifelong Learning. *EU Handbook and Glossary*. Updated version, April 2016. Online: www.lll-hub.eu/wp-content/uploads/2015/05/lllhub_handbookUPDATED_FINAL.pdf (Accessed February 2, 2017).

Lorey, Isabell. "Autonomy and Precarization." In *Mobile Autonomy: Exercises in Artists' Self-organization*. Edited by Nico Dock and Pascal Gielen, 47–63. Amsterdam: Valiz, 2015.

Lütticken, Sven, and Jorinde Seijdel. "Common Knowledge. A Virtual Round Table on the Crisis in Higher Education." *Open! Platform for Art, Culture & the Public Domain*, May 23, 2015. Online: www.onlineopen.org/common-knowledge (Accessed February 2, 2017).

Lütticken, Sven. "A Heteronomous Hobby: Report from the Netherlands." *E-flux Journal* 22, no. 1 (2011). Online: www.e-flux.com/journal/22/67753/a-heteronomous-hobby-report-from-the-netherlands/ (Accessed September 10, 2016).

Olssen, Mark. "Understanding the Mechanisms of Neoliberal Control: Lifelong Learning, Flexibility and Knowledge Capitalism." In *Foucault and Lifelong Learning: Governing the Subject*. Edited by Andreas Fejes and Katherine Nicoll, 34–48. New York: Routledge, 2007.

Osten, Marion von. "STOP MAKING SENSE: Some Reflections on Educational Reforms." In *Intersections: At the Crossroads of the Production of Knowledge, Precarity, Subjugation and the Reconstruction of History, Display, and De-Linking*. Edited by Lina Dokuzović, Eduard Freudmann, Peter Haselmayer, and Lisbeth Kovai, 39–54. Vienna: Löcker Verlag, 2009.

— — — "Unpredictable Outcomes/Unpredictable Outcasts. A Reflection After Some Years of Debates on Creativity and Creative Industries." *Eipcp* (November 2007). Online: www.eipcp.net/transversal/0207/vonosten/en (Accessed October 10, 2016).

Popovic, Katarina. "The Skills: A Chimera of Modern European Adult Education." In *Challenging the 'European Area of Lifelong Learning.'* Edited by George K. Zarifis and Maria N. Gravani, 17–31. Dordrecht: Springer, 2014.

Powell, Walter A., and Kaisa Snellman. "The Knowledge Economy." *Annual Review of Sociology* 30 (2004): 199–220.

Quijano, Anibal. "Coloniality of Power, Eurocentrism and Latin America." *Nepentla: Views From the South* 1, no. 3 (2000): 533–80.

Raunig, Gerald. *Factories of Knowledge. Industries of Creativity*. Semiotext(e) Intervention Series. Cambridge: MIT Press, 2013.

Rosenzweig, Ben. "International Student Struggles: Transnational Economies, Guest Consumers and Processes of Restructuring." *Mutiny* 48 (2010). Online: www.jura.org.au/files/jura/Mutiny%2048%20WebV3.pdf (Accessed October 4, 2016).

Masschelein, Jan, et al. "The Learning Society from the Perspective of Governmentality: An Introduction." *Educational Philosophy and Theory* 38, no. 4 (2006): 417–30.

Stoler, Ann Laura. *Race and the Education of Desire: Foucault's History of Sexuality and the Colonial Order of Things*. New York: Duke University Press, 1995.

Tlostanova, Madina V., and Walter D. Mignolo. *Learning to Unlearn: Decolonial Reflections from Eurasia and the Americas.* Columbus: The Ohio State University Press, 2012.

Tuschling, Anna, and Christoph Engemann. "From Education to Lifelong Learning: the emerging regime of learning in the European Union." *Educational Philosophy and Theory* 38, no. 4, (2006): 451–69.

UNESCO Report. *Learning to Be: The World of Education Today and Tomorrow.* Edited by Edgar Faure, et al. Paris: UNESCO, 1972. Online: www.unesco.org/education/pdf/15_60.pdf (Accessed October 4, 2016).

– – – – *Learning: The Treasure Within.* Edited by Jacques Delors, et al. Paris: UNESCO, 1996. Online: www.unesco.org/new/en/education/themes/leading-the-international-agenda/rethinking-education/resources/ (Accessed February 15, 2017).

Vishmidt, Marina. "Speculation as a Mode of Production in Art and Capital." PhD dissertation. London: Queen Mary University of London, 2012.

– – – – "The Politics of Speculative Labour." *Transformative Art Production,* 2012. Online: www.transformativeartproduction.net/the-politics-of-speculative-labour/ (Accessed November 12, 2016).

Wilder, Craig Steve. *Ebony and Ivory: Race, Slavery and the Troubled Histories of American Universities.* New York: Bloomsbury Press, 2013.

Wynter, Sylvia. "No Humans Involved: An Open Letter to My Colleagues." *Forum N.H.I.: Knowledge for the 21st Century I,* no. 1 (1994): 42–74.

– – – – "Unsettling the Coloniality of Being/Power/Truth/Freedom: Towards the Human, After Man, its Overrepresentation—An Argument." *The New Centennial Review* 3, no. 3 (2003): 257–37.

Adamson, Morgan. "The Human Capital Strategy." *ephemera: theory and politics in organization* 9, no. 4 (2009): 271–84.

Martin, Stewart. "The Pedagogy of Human Capital." *Mute: Culture and Politics after the Net* 2, no. 8 (2008): 32–45. Online: www.metamute.org/en/Pedagogy-of-Human-Capital (Accessed June 7, 2018).

Alexiadou, Nafsika, and Bettina Lange. "New Forms of European Union Governance in the Education Sector? A Preliminary Analysis of the Open Method of Coordination." *European Educational Research Journal* 6, no. 4 (2007): 321–35.

Boltanski, Luc, and Ève Chiapello. *The New Spirit of Capitalism.* Translated by G. Elliott. London: Verso, 2005.

Brown, Wendy. "Sacrificial Citizenship: Neoliberalism, Human Capital, and Austerity Politics." *Constellations* 23, no. 1 (2016): 3–14.

– – – – *Undoing the Demos: Neoliberalism's Stealth Revolution.* New York: Zone, 2015.

McRobbie, Angela. *Be Creative. Making a Living in the New Culture Industries.* Cambridge: Polity Press, 2016.

The Imperative for Self-Attainment: From Cradle to Grave

Blumenthal, Sidney. "A Short History of the Trump Family," *London Review of Books* 39, no. 4 (February 16, 2017).

Choi, Binna, and Annette Krauss. "Have You Had a Productive Day?" In *Unlearning Exercises: Art Institutions as Sites for Unlearning.* Edited by Binna Choi, Annette Krauss, and Yolande Zola Zoli van der Heide. Amsterdam: Casco Art Institute/Valiz, 2018.

Foucault, Michel. *The History of Sexuality.* Volume 1: An Introduction. Translated by Robert Hurley. New York: Random House, 1978.

Krauss, Annette. "Lifelong Learning and the Professionalized Learner." In "Sites for Unlearning: On the Material, Artistic and Political Dimensions of Processes of Unlearning." PhD dissertation. Vienna: Academy of Fine Arts Vienna, 2017.

Littler, Jo. "Meritocracy as Plutocracy: The Marketizing of Equality under Neoliberalism." *New Formations: a journal of culture/theory/politics* 80–81, (Autumn–Winter 2013): 52–72.

McNamee, Stephen, and Robert Miller. *The Myth of Meritocracy.* Lanham: Rowman & Littlefield, 2009.

Nye, Joseph. Chapter 4: "Wielding Soft Power." In *Soft Power: The Means to Success in World Politics.* Harvard Kennedy School

Belfer Center, 2004. Pdf. Online: www.
belfercenter.org/sites/default/files/legacy/
filesjoe_nye_wielding_soft_power.pdf,8
(Accessed July 5, 2017).

Rifkin, Adrian. "Inventing Recollection." In
*Interrogating Cultural Studies: Theory, Politics
and Practice.* Edited by Paul Bowman, 101–24.
London: Pluto, 2003.

Stengers, Isabelle, and Philippe Pignarre. *Capitalist
Sorcery: Breaking the Spell.* New York:
Palgrave Macmillan, 2011.

Vlaland Academy. "Let's Mobilize: What is
Feminist Pedagogy?" Tumblr. Online:
www.whatisfeministpedagogy.tumblr.com
(accessed July 5, 2017); andpublishing website.
Online: www.andpublishing.org/lets-
mobilise-what-is-feminist-pedagogy/
(Accessed July 5, 2017).

Willis, Paul. *Learning to Labour: How Working
Class Kids Get Working-Class Jobs.* Farnham:
Ashgate, 2000.

Young, Michael. *The Rise of Meritocracy.*
Hammondsworth: Penguin, 1958.

Sites for Unlearning
in the Museum

AFRO Magazine. "Decolonize The Museum
Conference April 16th 2016." *AFRO Magazine.*
Online: www.afromagazine.nl/agenda/
decolonize-museum-confer-
ence-april-16th-2016 (Accessed June 8, 2018).

Danius, Sara, Stefan Jonsson, and Gayatri
Chakravorty Spivak. "An Interview with
Gayatri Chakravorty Spivak." *boundary 2,*
vol 20, no. 2 (Summer, 1993): 24–50.

Esche, Charles, interviewed by Koen Kleijn and
Stefan Kuiper. "Musea lopen verschrikkelijk
achter" (museums are horribly behind),
De Groene Amsterdammer, May 14, 2008.
Online: www.groene.nl/artikel/mu-
sea-lopen-verschrikkelijk-achter (Accessed
June 8, 2018).

Framer Framed. "De koloniale blik" (the colonial
gaze). Debate, December 13, 2009, Centraal
Museum, Utrecht.

Hartman, Saidiya. "Venus in Two Acts," *Small Axe:
a journal of criticism,* no. 26 (2008): 1–14.

Hoffman, Alvina. "Interview—Walter Mignolo/

Part 2: Key Concepts." *E-INTERNATIONAL
RELATIONS* (January 21, 2017). Online:
www.e-ir.info/2017/01/21/interview-wal-
ter-mignolopart-2-key-concepts/ (Accessed
June 8, 2018).

Jacobs, Edwin, Meta Knol, and Stijn Huijts,
"Naar een mondig museum" (towards an
empowered museum), *NRC,* December 2006.
Online: www.nrc.nl/nieuws/2006/12/01/
naar-een-mondig-museum-11237877-a236037
(Accessed June 8, 2018).

Jans, Erwin. *An Offer You Can't Refuse;
Stimuleringsprijs voor culturele diversiteit*
(incentive prize for cultural diversity)
(Amsterdam: Mondriaan Fonds, 2011).

Knol, Meta, and Lejo Schenk, "Het onderscheid
tussen westerse en niet-westerse kunst is
achterhaald," (The distinction between
Western and non-Western art is outdated)
NRC, January 2, 2010. Online: www.nrc.nl/
nieuws/2010/01/02/het-onderscheid-tussen-
westerse-en-niet-westerse-kunst-
11832313-a176574 (Accessed June 8, 2018).

Knol, Meta, Nancy Jouwe. Interview, Museum
De Lakenhal, Leiden, August 20, 2010
(unpublished).

Knol, Meta. *Beyond the Dutch: Indonesië, Nederland
en de beeldende kunsten van 1900 tot nu*
(Indonesia, the Netherlands and the visual
arts from 1900 to now). Amsterdam:
KIT Publishers, 2009.

Krauss, Annette. *Sites for Unlearning: On the
Material, Artistic, and Political Dimensions
of Processes of Unlearning.* Colchester: Minor
Compositions, forthcoming–2019.

Legêne, Susan. Comment during symposium
"Omstreden geschiedenis. Een symposium
over de (re)presentatie van de Nederlands-
Indonesische geschiedenis in musea"
(concerned history: a symposium on the
(re)presentation of Dutch-Indonesian history
in museums. At Framer Framed, Amsterdam,
2012. Online documentation: www.
indischherinneringscentrum.nl/sites/www.
indischherinneringscentrum.nl/files/
afbeeldingenVerslag_Symposium_
Omstreden_Geschiedenis-lowres.pdf
(Accessed June 8, 2018).

Quijano, Aníbal. "Coloniality and Modernity/
Rationality." *Cultural Studies* 21, no. 2–3
(2007): 168–78.

Sternfeld, Nora. "Shaking the Status Quo*: Notes on Unlearning," Mezosfera.org, September 2016. Online: www.mezosfera.org/shaking-the-status-quo/ (Accessed September 10, 2018).

Tlostanova, Madina V., and Walter D. Mignolo. *Learning to Unlearn: Decolonial Reflections from Eurasia and the Americas*. Columbus: The Ohio State University Press, 2012.

Veldkamp, Fenneken. "Wat de Boer Niet Kent" (what the farmer does not know), *ZAM Africa Magazine* 11, no. 2 (2007): 16–19. Online: www.scribd.com/document/18233163/ZAM0702) (Accessed June 8, 2018).

Decolonizing Art Institutes from a Labor Point of View

Arts Collaboratory. "Arts Collaboratory Future Plan" (unpublished), 2018.

Choi, Binna, and Yolande Zola Zoli van der Heide. "Decolonizing Art Institutes from a Labour Point of View." *on-curating* 35 (December 2017). Online: www.on-curating.org/issue-35-reader/decolonizing-art-institutes-from-a-labor-point-of-view.html#.W7C5GC-2Q28o (Accessed June 14, 2018).

Gibson-Graham, J. K., Jenny Cameron and Stephen Healy. *Take Back the Economy: An Ethical Guide for Transforming our Communities*. Minneapolis, MN: University of Minnesota Press, 2013.

Haiven, Max, and Alex Khasnabish. *The Radical Imagination: Social Movement Research in the Age of Austerity*. London: Zed Books, 2014.

Harney, Sefano, and Fred Moten. *The Undercommons: Fugitive Planning and Black Studies*. Wivenhoe: Minor Compositions, 2013.

Krauss, Annette. "Unlearning." In *Sites for Unlearning: On the Material, Artistic and Political Dimensions of Processes of Unlearning*. PhD dissertation. Vienna: Academy of Fine Arts Vienna, 2017.

Luttikhuis, Bart. *Negotiating Modernity: Europeanness in Late Colonial Indonesia, 1910-1942*. PhD dissertation. Florence: European University Institute, 2014.

Mayer, Mark Paul, Tropenmuseum, Nederlands Filmmuseum. *Van de Kolonie Niets dan Goeds: Nederlands-Indië in Beeld, 1912–1942* (nothing but goodness in the colony: the Dutch Indies in pictures). DVD, 120 mins. Amsterdam: Filmmuseum, 2003.

Moshiri, Nazanine. "A Little-Known Massacre in Senegal." *Aljazeera.com*, 22 November 2013. Online: www.aljazeera.com/blogs/africa/2013/11/97751.html (Accessed June 15, 2018).

Sembène, Ousmane. *Camp de Thiaroye*. [1988] VHS tape, 152 min. New York: New Yorker Video, 1998.

Stakemeier, Kerstin, and Marina Vishmidt, "Unlearning to Unlearn." In *Unlearning Exercises: Art Organizations as Sites for Unlearning*. Edited by Binna Choi, Annette Krauss, and Yolande Zola Zoli van der Heide. Amsterdam: Casco Art Institute/Valiz, 2018.

————*Reproducing Autonomy: Work, Money, Crisis and Contemporary Art*. London/Berlin: Mute, 2016.

Toilet (T)issues #2

Antariksa, Binna Choi, Syafiatudina, Emily Pethick, and Ferdiansyah Thajib. "Curating Organisations (Without) Form: Toilet Tissue and Other Formless Organisational Matters." *Open Engagement* April 6, 2015. Online: www.openengagement.info/curating-organisations-without-form/ (Accessed June 13, 2018).

Choi, Binna, and Maiko Tanaka, eds. *Grand Domestic Revolution Handbook*. Amsterdam: Casco Art Institute/Valiz, 2014.

Afterword

Agamben, Giorgio. *The Highest Poverty: Monastic Rules and Form-of-Life*. Translated by Adam Kotsko. Redwood City, CA: Stanford University Press, 2013.

Federici, Silvia. "Feminism and the Politics of the Commons," *The Commoner*, January 24, 2012. Online: www.commoner.org.uk/?p=113 (Accessed June 2, 2018).

Fraser, Andrea. "An Artist's Statement (1992)." In *Museum Highlights: The Writings of Andrea Fraser*. Edited by Alexander Alberro. Cambridge: MIT Press, 2005.

Levine, Caroline. *Forms: Whole, Rhythm, Hierarchy, Network*. New Jersey: Princeton University Press, 2015.

Plotegher, Paolo et al., eds. *Nanopolitics Handbook: The Nanopolitics Group*. New York: Minor Compositions, 2013. Online: www.minor-compositions.info/wp-content/up-loads/2013/09/nanopolitics-web.pdf (Accessed April 4, 2017).

Spivak, Gayatri Chakravorty. *The Postcolonial Critic: Interviews, Strategies, Dialogues*. Edited by Susan Harasym. London: Routledge, 1990.

Stavrides, Stavros, and Mara Verlič. "Crisis and Commoning: Periods of Despair, Periods of Hope." In *Spaces of Commoning: Artistic Research and The Utopia of the Everyday*. Edited by Anette Baldauf et al., 48–60. Berlin: Sternberg Press, 2016.

Glossary of Terms

Ahmed, Sara. *On Being Included: Racism and Diversity in Institutional Life*. Durham, NC: Duke University Press, 2012.

Alexiadou, Nafsika, and Bettina Lange. "New Forms of European Union Governance in the Education Sector? A Preliminary Analysis of the Open Method of Coordination." *European Educational Research Journal* 6, no. 4 (2007): 321–35.

Chertkovskaya, Ekaterina, and Bernadette Loacker. "Work and Consumption: Entangled." *Ephemera Journal* 16, no. 3 (2016): 6.

Class War University. "Studying Through the Undercommons: An Interview with Stefano Harney and Fred Moten (by Stevphen Shukaitis)" (November 12, 2012). Online: www.undercommoning.org/studying-through-the-undercommons-stefano-harney-fred-moten-interviewed-by-stevphen-shukaitis/ (Accessed September 30, 2018).

Commission of the European Communities. *Communication from the Commission: Making a European Area of Lifelong Learning a Reality*, Brussels, 21.11.01 COM (2001) 678 final. Directorate-General for Education and Culture; Directorate-General for Employment and Social Affairs, Brussels, 2001. Online: www.viaa.gov.lv/files/free/48/748/pol_10_com_en.pdf (Accessed September 29, 2016).

————— Commission of the European Communities. *Commission Staff Working Paper: A Memorandum on Lifelong Learning*. Brussels, 30.10.2000 SEC(2000)1832: Luxembourg Publication Office, 2000. Online: www.arhiv.acs.si/dokumenti/Memorandum_on_Lifelong_Learning.pdf (Accessed December 3, 2016).

Dokuzović, Lina. *Struggles for Living Learning: Within Emergent Knowledge Economies and the Cognitivization of Capital and Movement*. Pdf. Vienna: transversal texts, 2016. Online: www.transversal.at/media/pdf/livinglearning.pdf (Accessed September 10, 2018).

Federici, Silvia. "Precarious Labor: A Feminist Viewpoint." Lecture presented as part of the discussion series "This is Forever: From Inquiry to Refusal." At Bluestockings Radical Bookstore, New York, NY, October 2006.

————— *Caliban and the Witch*. New York: Autonomedia, 2004.

Feiss, E. C. "Whiteness as Property: Reform as Material." In *White Paper: On Land, Law and the Imaginary*. Edited by Adelita Husni-Bey, Antonia Alampi, and E.C. Feiss. Amsterdam: Casco Art Institute/Valiz, 2017.

Gibson, Katherine. Presentation during "Forum I: Commoning Economy, with (Un)usual Business, Katherine Gibson, Martijn Jeroen ven der Linden and Philippe van Parijs." Casco Art Institute, Utrecht, January 17, 2016. Unpublished transcript.

Gibson-Graham, J.K., Jenny Cameron and Stephen Healy "Take Back Work: Surviving Well." In *Take Back the Economy: An Ethical Guide for Transforming our Communities*, 17–48. Minneapolis, MN: University of Minnesota Press, 2013.

Haraway, Donna. "Situated Knowledges: The Science Question in Feminism and the Privilege of Partial Perspective." *Feminist Studies* 14, no. 3 (Autumn, 1988): 575–99.

Haiven, Max, and Alex Khasnabish. *The Radical Imagination: Social Movement Research in the Age of Austerity*. London: Zed Books, 2014.

Harney, Stefano, and Fred Moten. *The Undercommons: Fugitive Planning and Black Studies*, 147. Wivenhoe: Minor Compositions, 2013.

Krauss, Annette. *Sites for Unlearning: On the Material, Artistic and Political Dimensions of Processes of Unlearning*. PhD dissertation. Vienna: Vienna Academy of Fine Arts, 2017.

Quijano, Anibal. "Coloniality of Power, Eurocentrism and Latin America." *Nepantla: Views from the South* 1, no. 3 (2000): 533–80.

Spivak, Gayatri. *An Aesthetic Education in the Era of Globalization*. Cambridge, MA: Harvard University Press, 2012.

Stakemeier, Kerstin and Marina Vishmidt, *Reproducing Autonomy Work: Money, Crisis and Contemporary Art*. London/Berlin: Mute, 2016.

Stavrides, Stavros, and Mara Verlič. "Crisis and Commoning: Periods of Despair, Periods of Hope." In *Spaces of Commoning: Artistic Research and The Utopia of the Everyday*. Edited by Anette Baldauf et al., 48–60. Berlin: Sternberg Press, 2016.

Tuck, Eve, and K. Wayne Yang. "Decolonization is not a Metaphor." In *Decolonization: Indigeneity, Education and Society* 1, no.1 (2012): 1–40.

Tlostanova, Madina V., and Walter D. Mignolo. *Learning to Unlearn: Decolonial Reflections from Eurasia and the Americas*. Columbus: The Ohio State University Press, 2012.

Ukeles, Mierle Laderman. "Manifesto for Maintenance Art, 1969!" In *Grand Domestic Revolution Handbook*. Edited by Binna Choi and Maiko Tanaka. Amsterdam: Casco Art Institute and Valiz, 2014.

Vishmidt, Marina. "Speculation as a Mode of Production in Art and Capital." PhD dissertation. London: Queen Mary University of London, 2012.

Vishmidt, Marina. *Speculation as a Mode of Production: Aesthetics and the Financialisation of the Subject*. Leiden: Brill, forthcoming–2018.

Wieger, Julia. "Kitchen Politics." In *In Spaces of Commoning: Artistic Research and The Utopia of the Everyday*. Edited by Anette Baldauf et al., 154–67. Berlin: Sternberg Press, 2016.

Zechner, Manuela. "A Politics of Network-Families? Precarity, Crisis and Careful Experimentations." In *Nanopolitics Handbook: The Nanopolitics Group*. Edited by Paolo Plotegher et al., 183–195. New York: Minor Compositions, 2013. Online: www.minorcompositions.info/wp-content/uploads/2013/09/nanopolitics-web.pdf (Accessed April 4, 2017).

Colophon

Phillips, Andrea. "The Imperative for Self-Attainment: From Cradle to Grave." In *Unlearning Exercises: Art Organizations as Sites for Unlearning*. Edited by Binna Choi, Annette Krauss, and Yolande Zola Zoli van der Heide. Amsterdam: Casco Art Institute/Valiz, 2018.

COLOPHON AND ACKNOWLEDGEMENTS

Who is "we"?
— Participant(s) during Site for Unlearning
(Art Organization)

The mechanisms that lead to authorship in (institutional) working processes determine which work is authored, which isn't, and why. The collaborative project and case study *Site for Unlearning (Art Organization)* has seen different phases, processes, and working groups.

As the years of experimentation have proceeded and the unlearning exercises have increased and decreased in number, and varied in their materializations, so has their content and form grown in such ways. Every contribution to this process has influenced its final form and given depth and acuity to its words.

What follows is a recounting of the many people and processes involved in the interconnection of *Site*

for Unlearning (Art Organization) with the publication that you hold in your hands and with Casco Art Institute's wider exhibitions program and research trajectory on the commons. Through acknowledging the collaborative embodiments and inclusive forms of attribution in *Unlearning Exercises: Art Organizations as Sites for Unlearning* we want to wholeheartedly thank the various contributors, and offer the colophon as part and parcel of thinking through and working towards collective authorship as a commoning gesture.

Unlearning Exercises: Art Organizations as Sites for Unlearning is a culminating node in Casco Art Institute's collaborative four-year project with Annette Krauss. This publication came out of the desire to center the Unlearning Exercises and share the unlearning project farther with other (arts) institutions. Below you will read the names of the people and organizations who have made this possible.

210

TEAM AT
CASCO ART INSTITUTE
2018

On June 9, 2018, Casco formally announced its change of name from Casco — Office of Art, Design and Theory to "Casco Art Institute: Working for the Commons." This change reflects a greater focus on its commitment to practices of commoning and its parallel culture of unlearning. During this time, work on the *Site for Unlearning (Art Organization)* project and the accompanying publication *Unlearning Exercises: Art Organizations as Sites for Unlearning* has been steadily underway, and the current team at Casco Art Institute consists of the following people:

OFFICE
director (since June 2008):
Binna Choi
deputy director (formerly head of publishing, publishing coordinator, production coordinator, and intern, since 2009):
Yolande Zola Zoli van der Heide
head of diverse economies (since March 2018):
Erik Uitenbogaard
curator (formerly curatorial fellow, intern, since 2015):
Staci Bu Shea
curator of language and dissemination (since March 2018):
Rosa Paardenkooper
production and logistics coordinator (formerly production assistant, volunteer, since 2015):
Marianna Takou

SUPPORT TEAM
installation:
Thomas de Kroon, Michael Klinkenberg, Jochem van Grieken
English language editors:
Liz Allan, Clementine Edwards, Cannach MacBride

English / Dutch translator:
Loes van Beuningen
interns:
Dohee Lee, Maria Sowter, Angeliki Tzortzakaki
hosts and volunteers:
Sanne Coopmans, Laura Cuzzocrea, Mafalda Gomes, Patricia Jiménez López, Una McAuley, Shona McCombes, Egoyibo Okoro, Paul Schmidt, Gentry Tsiatsiou, Roos van Unen, Jorge Vitorino, Tselenti Yota
graphic design:
David Bennewith / colophon.info with Zuzana Kostelanská
web programming:
Bram van den Berg
design support:
Ika Putranto
financial administration:
Elkin Willaert / Force Finance
photography:
Niels Moolenaar, Rachel Morón, Angela Tellier
cleaning (exhibition rooms):
Yara Agterberg

BOARD
Charles Esche (chair); Aetzel Griffioen; Tilly Janssen (secretary 2012–18); Martijn Jeroen van der Linden (treasurer); Wendelien van Oldenborgh

SITE FOR UNLEARNING (ART ORGANIZATION) PROJECT TEAM:

artist:
Annette Krauss
managing copyeditor:
Liz Allan
graphic design:
Rosen Eveleigh, Anja Groten
transcription and feedback:
Whitney Stark

FORMER TEAM MEMBERS AT CASCO ART INSTITUTE 2014–17

During the period of working on and putting *Site for Unlearning (Art Organization)* into practice, the composition of the Casco Art Institute team has been changing by adopting to different individual and collective situations. Here we acknowledge our former colleagues who have taken on other paths outside of Casco Art Institute but who shared some of the major and/or minor moments and processes around *Site for Unlearning (Art Organization)*.

OFFICE
Janine Armin (English language copyeditor, editor, 2012–16)
Cee Bakker (office coordinator, photographer, 2014–16)
Ester Bartels (office and communication coordinator, 2011–15)
Steyn Bergs (media and research coordinator, 2015–16)
Marleen de Kok (financial administration, 2012–16)
Roel Griffioen (media and research coordinator, 2014–15)
Sanne Oorthuizen (curator, development coordinator, 2012–16)
Jakob Proyer (maternity cover for project coordinator, 2016)
Anne Punt (community and office coordinator, intern, 2016–17)
Ying Que (maternity cover for project coordinator, community
    organizer and project organizer, 2012–16)
Suzanne Tiemersma (project and infrastructure coordinator, 2011–17)
Judith Torzillo (production coordinator, intern, 2017)
Niek van der Meer (office and mediation coordinator, 2016–17)
Jason Waite (curator, 2013–15)

SUPPORT TEAM
project coordinator for *Army of Love*:
Sven Engels
web programming:
Christoph Knoth

financial administration:
Erwin Nijholt
photography:
Coco Duivenvoorde
interns:
Simone der Kinderen, Lara Garcia Diaz, Fela Kim, Malcolm Kratz,
Ika Putranto, Deborah Sielert, Marieje Tordjo, Bjorn van de Logt,
Sofie Wierda
volunteers:
Charlotte Amrouche, Leana Boven, Zlil Busnach, Nisreen Chaer,
Sanne Coopmans, Laurel Cunningham, Laura Cuzzocrea, Mario Diaz,
Sven Engels, Patricia Jiménez López, Maria Karssenberg, Julija
Mockute, Tiva Pam, Christian Sancto, Paul Schmidt, Deborah Sielert,
Lygia van Sauers, Robby Wouters
cleaning (exhibition rooms):
Jessie Westgeest (2017), Sophie Sanders (2016–17), Paula Huijer (2016),
Maartje Verhagen (2014–15)

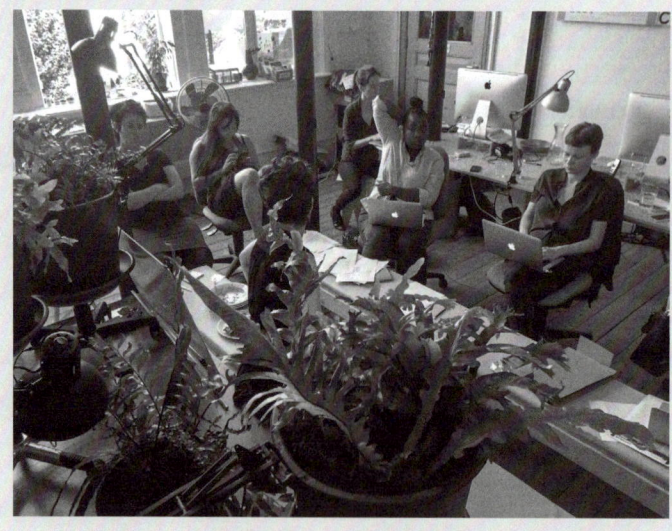

Unlearning meeting with the Casco Team and Annette Krauss as part of *Site for Unlearning (Art Organization)*, at Casco Art Institute, Utrecht, 2015. Photo: Binna Choi

PUBLIC MOMENTS OF
SITE FOR UNLEARNING
(ART ORGANIZATION)

A selection of public presentations of *Site for Unlearning (Art Organization)* in and around the context of Casco Art Institute. Elsewhere, *Site for Unlearning* has been presented at a number of symposia, seminars, lectures, and at other art and educational institutions nationally and internationally.

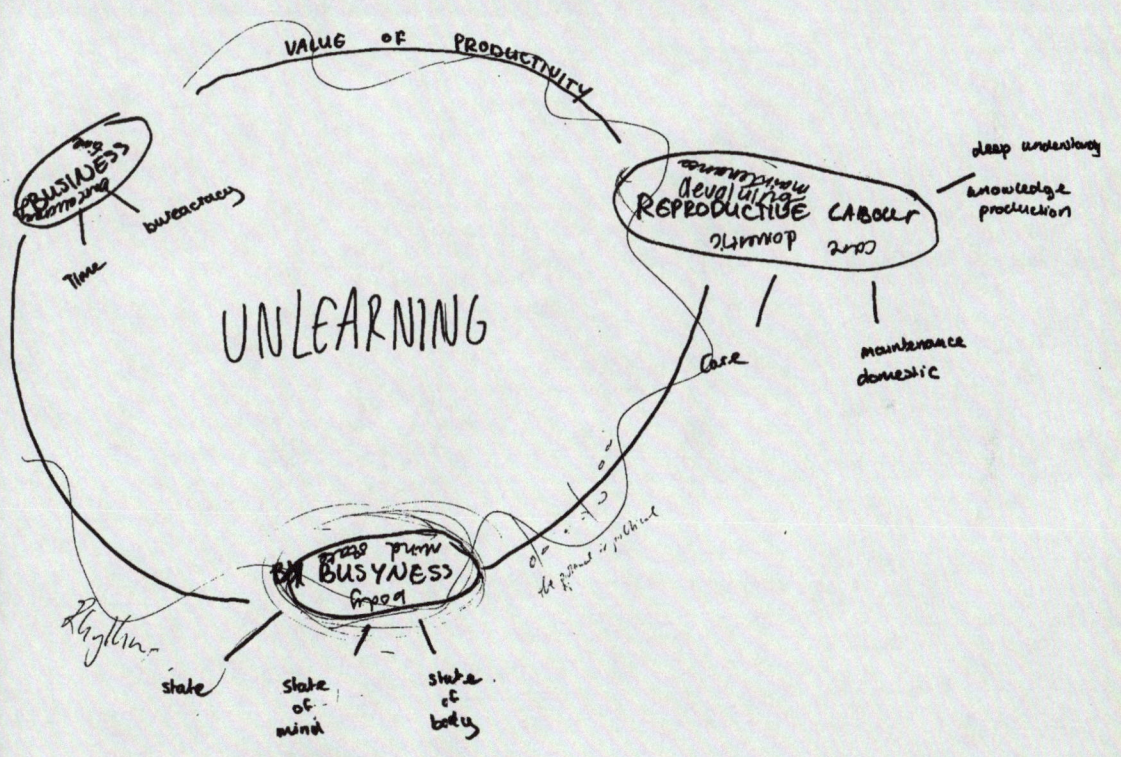

Schemes and diagrams from the "What to Unlearn?" workshop with the Casco Team and Annette Krauss as part of *Site for Unlearning (Art Organization)*, at Casco Art Institute, Utrecht, 2015. Photo: Casco archive

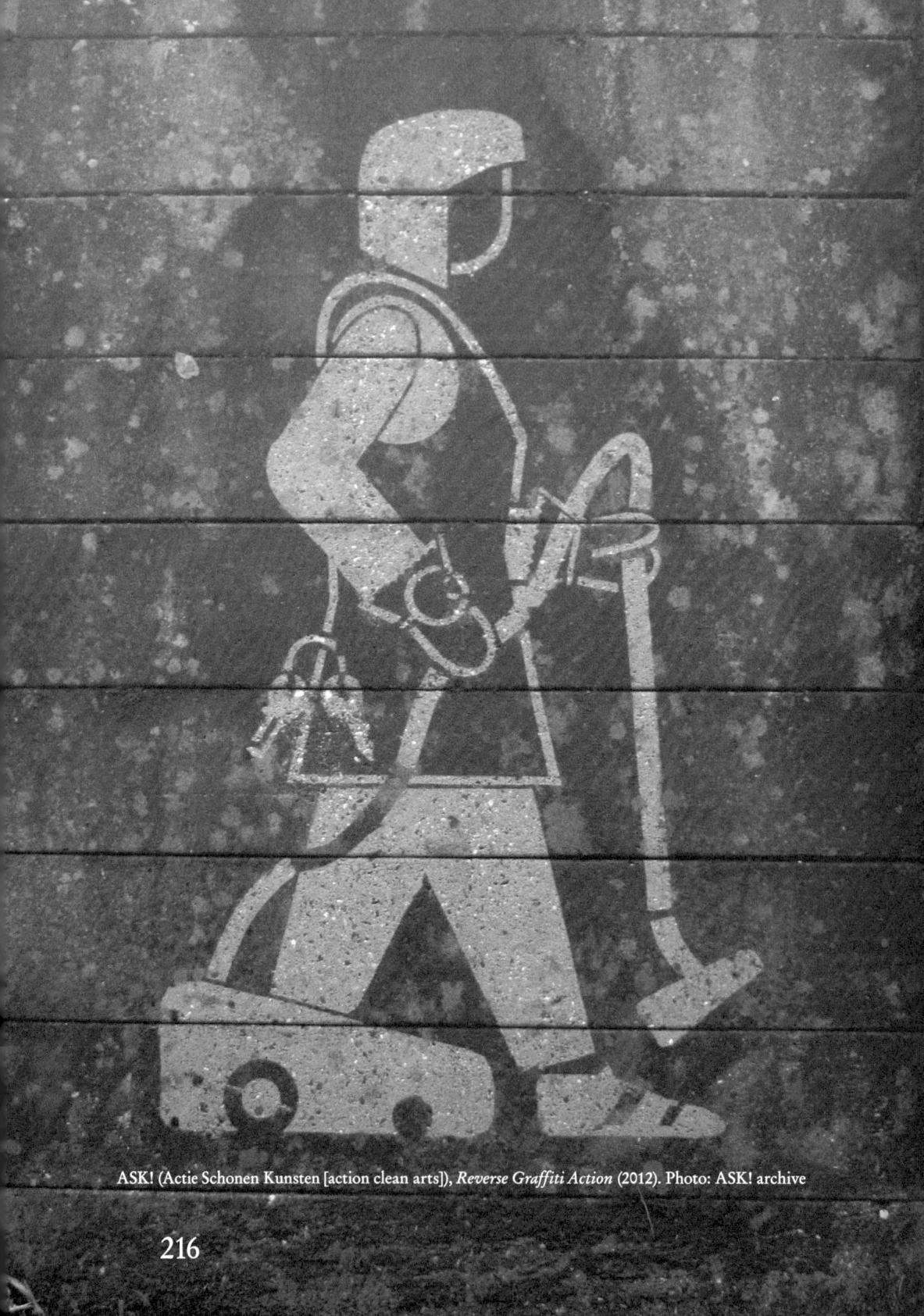

ASK! (Actie Schonen Kunsten [action clean arts]), *Reverse Graffiti Action* (2012). Photo: ASK! archive

216

Practicing Solidarity with Migrant Domestic Workers and Cleaners
Cultural and domestic workers find common ground, 2012–ongoing

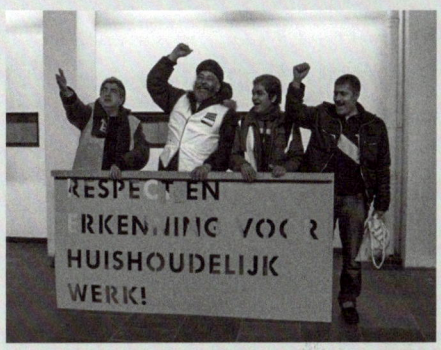

Members of the cleaners' union posing with the inverse graffiti stencil "Respect en Erkening voor Huishoudelijk Werk!" [respect and recognition for domestic work]. In 2012, thousands of cleaners organized a sit-in at Utrecht University along with hundreds of students and supporters, including ASK! (Actie Schonen Kunsten [action clean arts]), a group of cultural workers in support of migrant domestic workers. The sit-in was organized to demand fair working conditions and as a collaboration between the cleaners' union section of FNV Bondgenoten [a trade union that supports domestic workers], Kritische Studenten Utrecht [critical students Utrecht], and International Socialists. ASK! was initiated by Casco Art Institute in the context of its long term artistic and action research project *The Grand Domestic Revolution*, curated by Binna Choi and Maiko Tanaka, and had a few of the Casco Art Institute team and Annette Krauss as its members. The inverse graffiti with the figure of domestic workers—designed by artist Andreas Siekmann—was its main action. Photo: Marc Roig Blesa

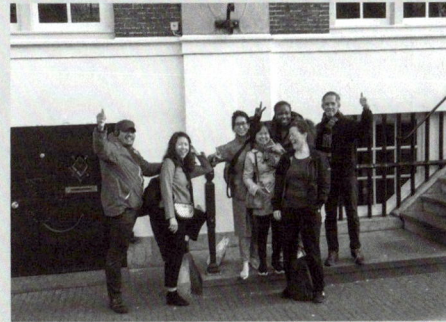

Left to right: Faisol Iskandar, Binna Choi, Sakiko Sugawa, Yolande Zola Zoli van der Heide, Jack Apostal, Joy Melanie Escano, and Annette Krauss posing outside of Wereldhuis in Amsterdam, after the conversation "Toilet Tissue #3 Against All Odds—Migrant Domestic Labor Struggle and Forms of Organizing," with Casco Art Institute, Indonesian Migrant Workers Union (IMWU), Filipino Migrants in Solidarity (FILMIS), Sugawa, and Krauss. April 2018. Photo: Casco Art Institute archive

217

Transcription Booklets—Site for Unlearning (Art Organization)
In the context of *New Habits,* a project exhibition at Casco Art Institute, 2014

In 2014, during the development of the exhibition and program *New Habits*, the team at Casco Art Institute and Annette Krauss initiated *Site for Unlearning (Art Organization)* together, and worked on articulating a basic understanding of "what to unlearn," "what's at stake in collaboration," "deinstitutionalization," and "business/busyness." These articulations resulted in four transcription-booklets with the same titles, accompanied by four audio pieces.

With: Janine Armin, Ester Bartels, Binna Choi, Marleen de Kok, Anja Groten, Malcolm Kratz, Annette Krauss, Laura Pardo, Ying Que, Deborah Sielert, Suzanne Tiemersma, and Yolande Zola Zoli van der Heide, Sofie Wierda.

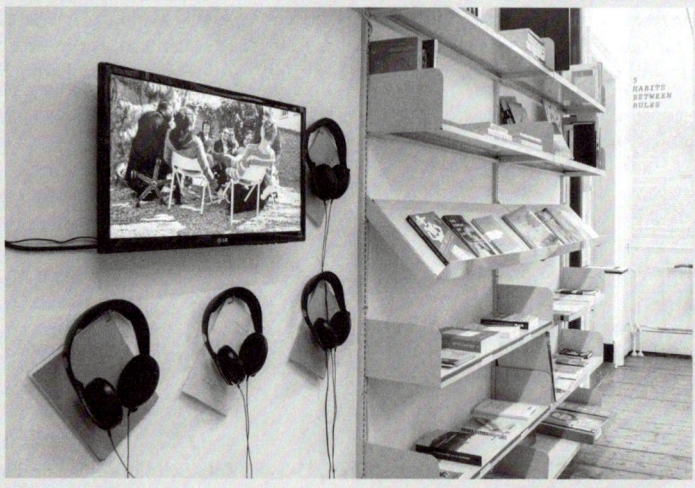

Site for Unlearning (Art Organization), installation view (four booklets, four audio pieces, Unlearning Exercises slideshow), as part of the exhibition *New Habits,* curated by Binna Choi with Sanne Oorthuizen and Jason Waite, at Casco Art Institute, Utrecht, 2014. Photo: Niels Moolenaar

218

BUSINESS/BUSYNESS

TRANSCRIPTIONS
STE-012-17.3.14.wav

PART OF:
SITE FOR UNLEARNING #3 (ART ORGANIZATION)
UTRECHT 2014

1

DEINSTITUTIONALIZING

TRANSCRIPTIONS
STE-029-14.4.14.wav

PART OF:
SITE FOR UNLEARNING #3 (ART ORGANIZATION)
UTRECHT 2014

1

WHAT TO UNLEARN?

TRANSCRIPTIONS
STE-004-10.3.14.wav

PART OF:
SITE FOR UNLEARNING #3 (ART ORGANIZATION)
UTRECHT 2014

1

WHAT'S AT STAKE
IN OUR COLLABORATION?

TRANSCRIPTIONS
STE-019- 23.3.14.wav
STE-029-14.4.14.wav

PART OF:
SITE FOR UNLEARNING #3 (ART ORGANIZATION)
UTRECHT 2014

1

Casco Team and Annette Krauss, the four transcription booklets for *Site for Unlearning (Art Organization)*, at Casco Art Institute, Utrecht. Design by Anja Groten

Casco Case Study #2—Site for Unlearning (Art Organization) 2014–15

At Casco's by-then new home at Lange Nieuwstraat, Casco initiated the "Casco Case Study" format to present research threads of its program and its work in process that ran parallel to the main exhibition upstairs. These case studies were presented in a display case in a corridor outside of Casco's office and bookshop area, and were an attempt to articulate and make processes of research visible; the first case study in the series was dedicated to the *Site for Unlearning (Art Organization)* project.

Up until then, in weekly "unlearning" discussions, we had been exploring what could be unlearned to institute a more communal way of working. Further questions included how to go about this prefiguratively while facing the contradiction of our responsibility to the public in a neoliberal society, whereas also acknowledging that Casco Art Institute is itself a public institution. For this "Case Study" moment, we staged one of our regular unlearning exercises, that is, cleaning our office and kitchen area, and made photo documentation of this "performance"-cum-"new habit." These photos were presented with a selection of diagrams and notes from our meetings, along with relevant quotes from our literature.

Specifically with: Cee Bakker, Ester Bartels, Staci Bu Shea, Binna Choi, Annette Krauss, Sanne Oorthuizen, Ika Putranto, and Ying Que. Transcriptions: Whitney Stark.

Casco Team and Annette Krauss, *Site for Unlearning (Art Organization)*. Diagrams, photograph, reference material. In "Casco Case Study #2," at Casco Art Institute, Utrecht, 2015. Photo: Niels Moolenaar

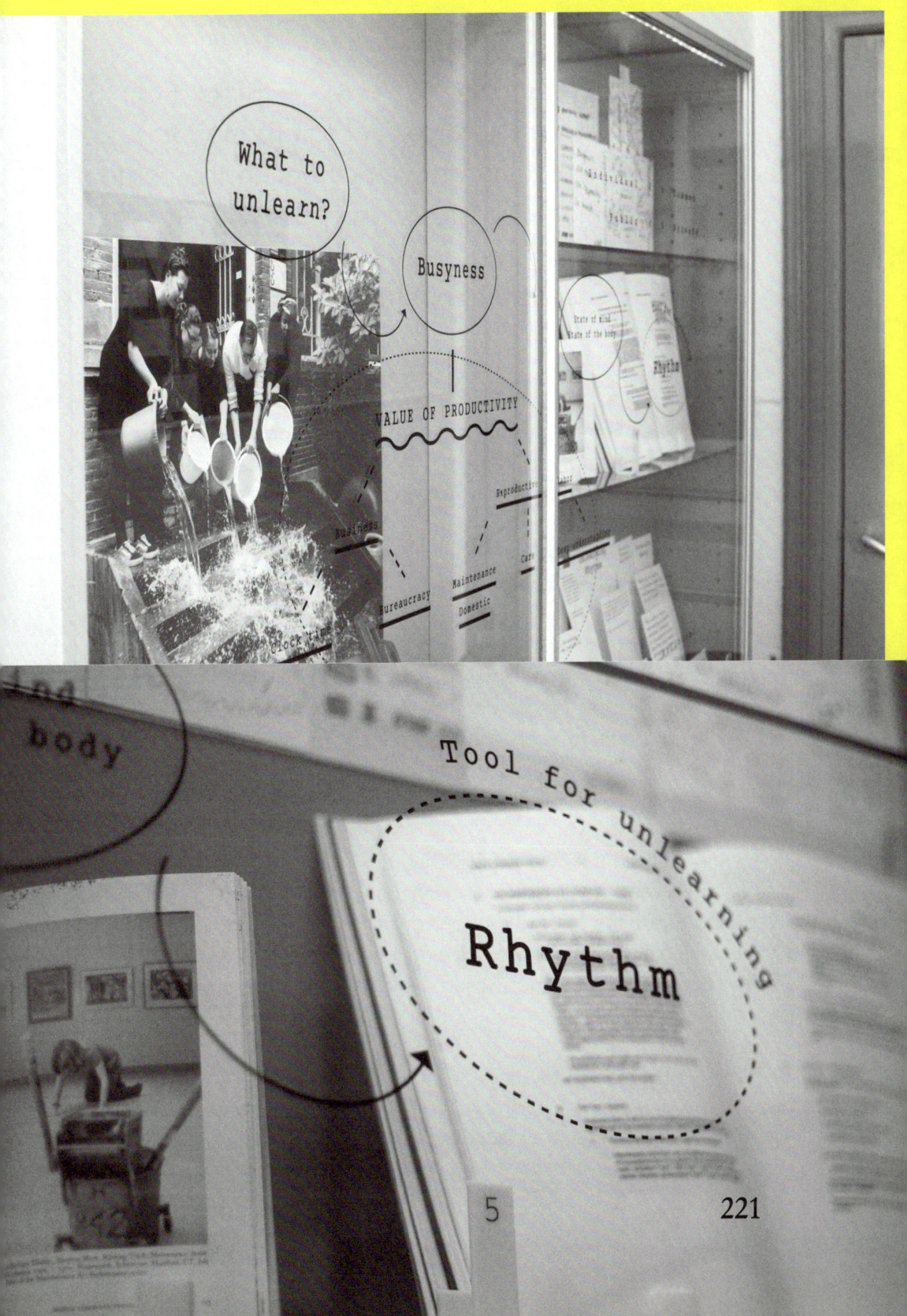

Unlearning Exercises — Site for Unlearning (Art Organization)

Tear pads, installation, and workshop. In the context of the exhibition and study program *We Are the Time Machines: Time and Tools for Commoning*, at Casco Art Institute, 2015–16.

From November 15, 2015–March 13, 2016 Casco Art Institute began to generate "tools" for practicing the commons as part of the exhibition project and study program *We Are the Time Machines: Time and Tools for Commoning*. It was in this context that the Unlearning Exercises were first exhibited.

The Casco team with Annette Krauss was divided into three working groups, which partly developed the structure and produced content and materials for parts of the exhibition. The working groups were involved in creating content for the workshop, which was concerned with commoning art organizations, alongside the thematic concerns of commoning aesthetics, commoning economy, and commoning governance. The subsequent working rhythm provided the basis of a working method for the the following phase of the project. The working groups were:

UNLEARNING EXERCISES / METHODOLOGY
This working group revisited transcriptions from the already articulated Unlearning Exercises to find overarching clusters, methods, and practices within the set. The aim being to make the exercises public with the support of designer Rosen Eveleigh. With: Cee Bakker, Binna Choi, and Annette Krauss.

TEXTUAL MATRIX
This working group produced texts for both the Casco website and the *We Are the Time Machines* exhibition program, as wellas articulating

222

an initial structure for this publication. With: Steyn Bergs, Annette Krauss, and Yolande Zola Zoli van der Heide.

GENERAL STRUCTURE
This working group coordinated and revisited the rhythms of meeting each other for *Site for Unlearning (Art Organization)* and met every three weeks as a new structure to continue collective unlearning processes and develop "study" moments. With: Sanne Orthuizen, Ying Que, and Suzanne Tiemersma.

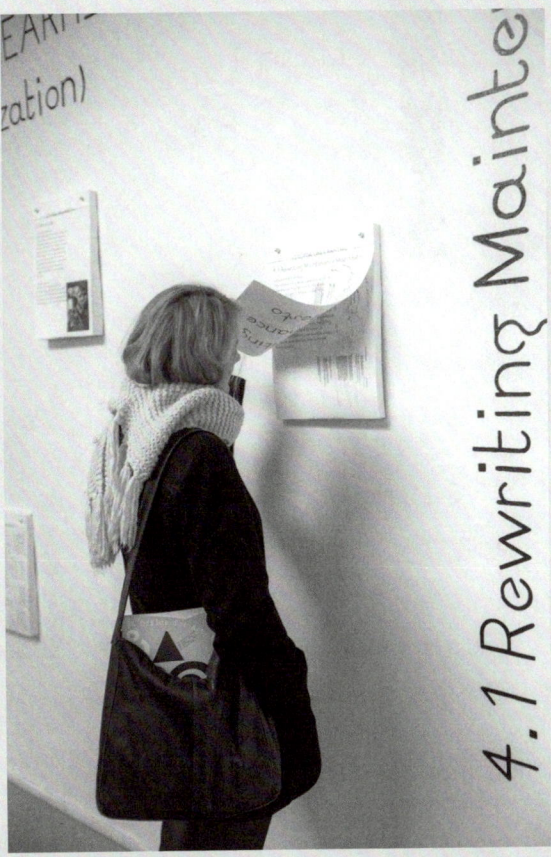

This and next page: Casco Team and Annette Krauss, Unlearning Exercises, installation view. At the exhibition *We Are the Time Machines: Time and Tools for Commoning*, curated by Binna Choi, Casco Art Institute, Utrecht, 2016. Design by Rosen Eveleigh. Photo: Niels Moolenaar

223

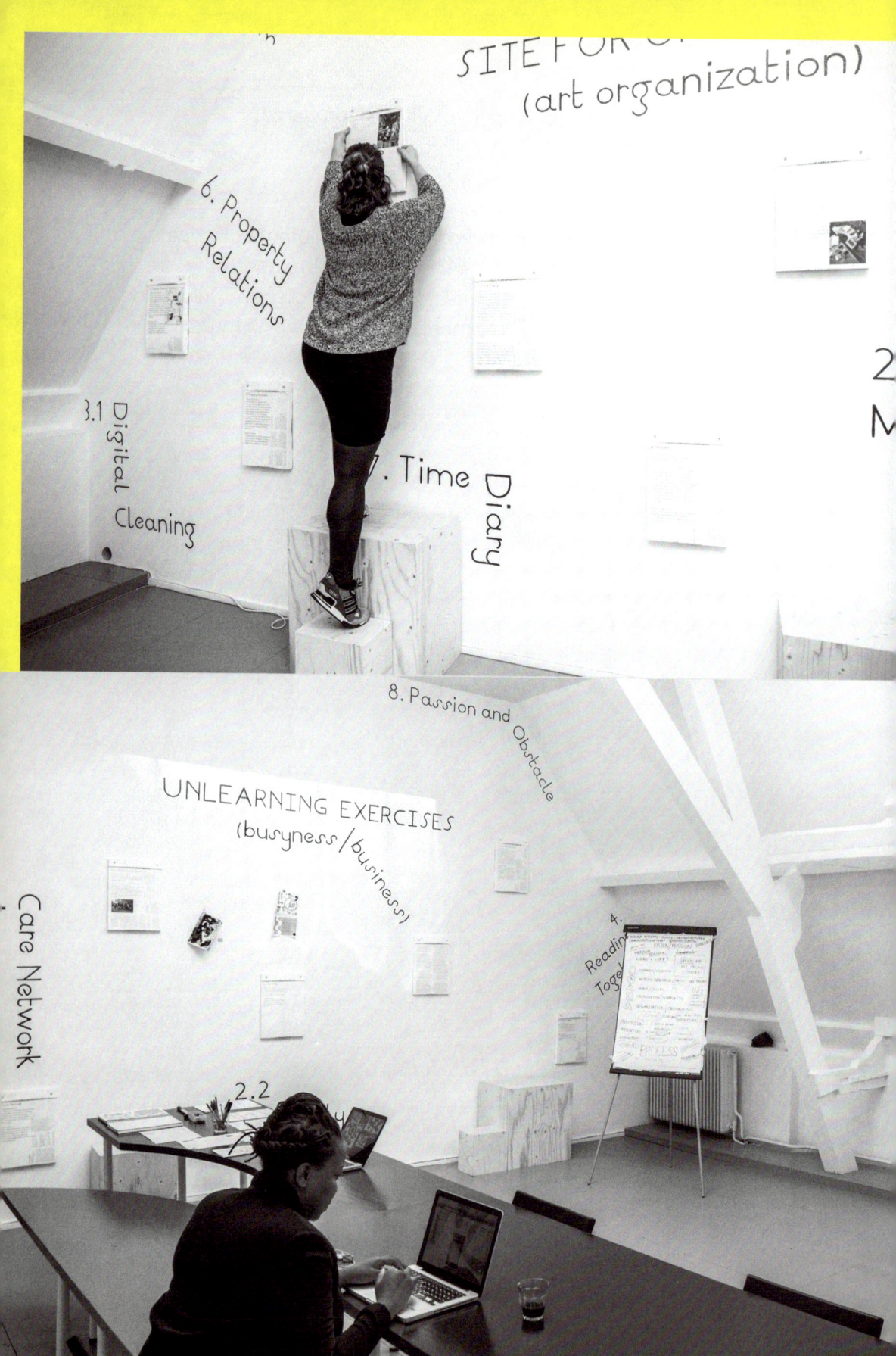

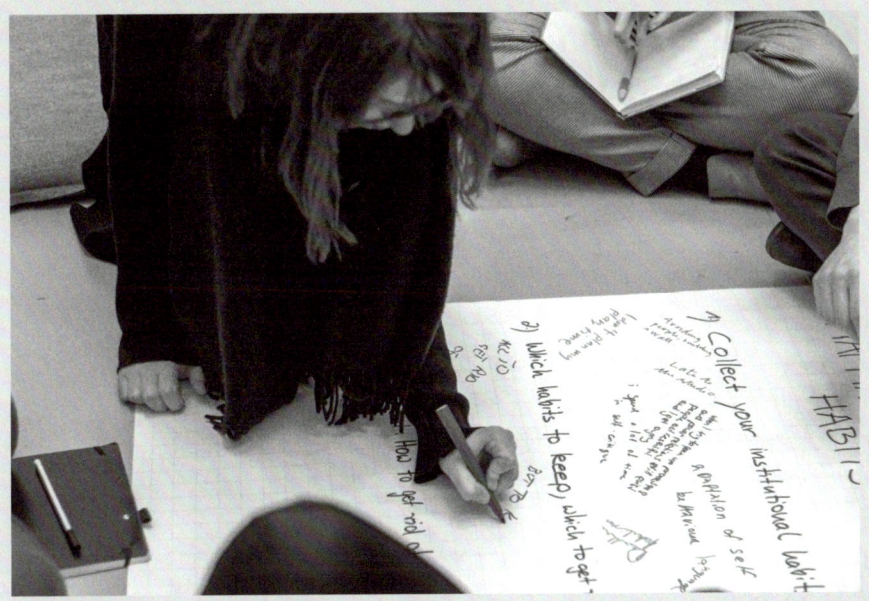

Unlearning workshop during the forum "WTM II: Commoning Art Organization." As part of the *We Are the Time Machines: Time and Tools for Commoning* exhibition program, at Casco Art Institute, Utrecht, 2016. Photo: Cee Bakker

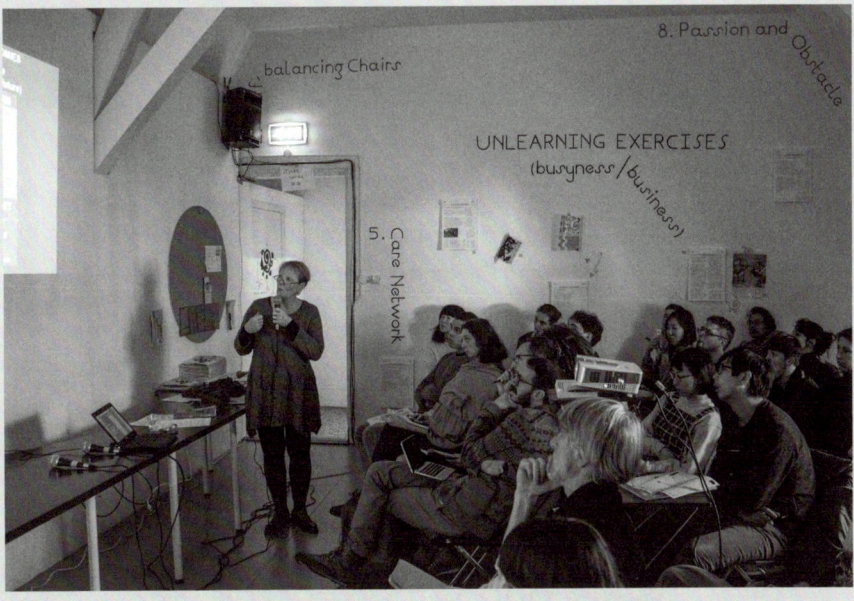

Katherine Gibson presenting in the Unlearning Exercises installation during the forum "WTM III: Commoning Economy," as part of *We Are the Time Machines: Time and Tools for Commoning*, at Casco Art Institute, Utrecht, 2016. Photo: Niels Moolenaar

Unlearning Exercises:
Art Organizations as
Sites for Unlearning
Book team, 2018

general editors:
Binna Choi, Annette Krauss, Yolande Zola Zoli van der Heide
managing editors:
Liz Allan, Yolande Zola Zoli van der Heide
graphic design:
Rosen Eveleigh
editorial advice:
Astrid Vorstermans
copyediting:
Liz Allan
proofreading:
Cannach MacBride
transcription and feedback:
Whitney Stark

authors:

Foreword: Unlearning to Unlearn
Kerstin Stakemeier and Marina Vishmidt
Introduction
Liz Allan and Yolande Zola Zoli van der Heide
Unlearning Exercises
The shifting team at Casco and Annette Krauss, re-workshopped
by Binna Choi, Annette Krauss, Anne Punt, Ying Que, Yolande Zola
Zoli van der Heide, Niek van der Meer
Toilet (T)issues #1:
Toilet Tissue and Other Formless
Organizational Matters
Antariksa, Ferdiansyah Thajib, Syafiatudina (KUNCI Study

Colophon and Acknowledgments

Liz Allan, Binna Choi, Annette Krauss, Yolande Zola Zoli van der Heide, with Judith Torzillo. Photography: ASK! archive, Cee Bakker, Coco Duivenvoorde, Annette Krauss, Niels Moolenaar, Marc Roig Blesa

images:
Unlearning Exercises contributors, unless otherwise mentioned
printing:
Drukkerij Raddraaier SSP, Amsterdam
paper:
Cyclus print 90gsm and Gmund Colours Matt 44 300gsm
typefaces:
Garamond no. 8, and Geranium by Rosen Eveleigh

Co-published by Casco Art Institute and Valiz

Casco Art Institute: Working for the Commons
Lange Nieuwstraat 7
3512 PA Utrecht, The Netherlands
www.casco.art

Valiz, book and cultural projects
Het Sieraas, Studio K34–K36
Postjesweg 1
NL 1057 DT Amsterdam
www.valiz.nl

Printed and bound in the Netherlands, 2018

This book was made possible with the financial support of Mondriaan Fund, Utrecht City Council, Stichting DOEN via Arts Collaboratory, and Foundation for Arts Initiatives. Annette Krauss' involvement in the project was supported by the Academy of Fine Arts Vienna in the framework of her postdoctoral grant, financed by the Austrian Science Fund (FWF): 495.

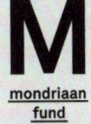
mondriaan
fund

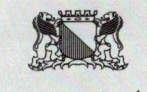
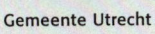
Gemeente Utrecht

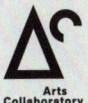
Arts
Collaboratory

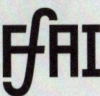

Unlearning Exercises: Art Organizations as Sites for Unlearning
Reprint, 2025

The reprint of *Unlearning Exercises: Art Organizations as Sites for Unlearning* is published together with its younger sister *Unlearning Routines of the Impossible*. For this occasion, the typeface designed by Rosen Eveleigh has been updated, name changes adapted, and the covers newly designed.

The reprint was collated by Rosen Eveleigh, Aline Hernández, Annette Krauss, Marianna Takou, and Stevphen Shukaitis, in conversation with Binna Choi and Yolande Zola Zoli van der Heide.

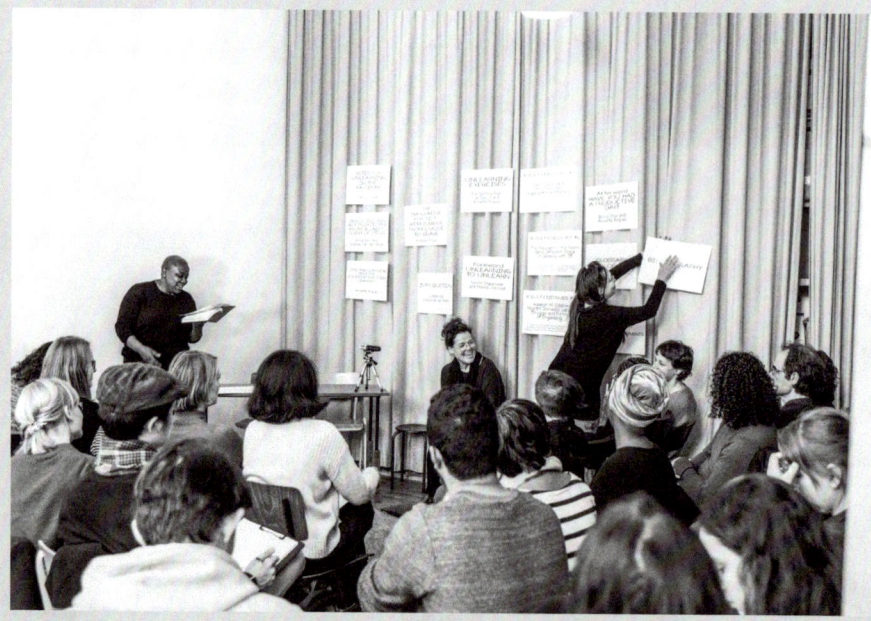

Book launch of *Unlearning Exercises* during the Assembly *Elephants in the Room*, at Casco Art Institute, Utrecht, 2018. Photo: Filippo Guiseppe Iannone

Co-published by Casco Art Institute and Minor Compositions
Distributed by Casco Art Institute and Autonomedia

design:
Rosen Eveleigh
design assistance:
Carlo Canún
typeface assistance:
Karl-Emil Bengtson

printing:
Drukkerij Raddraaier SSP, Amsterdam
paper:
90 gsm Arena Natural Smooth and 210 gsm Stucco Old Mill
typefaces:
Garamond no. 8, and Geranium by Rosen Eveleigh

Casco Art Institute: Working for the Commons
Lange Nieuwstraat 7
3512 PA Utrecht, The Netherlands
www.casco.art

Minor Compositions
Colchester / New York / Port Watson
www.minorcompositions.info

Autonomedia
PO Box 568 Williamsburgh Station
Brooklyn, NY 11211, USA
www.autonomedia.org

ISBN 978-1-57027-425-1
Printed and bound in the Netherlands, 2025